UNDERSTANDING VERTEBRATES

UNDERSTANDING VERTEBRATES

By

Dr. Amita Sarkar

Dept. of Zoology

Agra College

Agra (U.P.)

(India)

DPH

DISCOVERY PUBLISHING HOUSE PVT. LTD.

NEW DELHI-110 002

Published by:
Namit Wasan
DISCOVERY PUBLISHING HOUSE PVT. LTD.
4383/4B, Ansari Road, Darya Ganj
New Delhi-110 002 (India)
Phone : +91-11-23279245; 23253475; 43596065
E-mail : discoverybooksindia@gmail.com
discoverypublishinghouse@gmail.com
namitwasan9@gmail.com
web : www.discoverypublishinggroup.com

First Edition: **2010**

ISBN: 978-81-8356-546-2

Understanding Vertebrates

Preface

The present title "Understanding Vertebrates" has been written for those students interested in careers in diverse fields of biological sciences. It provides a structured approach to learning by covering all the important topics in a uniform, systematic format. The book has been comprehensively designed incorporating recent advances in this fast moving field. It also provides accessible information on molecular biology in compact form for undergraduate students in biology and related life sciences. It is intelligible to the educated layman, though it deals with some complex ideas. It is an adequate text for all the requirements of students in this area. In addition, busy lecturers who require a quick reference compendium will find it useful, particularly for tutional planning. Simple, yet hopefully clear figures and tables are provided throughout the book.

The over-riding goal of this book, and indeed of the whole *Understanding series,* is to present the essential information concering molecular biology in a compact, readily accessible form which leads itself to student learning and revision. The convergence of various approaches has generated a rich panorama of detail, the significance of which we are still attempting to unraval. The present text has been written as an introduction to this rapidly growing field.

To make the work more comprehensive and informative, the author has consulted many authoritative books, research journals, abstracts, monographs etc., so there can be no claim to originality except in the manner of treatment.

The author expresses his thanks to his friends and colleagues whose continue inspirations have initiated him to bring out this book.

The author expresses his gratitude to Mr. Wasan and staff of M/s Discovery Publishing House Pvt. Ltd. for their whole hearted cooperation in the publication of this book.

In the mean time, the author will remain sincerely responsible for any shortcomings of the book and be grateful to the readers for their suggestions and constructive criticism for the continuous betterment of the book. He takes this opportunity to appeal to the readers to send their suggestions straightaway to his Publisher.

Author

Contents

1

Chordate Morphology and Evolution

The Phylum Chordata will serve as our introduction to one type of data that convinced Darwin and others that evolution had occurred. We shall follow the usual scientific procedure by assuming our hypothesis, in this case evolution, to be true. We shall make deductions from the hypothesis. Next we shall see if the data substantiate the deductions.

If evolution has occurred, these are some inferences a biologist could make:

1. In a taxonomic group, such as the Phylum Chordata, all species are descended from a common ancestral type.
2. If all chordates are related by descent from a common ancestor, there should be indications of this in their structure. There should be a basic morphological plan, or *archetype*, from which all forms could be derived.
3. The over-all trend of evolution should be from the simple to the complex. We would expect to find the simple or primitive chordates appearing at an earlier time in geological history than the more complex forms. If our hypothesis is correct it is absolutely essential that species assumed to be ancestral precede their assumed descendants in time.

We shall study the Phylum Chordata, our own taxonomic category, with these deductions in mind. We shall attempt to trace the evolution of the chordates from the most primitive forms to modern man. The end point we have chosen is, of course, a prejudiced one. The story is somewhat more complete for other animals, but an interest in our own species might outweigh all other considerations. Our species, *Homo sapiens*, is a comparative newcomer in the world of life.

The best available evidence indicates that our non-human predecessors, however, have been a part of the biological scene for a very long time. Our ancestral line extends back to the origin of life on this planet. During the last 180 million years our ancestors have been mammals.

For 50 million years before, that they were reptiles. During the previous 40 million years they were amphibians, and earlier than that they spent at least 180 million years as fish of one sort or another.

This is a total elapsed time of approximately 450 million years. Our ancestry in more remote times is shrouded in mystery, but it is highly probable that some group of invertebrates gave rise to our phylum, the Chordata, approximately 500 million years ago.

Many zoologists who have made a careful study of the matter believe the Chordata arose from some echinoderm-like invertebrate. The point should be emphasized, however, that our ancestral line is fairly well known only for the past 450 million years, and that during this period the ancestors have always been chordates.

For the present we shall not be concerned with the evidence for these time estimates. That will come in Chapters D-9 and D-10.

Methods of Studying Evolution

Our task now will be an attempted reconstruction of the evolution of human body structure. This would be a fairly routine endeavor if we had complete specimens of ancestral types taken at short intervals, say every million years, for the last 500 million years.

Material of this sort, however, is not available. What we do have are fossils with the hard structures-bones, teeth and scalespreserved. We can study these and learn a great deal about bones, teeth and scales, but in only a few exceptional cases do we have direct information on the soft parts of extinct animals. If most of the evidence has been destroyed, how can we reconstruct the past history of our body form?

The answer is, in part, through the methods of comparative anatomy. We can apply such methods because of certain chance events in the evolution of the chordates. Let us suppose, in order to emphasize how fortunate we are, that evolution in the chordates had been very different from the way it actually was, and that what happened was something like this:

The first chordates gave rise to fish-like forms and then became extinct; the fish gave rise to the amphibians and then became extinct; the amphibians vanished after giving rise to the reptiles, and the reptiles died out after the mammals arose.

In short, let us suppose that there was a sequence of the appearance and extinctionof the main chordate types. If this had been the story, our knowledge of evolution of the human body form would be restricted to what we can learn from fossil bones, teeth, and scales.

But it so happens that all of the major groups of chordates, except one (the placoderms), have living representatives. There is no special reason why this should be so; but those interested in evolution can count it as a blessing that it is so.

The earliest known chordate remains are the ostracoderms, which appeared about 450 million years ago. In structure, the ostracoderms are so similar to the living lampreys and hagfish that all are put in the same class, the Agnatha.

Now, this is a very interesting phenomenon. You, I, and the lamprey can all trace our ancestry back to the same common ancestor, the ostracoderms. The line from ostracoderm to lamprey has been almost static in its rate of evolution; the present-day lamprey is different from the ostracoderms, but not enough to be put in a separate taxonomic class.

In the same interval of time another group of descendants of the ostracoderms passed through all the stages leading up to man. We study the lamprey of today for what it can tell us about body structure when we were in the agnathan stage of evolutionary development. A word of caution should be interjected at this point.

Although the lamprey resembles the ostracoderms in being built on the same fundamental plan, there are many points in which the two types differ. It will be necessary to disregard the specializations peculiar to the lamprey, but this is not always easy. To do so, we must be in a position to distinguish between primitive and specialized features.

The former are of great significance in the evolution of the higher forms, while the latter are of no importance in this respect. How do you think this can be done? Perhaps this consideration will help you to answer the question: Most mammals have five toes on each foot.

The horse has only one toe. Which condition would you suppose to represent the primitive mammalian condition—and why? There is nothing unusual about the fact that the Class Agnatha has living representatives. All along our ancestral line, branches were given off that changed relatively little in subsequent ages. By a proper selection of living forms, therefore, we can obtain some insight into what our ancestors were like.

This is the method of comparative anatomy. Another source of data is the study of embryonic development. Evidence of this sort has been most important in shaping our conception of the structure of the earliest chordates.

Embryos show many characteristics that appear to be primitive. Thus, at one stage the mammalian embryo possesses a notochord and pharyngeal pouches, characters common in the most primitive living chordates but absent in adult mammals. During development these structures are lost or become highly modified.

The fact that they are present at all calls for explanation. At one period in the history of biology, it was believed that the development of an individual is merely a much abbreviated repetition of what took place in evolution.

This view was expressed as 'ontogeny recapitulates phylogeny' in Haeckel's Biogenetic Law. Today this is taken as not more than the most general of approximations. As embryos, we did not pass through a sequence of agnathan, fish, amphibian, and reptilian stages.

There is, however, a certain element of truth in this point of view. The embryos of all chordates resemble one another in the earliest stages.

There is a similar ground plan and in every class this plan is modified in a different manner. In one case the end product is a bird, in another a frog, and in still another a mammal. Perhaps it would be more accurate to say that ontogeny seems to recapitulate some developmental features of lower forms.

This similarity of embryonic beginnings has suggested that the first chordates were organized along much the same lines as the embryos of present-day forms.

We shall use data from embryology frequently to reconstruct a chordate archetype, but the indirect nature of the data should be kept constantly in mind. We can gain some conception of what the earliest chordates must have been like merely by listing the essential characteristics of the Phylum Chordata.

By definition, the early chordates must have exhibited these essential characteristics, which we shall now list, or they would not have been chordates.

CHARACTERISTICS OF THE PHYLUM CHORDATA

The members of the Phylum Chordata resemble one another and differ from all other animals in possessing the following structures at some period of their life:

A Notochord

This is a rod of tissue, functioning primarily for support, that is situated ventral to the nerve tube and dorsal to the alimentary canal. In most chordates its anterior tip reaches the level of the midbrain. Posteriorly it extends to the end of the body.

In development, it is derived from the mesoderm and its role as an embryonic organizer for the neural plate should be recalled. The notochord is found in the embryonic stages of all chordates, but it is present in the adult of only the most primitive forms, such as amphioxus, the lamprey, and the hagfish.

In most sharks and bony fish, at least remnants of it are present in the adult. In all higher chordates (amphibians, reptiles, birds, and mammals) it is present in the early embryo, but it is replaced during development by the vertebral column. The name of the phylum, 'Chordata,' is in reference to the notochord.

A Dorsal Nerve Tube

This organ is dorsal to the notochord and in the mid-line of the body. In most chordates, the anterior portion of the nerve tube is

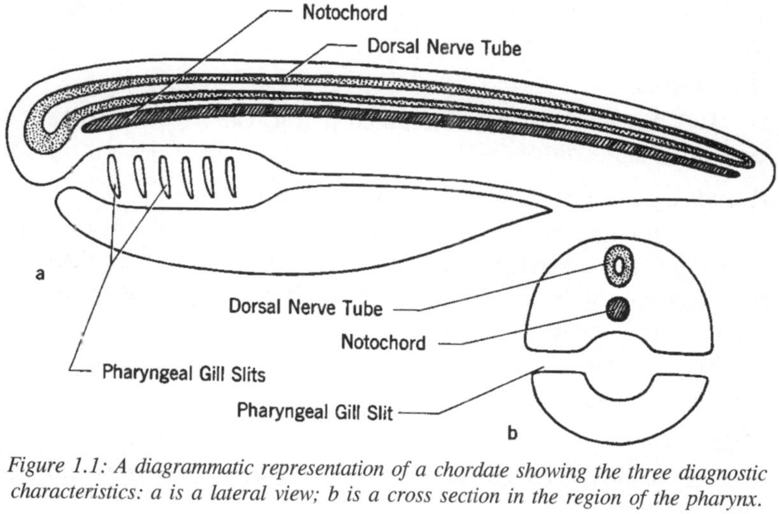

Figure 1.1: A diagrammatic representation of a chordate showing the three diagnostic characteristics: a is a lateral view; b is a cross section in the region of the pharynx.

enlarged to form a brain and the remainder is the spinal cord.

The dorsal position and tubular structure are in contrast to the nervous system in other phyla. For example, the main longitudinal nerve of annelids and arthropods is ventral in position and it is-solid.

Pharyngeal Gill Slits or Pouches

In the lower chordates (tunicates, amphioxus, and most fish) there are openings from the pharyngeal portion of the alimentary canal to the outside. These are the gill slits, which have an important respiratory function.

The embryos of higher forms (amphibians, reptiles, birds, and mammals) possess gill slits or pouches. These are lost or become highly modified in the adult.

In addition to these three diagnostic characteristics, most chordates show the following features that are usually, but not always, characteristic of this phylum alone.

A Tail

The alimentary canal terminates some distance from the hind end of the body. The portion posterior to the anus, or to the cloacal opening, forms the tail.

A Closed Blood System with a Heart

The blood vessels form a continuous tubular system of a type first observed in the annelids. This is in contrast to the open blood system of the arthropods. The chief distributing vessel is the dorsal aorta. In it blood travels posteriorly. A heart is located on the ventral side posterior to the pharynx.

Endoskeleton

The skeleton, which is composed of cartilage, bone, or both, is internal. Contrast this with the encasing exoskeleton of the arthropods.

Paired Appendages Derived from Many Segments

Not all chordates possess paired appendages (paired fins or legs). If they do, the appendages are formed by tissue from more than one body segment. In the annelids and arthropods each appendage is derived from a single segment.

The chordates share with some of the other advanced phyla the following characteristics:

Metamerism

The body is divided into segments showing some repetition of similar structures.

A Well-developed Coelom

The spacious body cavity is lined by a mesodermal epithelium and is, therefore, a true coelom.

Bilateral Symmetry

The body of a chordate can be divided into two similar halves by a. cut in only one plane. This plane would be longitudinal and include the dorsal and ventral mid-lines.

THE SUBPHYLA AND CLASSES OF CHORDATES

There are approximately 40,000 different species in the Phylum Chordata. These are placed in four subphyla (the first of which may not even belong to the Chor.Clata).

Subphylum Hemichorda ('half-chord')

This taxonomic group includes a relatively small number of marine species, which are wormlike in appearance. They live in burrows in shallow water along the seacoasts. The more frequently mentioned genera are Balanoglossus and Saccoglossus.

Some of the early investigators believed that these forms possessed a structure homologous with the notochord. Recent workers seriously doubt if the structure in question has anything to do with a notochord.

The best claim to relationship with the chordates is the presence of gill slits in the pharynx. The name of this subphylum refers to the shortness of the structure which is supposed to be a notochord. Most present-day workers regard the hemichordates as early offshoots of the evolutionary line leading up to the chordates.

If this view is accepted, the hemichordates are pre-chordates and should not be included in the Phylum Chordata at all.

Subphylum Urochorda ('tail-chord')

This is another group of marine animals. They are commonly known as tunicates, ascidians, or sea-squirts. In most species the adults are permanently attached to rocks or some other supporting structure. Many are colonial.

A major portion of the body is taken up by the pharynx, the walls of which are perforated by numerous gill slits. A continuous stream of water passes through the mouth, into the pharynx and then out through the gill slits.

The water is then in a spacious cavity, the atrium. It leaves the atrium through the atriopore to reach the outside. The mouth is

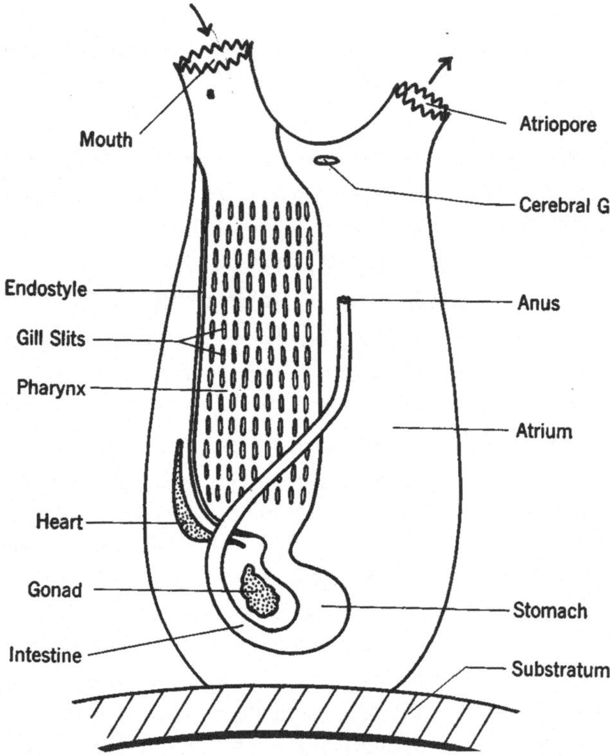

Figure 1.2: Subphylum Cephalochorda: Amphioxus. A cross section through the pharyngeal region.

considerably larger than the gill slits, and many small animals and plants are swept into the pharynx but are unable to pass through the gill slits. In this manner the pharynx acts as a strainer.

The trapped organisms are used for food by the tunicate. Some of the common genera along the Atlantic Coast are Ciona, Molgula, Amaroecium, and Botryllus.

The larval stage is of great interest. It has the appearance of a tiny tadpole. The tail contains a dorsal nerve tube and a well-developed notochord. When a larva changes into the adult stage, the tail is lost. The group name 'Urochorda' refers to the presence of a notochord in the tail.

If you were able to study only an adult tunicate, there would probably be considerable doubt in your mind regarding its chordate affinities. An examination of the developmental stages would quickly dispel any uncertainty.

Subphylum Cephalochorda (head-chord)

This subphylum contains relatively few species, most of them belonging to the genus Branchiostoma. The formerly employed generic term amphioxus has become a commbn,name for all forms. These animals are marine, and are restricted to the coastal waters of the tropical and temperate zones.

One species extends as far north as Chesapeake Bay on the Atlantic Coast of North America. The adults are elongate and never reach a length of more than a few inches. They are capable of swimming, but spend most of their time buried in the ocean bottom with only the head protruding.

The adult possesses the three diagnostic characters' 'of the chordates, and for this reason is of considerable interest. The dorsal nerve tube is similar in size throughout its entire length; there is no enlargement that we could call a brain.

It is highly probable that the absence of the brain is not a primitive character, but is the result of degeneration (this implies, of course, that the ancestors of amphioxus possessed a brain). Associated with the absence of the brain, we find that olfactory organs, eyes, and ears are likewise lacking.

Can you think of any reason why the absence of a brain might result in the absence of the sense organs just mentioned? Do you think it would be possible for well-developed olfactory organs, eyes, and ears to be present in an animal having no brain?

The notochord extends from the extreme anterior to the extreme posterior end of the body. In nearly all chordates, the anterior terminus of the notochord is in the region of the midbrain. The extreme anterior extension of the notochord in amphioxus is the basis of the subphylum name, '*Cephalochorda.*'

The gill slits of amphioxus are very numerous. They act as strainers in capturing the tiny marine organisms that form the food of amphioxus.

These three subphyla, the Hemichorda, Urochorda, and Cephalochorda, are sometimes known as the protochordates ('first-chordates') or the acraniates ('without a skull'). All are marine.

Their structure is a combination of primitive, degenerate, and specialized characters. All lack a well-developed brain, eyes, ears, olfactory organs, limbs, and skeleton of the vertebrate type. Their chief interest lies in the possibility of their shedding some light on the nature of the first chordates that appeared on the earth.

Subphylum.Vertebrata

Most of the chordates belong to this group. A vertebral column is present, it being responsible for the name of 'the subphylum. There is usually a well-developed endoskeleton composed of cartilage or bone. There is a brain, which is enclosed by a skull.

Olfactory organs, eyes, and ears are found in nearly all vertebrates. The following classes are recognized: *A. Class Agnatha ('without jaws').* The lamprey (Petromyzon, Entosphenus) and the hagfish (Bdellostoma) belong to this class. Morphologically, these are the most primitive of living vertebrates.

A well-developed notochord is present in the adult. The vertebral column is rudimentary. Paired limbs and jaws are lacking. The olfactory organs communicate with the outside through a single median opening. *B. Class Chondrichthyes ('cartilaginous fish').* Also known as the elasmobranchs.

This class includes the sharks, dogfish, skates, chimaeroids, and rays. These forms show an advance over the Agnatha in possessing paired appendages, jaws, and better differentiated vertebrae (with corresponding restriction of the notochord). Tiny scale-like structures, the dermal denticles, are present.

C. Class Osteichthyes ('bony fish'). The remaining fish living today belong to this class. True bone, scales, and an air bladder are present. The three classes—Agnatha, Chondrichthyes, and Osteichthyes-are frequently combined as the Superclass Pisces. They are known by the common name 'fish.'

The remaining four classes, Amphibia, Reptilia, Aves, and Mammalia, are predominantly terrestrial. Collectively they are known as the Tetrapoda ('four feet'). The paired appendages, which were in the form of fins in the Pisces, are modified as limbs for travel on land.

Living on land has resulted in pronounced physiological and morphological changes that help to adapt these forms to live in a relatively dry environment.

D. Class Amphibia ('double life'). Salamanders, frogs, and toads. The developmental stages, and in some cases the adults, must live in water. Arms and legs make their appearance. A threechambered heart (two atria and one ventricle) is present, as are lungs.

E. Class Reptilia ('creeps'). Snakes, lizards, turtles, and alligators. The developmental stages are not dependent on an aquatic environment. The body usually is covered with scales.

F. Class Aves ('birds'). The body is covered with feathers. Birds are homothermic, which means they have a nearly constant body temperature (all lower forms are poikilothermic, that is, they are unable to control their temperature). They have a heart with four chambers (two atria and two ventricles).

G. Class Mammalia ('having breasts'). These are the mammals. The body is covered with hair. In nearly every case the young are born free and not encased in a shell and membranes. They are nursed by the mother. The mammals are homothermic and possess a four-chambered heart. A well known example is shown in Figure elsewhere in this chapter.

The sequence of the subphyla and classes of the chordates whic has just been given is not arbitrary. It is based on increasing morph logical complexity and, except for the Chondrichthyes, it reflec evolutionary descent.

The living protochordates are certainly the leas complex of all the chordates in general morphology. Among the living Vertebrata the sequence is one of increasing structual complexity.

Aves Mammalia
↖ ↗
Reptilia
↑
Amphibia
↑
Osteichthyes
↑
Chondrichthyes
↑
Agnatha

The fossil history of the Chordata begins with the Agnatha-there are no indications of what came before. (Perhaps earlier forms were soft-bodied and therefore failed to leave fossil remains.) The first Agnatha were the Ostracodermi.

From them all living vertebrates, including the lamprey and hagfish, are descended. There were innumerable steps in this diversification, but by concentrating on the broader aspects of the line leading to mammals, we find that the Ostracodermi first gave rise to a group of primitive fish, the Placodermi.

These evolved into the Chondrichthyes and Osteichthyes. After a very long time, one group of Osteichthyes gave rise to the early Amphibia. One line of the early Amphibia evolved into the Reptilia, which gave rise to both the Aves and the Mammalia. The evolutionary sequence, therefore is:

Aves   Mammalia
↖   ↗
Reptilia
↑
Amphibia
↑
Chondrichthyes   Osteichthyes
↖   ↗
Placodermi
↑
Agnatha

The close correspondence between this and the sequence based on increasing structural complexity should be noted. Since the classification of the chordates is based on evolutionary developments, it is highly probable that all chordates are descended from one, or at most a relatively few, species of pre-chordates that existed approximately half a billion years ago.

In short, there is a real genetic relationship among the various members of the phylum. The underlying similarity in structure and body plan is the result of this descent from a common ancestor. It might be noted, somewhat parenthetically, that the chordates were recognized as a group long before we knew of Darwinian evolution.

In the pre-evolution days, animals were grouped as chordates because of their morphological similarity. We realize now that this morphological similarity is based on descent from a common ancestor.

THE AMMOCOETE LARVA

In this chapter and the next we shall study in detail two forms, the ammocoete larva of the lamprey and the dogfish. The purpose of this is to gain a foundation for the discussion of the anatomy of the chordates.

Both the ammocoete larva and the dogfish are generalized forms and the specializations of higher chordates can be understood as modifications of their more basic structure. There is no better way of introducing the chordates than by a study of the ammocoete larva.

This form has long been regarded as one of the closest approaches to the archetypal chordates that we possess. We have previously noted these two facts: the Agnatha are the most primitive living chordates, and embryos frequently exhibit characteristics believed to be of a primitive type.

Since the ammocoete larva is the embryonic stage of the lamprey, which is a member of the most primitive vertebrate class, it is small wonder that we consider it of such importance in understanding the basic structural plan of the phylum to which we humans belong.

The larva of the lamprey is an eel-like organism that spends most of its time buried in the muddy bottoms of streams. When it was first discovered, the true nature of this little animal was not appreciated. It was given the generic name Ammocoetes.

Somewhat later, when it was realized that this was merely the larval stage of the lamprey, the name Ammocoetes was replaced by the proper generic name of the adult. Ammocoetes is now used as a common name for the larval stages of all genera of lampreys.

Petromyzon is a common genus of lampreys. The adults, which may be several feet in length, spend most of their life in the ocean. Shortly before breeding, they enter rivers and swim upstream in their search for spawning grounds.

They generally select small streams with sand or gravel bottoms, and fashion a crude nest by removing the stones. The male encircles the body of the female and sheds sperm when the eggs pass out of her body. The developing embryos usually become buried in the sand.

Death comes to the adults shortly after spawning, and their bodies are washed down toward the sea. The embryonic stages require several years and it is not until this time has passed that the ammocoete larva metamorphoses into an adult.

A return migration to the sea then occurs. The brook lamprey, Entosphenus, spends its entire life in fresh water. It is much smaller than Petromyzon, but its breeding habits are essentially the same.

Many important features can be seen in the stained ammocoete shown in Fig. D4-1. The three diagnostic characters of the chordates are prominent. The *dorsal nerve tube* occupies its usual position, and its anterior portion is enlarged to form the brain.

The *notochord* is very large. The *pharyngeal gill slits* are seven pairs of openings between the pharynx and the outside. Indications of segmentation can be seen in the muscular system. In ammocoetes, the muscles in the dorsal part of the body are in the form of blocks extending from the head to the tail.

This muscular segmentation can be best observed at the level of the notochord. (The notochord is beneath the muscles, though in the nearly transparent specimen the two appear to be at the same level.)

The remaining structures will be discussed in relation to the organ system of which they form a part.

THE DIGESTIVE AND RESPIREATORY SYSTEMS

The alimentary canal is a straight tube, nearly as long as the body, that extends from the mouth to the opening of the cloaca. It develops from the archenteron. Its mucosa lining and the glands derived from it are endodermal.

The connective tissue, parts of the circulatory system, and smooth muscle that make up much of the wall of the alimentary canal are mesodermal. Its nerve supply is ectodermal. The mouth is located slightly behind the anterior end of the body.

It is overhung by the *oral hood.* The *oral tentacles*, which have a sensory function, surround the mouth. A considerable part of the alimentary canal is taken up by the *pharynx.*

This division has important respiratory as well as digestive functions, which is why the two are treated together in this section. The *velum* is located in the anterior part of the pharynx. Its movements help to create a current of water that enters the mouth, passes through the pharynx and then leaves the body through the gill slits.

There are seven pairs of *gill slits*, which are openings extending from the pharynx to the outside. The wall of the pharynx between adjacent gill slits is strengthened by rods of cartilage, the *gill bars.*

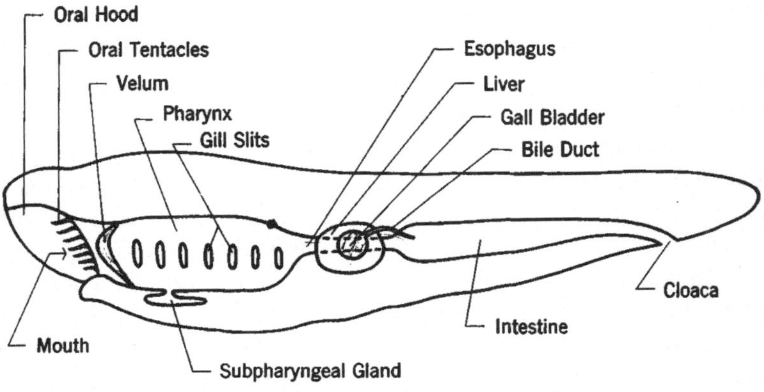

Figure 1.3: The digestive and respiratory systems of ammocoetes.

Each gill slit has *a gill* on both its anterior and its posterior surface.

The gills, which are constantly bathed by a current of water, are richly supplied by capillaries. It is here that the blood loses carbon dioxide and gains oxygen. The *sub pharyngeal gland*, or endostyle, is ventral to the pharynx. It opens into the lumen of the pharynx by a small duct.

One of its functions is to secrete mucus, which passes into the pharynx. Because mucus is sticky, tiny particles of food adhere to it. Both food and mucus are forced posteriorly into the intestine by cilia lining the pharynx.

The subpharyngeal gland has some resemblance to the endostyle found on the floor of the pharynx in amphioxus. When metamorphosis occurs, a portion of the subpharyngeal gland is converted into the *thyroid* which, as in all vertebrates, is able to accumulate iodine.

At its posterior end, the pharynx narrows to form the *esophagus*. This portion, which is relatively short, terminates in the *intestine*. In the embryo, the *fiver*, arises as an outgrowth from the gut wall in the region that will form the anterior part of the intestine.

It maintains a connection by means of the *bile duct*. Note that the *gall bladder* in ammocoetes is unusually large. The *pancreas is* not present as a separate organ, but cells similar to those found in the pancreas of higher forms are present in the anterior part of the intestine.

In higher forms the pancreas has two main functions: digestive enzymes are secreted by zymogen cells; and the hormone insulin, which helps to regulate the amount of glucose in blood, is secreted by the islets of Langerhans.

In ammocoetes, the zymogen cells are found in the mucosa of the anterior portion of the intestine. The islet cells bud off from the intestine and form clusters in the submucosa. It is interesting that these cells have the same physiological function as they do in higher vertebrates, namely, the regulation of sugar concentration in the blood.

It is probable that nearly all digestion and absorption occur in the intestine. Can you think of any reason why the extent of digestion might be limited in the pharynx? The intestine is horseshoe shaped when seen in cross section.

At the posterior end the kidney ducts join the intestine, thus forming a *cloaca*. The alimentary canal of ammocoetes is of interest not only for its simplicity but also for the structures it lacks. There are no teeth of the typical vertebrate type.

The adult possesses horny tooth-like structures that are formed entirely by the ectoderm, while the true teeth of higher vertebrates are entirely different structures, which are derived from both ectoderm and mesoderm.

There are no jaws in the larval or adult lamprey. The alimentary canal shows relatively little regional differentiation in the post-pharyngeal portion. There is no stomach, no separate pancreas, and no division of the intestine into a small intestine and large intestine. The alimentary canal of the ammocoete larva is probably of as simple a type as we could expect in the early chordates.

THE CIRCULATORY SYSTEM

The blood system of ammocoetes appears to be very primitive, and once again we lean heavily on this form for our concept of what the circulatory system may have been like in the early chordates.

The Basic Plan of the Circulatory System

The basic plan of the circulatory system of the hypothetical early chordates might be imagined to consist of four longitudinal vessels with two types of interconnection. The four longitudinal vessels would be:

1. *The dorsal aorta*, which extends along the dorsal side of the alimentary canal immediately below the nerve tube.
2. *The subintestinal vessel*, which runs along the ventral side of the alimentary canal.
3. *The right cardinal vein*, which is in the body wall on the right side.
4. *The left cardinal vein*, which occupies a similar position on the left side.

The two types of connections, excluding capillaries, are:

1. *The right and left ducts of Cuvier.* These carry blood from the cardinal veins to the subintestinal vessel. That portion of the cardinal vein anterior to the duct of Cuvier is the *anterior cardinal.* The portion that is posterior is the *posterior cardinal.*
2. *The aortic arches.* These vessels are found in the region of the pharynx. They carry blood from the subintestinal vessel to the dorsal aorta. In the lower chordates the aortic arches form a capillary network in the gills, and it is here that oxygen is obtained and carbon dioxide lost.

The Circulatory System of Ammocoetes

The general plan just given applies more-or-less to the embryos of

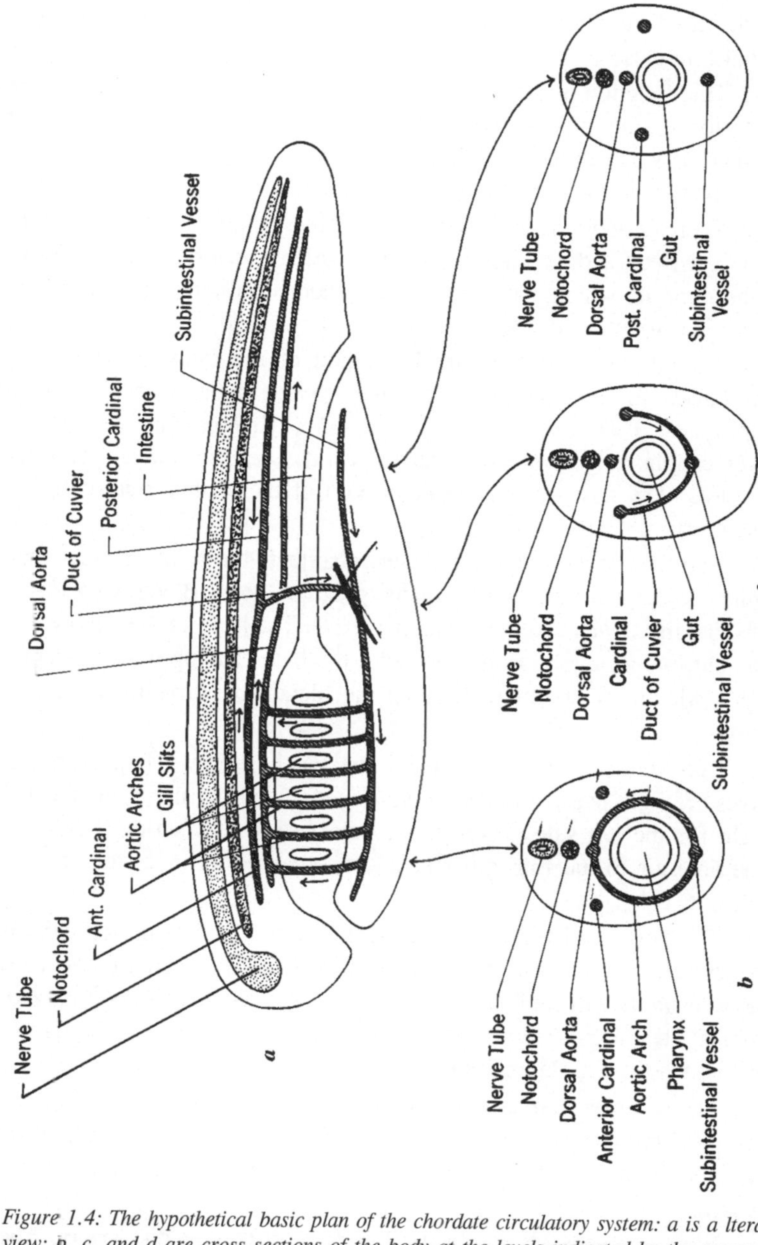

Figure 1.4: The hypothetical basic plan of the chordate circulatory system: a is a lteral view; b, c, and d are cross sections of the body at the levels indicated by the arrows.

all chordates, including ammocoetes. In ammocoetes, the *dorsal aorta* is the chief distributing vessel. It carries oxygen and digested foods to all the tissues.

The direction of blood flow is toward the tail, except in the region anterior to the gills where it flows toward the head. It gives off numerous small branches. These are evenly spaced and correspond to the myotomes, thus exhibiting segmentation.

There is only one large vessel branching from the aorta. It supplies the intestine, and is known as the *intestinal artery*. The primitive condition, in which there was a continuous subintestinal vessel, is modified in ammocoetes.

The posterior portion, in the region of the intestine, begins in capillaries in the gut wall and runs 'to the liver, where it forms capillaries. This is the *hepatic portal vein*. After passing through the liver capillaries, the blood is carried by the *hepatic vein* to the sinus venosus. The next more anterior portion of the subintestinal vessel is the heart.

The first portion is a thin-walled chamber, the *sinus venosus*, into which the hepatic vein and the ducts of Cuvier open. Blood passes from this into the *atrium* and then to the *ventricle*. The heart of the ammocoete has but one atrium and one ventricle, the latter having thick muscular walls which, by contracting, force the blood out through the *ventral aorta*.

The ventral aorta is located immediately below the pharynx. It gives off eight pairs of *aortic arches-eight* vessels for the right side and eight for the left side. There is a single vessel between each gill slit, one anterior to the first gill slit, and another posterior to the seventh gill slit.

The portion of the aortic arch that carries blood to the gill slits is the *afferent branchial artery*. The portion of the aortic arch that carries blood from the gill capillaries to the dorsal aorta is the *efferent branchial* artery. The cardinal veins collect blood that was carried to the tissues by branches of the dorsal aorta.

The *anterior cardinals* are lateral-to the notochord and the *posterior cardinals* are lateral to the dorsal aorta. Blood from the cardinals flows into the right and left *ducts of Cuvier*, which carry it to the sinus venosus.

Finally, in the late larva the left duct of Cuvier disappears. The anterior and posterior cardinal on this side then open into the right duct

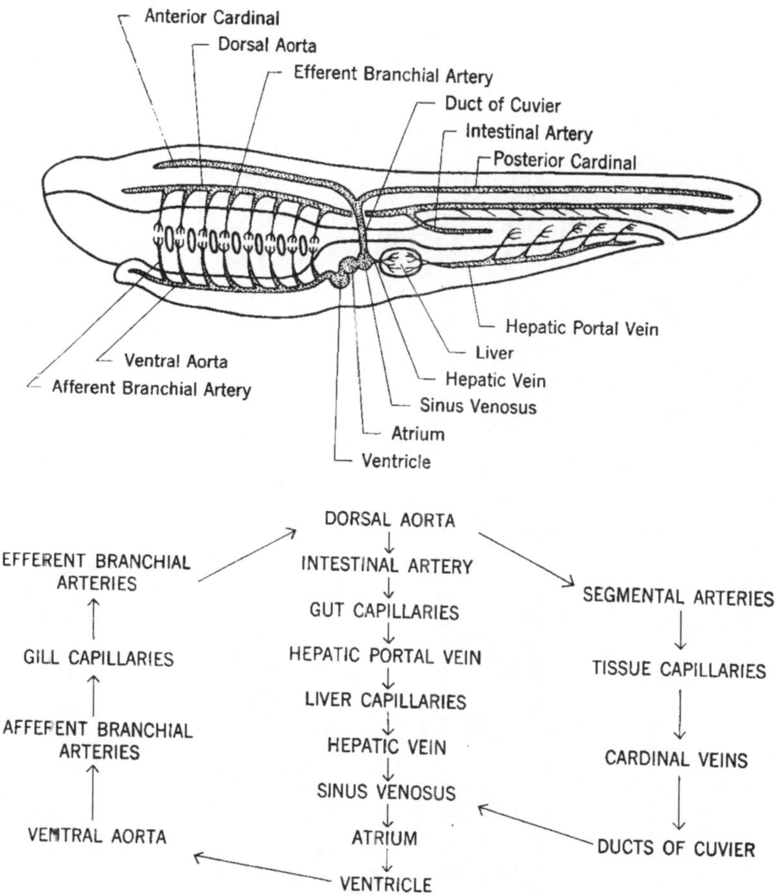

Figure 1.5: The principal blood vessels and the route of blood movement in ammocoetes.

of Cuvier. This change is a specialized feature of the lamprey and has no phylogenetic significance.

EXCRETORY SYSTEM

The excretory organs of the vertebrates are derived from the mesoderm. For this reason a study of this embryonic layer will aid in understanding the morphology of the kidneys and their ducts.

The Derivatives of the Mesoderm

Figure elsewhere in this chapter is a schematic representation of the trunk of a chordate embryo. It approximates the structure of the ammocoete and other primitive vertebrate embryos. The dorsal portion

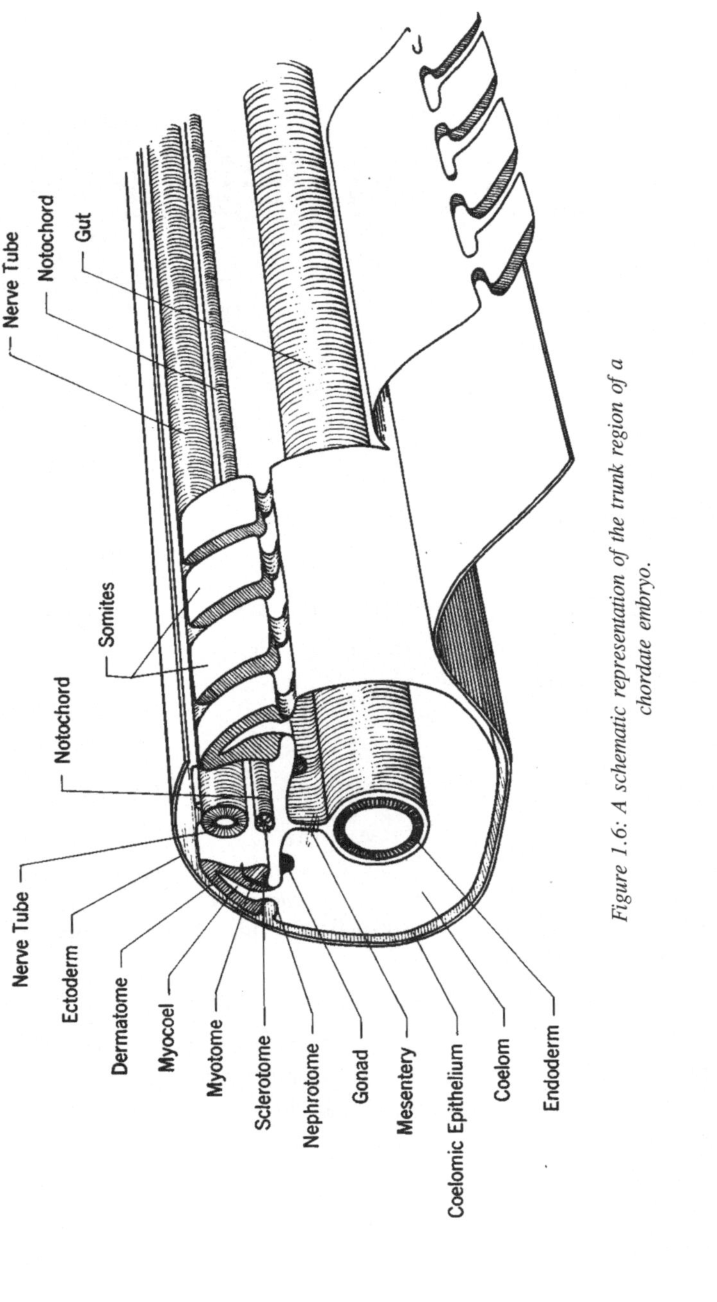

Figure 1.6: A schematic representation of the trunk region of a chordate embryo.

of the mesoderm is segmented, each block of tissue being known as *a somite*. The greater portion of the somite is the *myotome* region, which will give rise to most of the striated muscles.

The outer portion of the somite is the *dermatome*. The dermis layer of the skin comes from it. There is much evidence suggesting that the somite had a cavity, the *myocoel*, at an early stage in its evolution and it is found in the embryos of some chordates.

The inner, ventral portion of the somite is the *sclerotome*. The vertebrae develop from its cells. The *nephrotome* area consists of a series of connections between the somites and the ventral portion of the mesoderm.

The kidneys and their ducts originate from the nephrotome. The mesoderm of the ventral region forms the *coelomic lining* and the *mesenteries* that cover the organs suspended in this body cavity.

There is some evidence to suggest that the coelom may have been segmented at a very early evolutionary stage, but the primitive vertebrates living today have an unsegmented coelom except for the myocoel.

The Excretory Organs of Ammocoetes

The excretory organs of ammocoetes first develop from the nephrotomes in the heart region. The most anterior nephrotome involved breaks its connection with the somites and grows backward as a duct. The next posterior nephrotome connects with this duct.

This process occurs on both sides of the body; a total of four pairs of nephrotounes are involved. They form the *pronephros* (*'first kidney'*), which is the functional kidney of the early embryo. The ducts, which are known as the *pronephric ducts*, grow posteriorly and enter the cloaca.

Later in development additional tubules are formed in, a more

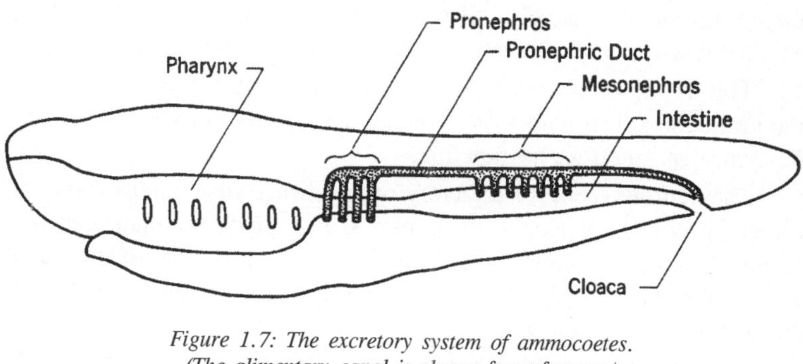

Figure 1.7: The excretory system of ammocoetes. (The alimentary canal is shown for reference.)

posterior region, opposite the intestine. These are the *mesonephric tubules*. They open into the already formed pronephric duct, which then becomes known as the *mesonephric duct*. Eventually, the pronephros degenerates leaving the mesonephros as the functional kidney of the adult.

REPRODUCTIVE SYSTEM

The gonads arise as paired ridges on the dorsal side of the coelom. They fuse subsequently to form a median structure. It is thought that this fusion is a specialization of the lamprey, since in all other vertebrates the gonads are paired.

The lamprey lacks genital ducts, the gametes being shed directly into the coelom. In sexually mature individuals, there is an opening from the coelom into the posterior part of the mesonephric duct. It is through this opening that the gametes leave the coelom.

The mesonephric ducts break their connection with the alimentary canal at the time of metamorphosis, and the right and left ducts unite, forming a urinogenital papilla. It is through this that urine and gametes leave the body. The urinogenital papilla and the intestine open separately into a shallow depression on the ventral side of the body.

The adult, therefore, does not have a cloaca. We shall study the urinogenital system in more detail in the dogfish. The ammocoete is, after all, an embryonic stage, and the organs of excretion and reproduction do not reach their full development.

NERVOUS SYSTEM

The central nervous system of ammocoetes consists of the brain and spinal cord. The brain exhibits the basic chordate plan. It is composed of three main divisions: forebrain, midbrain, and hindbrain.

These three divisions are functionally associated with the three main sense organs, namely, olfactory organs, eyes, and auditory organs. The *forebrain* consists largely of the *olfactory lobes*.

This is the center for the olfactory nerves. A *center* is an area in the brain concerned with a particular function. The olfactory center has the sense of smell as its function.

The neurons from the olfactory organs bring their impulses into the olfactory center, where connections are made with other neurons. Outgrowths on the dorsal side of the forebrain give rise to the *pineal eye* and *parapineal eye*, both of which appear to be concerned with color changes in the ammocoete.

The paired *eyes* develop from the forebrain of the embryo. The

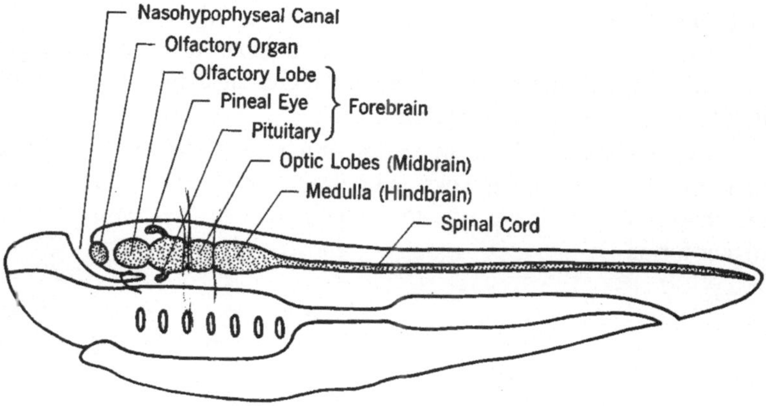

Figure 1.8: A schematic representation of the central nervous system of the ammocoete larva.

infundibulum is formed from the ventral portion of the forebrain. The *hypophysis* is formed of cells pinched off from the posterior portion of the nasohypophyseal canal, and it is an ingrowth of the superficial ectoderm.

The infundibulum, together with the hypophysis, forms the *pituitary gland*. The *midbrain* is composed largely of the *optic lobes*. These are the center for the nerves originating in the retina of the eye.

The *hindbrain* consists largely of the *medulla. A* tiny *cerebellum* is formed from the hindbrain roof. The hindbrain is a center for nerves coming from the *ears* which, in the lamprey, are organs of balance.

The *spinal cord* begins at the hindbrain and extends to the tip of the tail. In every segment a pair of *dorsal roots* and a pair of *ventral roots* connect with the spinal cord.

The dorsal roots consist mainly of sensory neurons, while the ventral roots consist of motor neurons. The nucleus of each sensory neuron is located in a ganglion on the dorsal root. In contrast to the condition in higher vertebrates, the dorsal and venal roots of the spinal nerves do not join.

The nerves of the lamprey have no myelin covering. The nervous system will also be considered in more detail when we discuss the dogfish.

SKELETAL SYSTEM

The skeleton of the adult lamprey is very poorly developed, as compared with higher chordates. This is in part the result of degeneration. The skeleton consists of cartilage cases that partially surround the brain and sense organs.

The gill region is supported by cartilaginous bars that form the branchial basket, and the vertebrae are represented by tiny pieces of cartilage adjacent to the notochord.

The notochord is the main portion of the trunk skeleton of both the ammocoete and the adult. Jaws and paired appendages are lacking, as are those portions of the skeleton associated with these structures in higher forms.

2

PROTOCHORDATES: VERTEBRATE RELATIVE

This book is about vertebrates, which, as you will see if you look at the classification above, are one of three groups within the phylum Chordata. To put them in context within the Animal Kingdom as a whole, we shall use this chapter to describe some animals which are chordates, but not vertebrates, for they throw some light on the origin of vertebrates themselves.

Urochordates and cephalochordates are often known collectively as 'protochordates'. How can living protochordates be useful in determining vertebrate origins, which must lie millions of years in the past?

The assumption is that if evolution proceeds by modification of pre-existing groups, then living animals should reflect their ancestry. Zoologists search for structures with the same origin in a group of animals; such structures are said to be 'homologous' to each other.

The problem lies in determining which structures are truly homologous and which are simply similar for functional reasons. What zoologists do is to combine the study of comparative anatomy, morphology, and embryology of living animals with data from the fossil record.

From this, a set of characteristics can be defined which is common to, in this case, all members of the phylum Chordata. It is then possible to look for these essential characteristics both in fossils and in other groups of living animals—invertebrates, for example. Hypotheses have gradually emerged about the origin of vertebrates from protochordates, and of protochordates from other invertebrates. This chapter concentrates on those features of protochordates that seem to be most relevant to vertebrate origins.

Material required

- Live *Ciona* and *Ascidiella* (or other appropriate solitary sea squirts) for observation. (The structure of the pharynx is easier to see in *Ascidiella*.)
- Slides of the ascidian tadpole.
- Whole, preserved adult *Branchiostoma.*
- Slides of whole mounts of larval *Branchiostoma.*
- Slides of transverse sections of the pharynx of *Branchiostoma.*

CHORDATE CHARACTERISTICS

Members of the phylum Chordata have five distinguishing characteristics:

1. The pharynx at the anterior end of the gut is perforated by gill slits, and has a ventral groove called the endostyle, which produces mucus and sequesters iodine. The endostyle is thought to be the forerunner in protochordates of the thyroid gland of vertebrates.
2. There is a long dorsal rod called the notochord (hence 'chordate'), running from head to tail and providing the main support for the body in primitive chordates.
3. A dorsal hollow nerve cord lies above the notochord.
4. A post-anal tail is present.
5. Primitive chordates are deuterostomes; that is, the coelom develops as pouches pushing out from the embryonic gut, and the blastopore of the embryo forms the anus, not the mouth which is a new opening.

If we add onto these five features a sixth - the presence of an internal skeleton around brain and spinal cord - we have defined not only a chordate, but a vertebrate.

UROCHORDATES

We shall concentrate here on the ascidians (also called tunicates), because they are most obviously relevant to discussions about vertebrate origins. Live sea squirts can readily be studied in the laboratory. They are at first sight unlikely looking chordates, being sessile and sac-like, but they have one important feature—the large perforated pharynx, which they use for filter feeding.

The best way to study its structure and function is to allow live animals to take in a suspension of particles, which can then be seen either with the naked eye or under a microscope. Dissection of the pharynx reveals the destination of the particles after filtration, and it is then possible to deduce certain aspects of the filtering process.

Ciona and *Ascidiella* are two genera of solitary sea squirts found around the British Isles. Small individuals of *Ciona* often reveal details of their internal anatomy because the tunic is transparent. Much can therefore be seen by transmitted light under a low-power dissecting microscope.

Ascidiella has a more opaque tunic, and less of its internal structure can be seen without dissection. Before proceeding, allow your animals to take in a suspension of carmine particles in sea water (India ink or algal suspensions are other possibilities). This can be introduced by discharging the suspension gently from a pipette, near the inhalant siphon (avoid touching the animal—it will close up).

As you then watch your animal, a red line of accumulated carmine particles should appear down one side of the pharynx. But meanwhile, look at the general layout of the animals.

General Features

1. Notice that the animals have two siphons at one end—one inhalant and one exhalant. Find out which is which. The other end of the animal is the attachment point.
2. The inhalant siphon passes into a large pharynx, which takes up most of the volume of the body. Water passes through the slits in its wall into the surrounding space or atrium, and so out via the exhalant siphon.
3. Down one side of the pharynx is a deep groove, heavily ciliated, called the endostyle. This sometimes appears (e.g. in small *Ciona)* as a wavy line visible through the tunic and body wall. It allows you to orientate the animal, as do the siphons—the endostyle is ventral, the exhalant siphon is dorsal.
4. Below the pharynx, at the base of the animal, are the intestine, the reproductive organs, and the heart. The intestine loops around and runs up one side of the pharynx to open into the atrium below the exhalant siphon. You can usually see it through the tunic.

   Ascidians are hermaphrodite, and have a single ovary and testis lying in the intestinal loop. The genital ducts also open

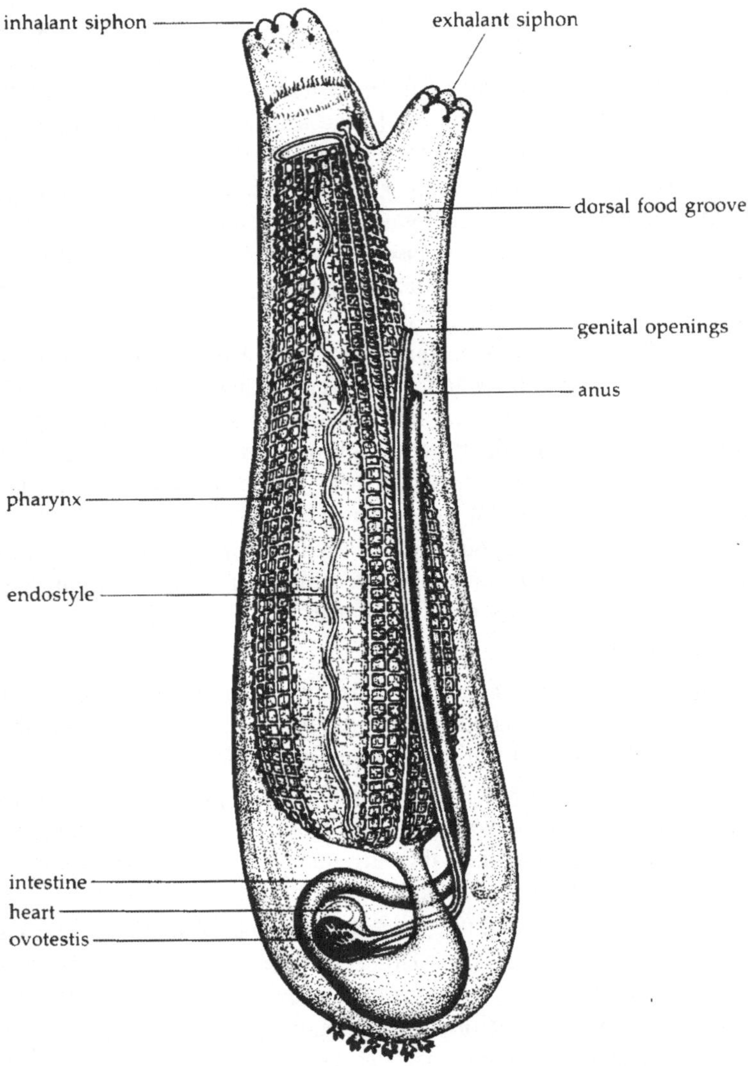

Figure 2.1: General Anatomy of Ciona.

below the exhalant siphon, but beyond the anus.

5. The heart and circulatory system are interesting, because the direction of blood flow reverses from time to time. You will not see the heart without dissection, but you may come across it as you investigate pharyngeal function.

   It is a transparent structure, shaped like a blunt finger, and lies in the intestinal loop, between intestine and gonad. The blood is also transparent, but has cells floating in it, which you can see moving as the heart beats. It is by looking at them that you will see the reversal of blood flow.

Internal Features

The object of this section is to see the structure and extent of the pharynx, and to gain an idea of how it functions. Sea squirts obtain their food entirely by filtering vast quantities of water through the pharynx—hence its size.

The best animal to use for investigation is *Ascidiella* because its pharyngeal structure is very clear upon dissection.

1. By the time you have looked at external features, your animal will have been able to take up some carmine particles and concentrate them in its pharynx. This will help you to see what is going on when food is processed.
2. Cut off the thick outer covering, or tunic, around the animal. Note its consistency as you do so—there is a cellulose-like substance in the tunic.
3. The general distribution of organs will now be clearer. Note the arrangement of siphons, pharynx, intestine, and gonads.
4. Cut open the pharynx from anterior to posterior end, passing half way between the exhalant siphon (dorsal) and the opposite side of the animal (ventral). The orientation of sea squirts is confusing, so look at Figure elsewhere in this chapter first.
5. Carefully pin out the pharynx, so that you can look at one complete side of it. Using a dissecting microscope, locate the following:
   (a) The endostyle. Can you see that it is a groove? It contains cilia, and secretes mucus, which passes out of the groove and onto each side of the pharynx as a continuous sheet. (You are unlikely to see this, because mucus secretion is usually interrupted as soon as an animal is disturbed.)
   (b) The gill slits in the walls of the pharynx.
   (c) The dorsal food groove, where food is collected into a mucous string for passing back into the intestine. You should see a string of carmine particles in the dorsal groove if your animal has processed them. Does the dorsal groove have the same appearance as the endostyle?
   (d) The entrance from pharynx to intestine. This is dorsal.

Follow the dorsal groove back until it passes into the intestine.

6. Filter-feeding involves a combination of ciliary currents and mucus secretion. The presence of a cord of accumulated carmine particles in the dorsal groove tells you that food particles are filtered by the pharynx, and concentrated dorsally.

   The food cord is then moved back along the dorsal groove to the intestine. What filters the food out of the water? And where are the cilia? You can investigate to some extent by cutting out a small piece of the pharynx wall, and mounting it on a slide, stretched under a coverslip.

   Look at it under a microscope with a x20-40 phase-contrast objective. You may see cilia beating, but in any case, you will see their arrangement on the edges of the pharyngeal slits.

   The fine filter is actually the mucous sheet, not the slits, and it is the endostyle that is responsible for secreting it. Cilia then move it up over the sides of the pharynx, so that water has to pass through it in order to exit through the gill slits. It is collected, with its filtered food particles, in the dorsal food groove. This feeding process is a fundamental chordata characteristic. Feeding occurs in a very similar way in the cephalochordate, *Branchiostoma,* and also in larval lampreys.

Ascidian Larvae

Clearly, the organisation of adult sea squirts is dominated by the large surface area of the pharynx required to collect enough food. Apart from the perforated pharynx, little else qualifies these animals for membership of the chordates.

However, if we look at their development, an altogether different picture emerges. The fertilised egg of ascidians develops into a swimming, tadpole-shaped larva with a dorsal tubular nerve cord, a notochord, and a post-anal tail.

Living larvae are hard to observe and collect, because they are tiny and may be very short-lived. Look at a prepared slide instead. Note the general structure. The tadpole larva shows, at a very basic level, some important features of chordate organisation.

These are the presence of a post-anal tail, supported by a notochord, which provides the force for locomotion; and a dorsal nerve cord running along into the tail above the notochord. Rows of muscle cells surrounding the notochord contract and, because the notochord is incompressible, their forces are translated into undulations of the tail.

Structures concerned with feeding and other bodily functions are concentrated at the anterior end in chordates, and do not extend into the tail, whose function is to move the animal through the water. The role of the tadpole larva is to select a site for the adult to settle.

It is also a dispersal mechanism, because the adult does not move. Attachment occurs by adhesive glands at the anterior end; the tail and notochord are resorbed, and eventually the adult form develops.

Note that a functional perforated pharynx is not present in the larva, which does not feed, although gill slits begin to appear. The larva is quite different from the adult, and its development up to metamorphosis is very like that of the next group—the cephalochordates—to which we shall now turn.

CEPHALOCHORDATES

Cephalochordates - lancelets - used to belong to the genus *Amphioxus* until it was discovered that the name *Branchiostoma* had precedence. Many people still use 'amphioxus' as a common name for these animals.

Branchiostoma looks like a small, laterally flattened fish, pointed at both ends. It spends its adult life semi-embedded in sand with its head sticking out into the water.

It possesses all the features that are considered basic to chordate organisation, but it is not a vertebrate because it has no internal skeleton like theirs.

Branchiostoma is a difficult animal to dissect successfully, but a combination of whole preserved adults and prepared slides of younger stages should reveal most of the essential aspects of its structure.

External Features

1. The head has no eyes, ears, or jaws; but a group of buccal cirri extend outwards from around the mouth.
2. The skin is transparent, and through it may be seen the V-shaped segmental muscles used in locomotion.
3. Look along the ventral side of the animal for an opening. Behind it, the body narrows. This atrial pore marks the posterior end of the pharynx, which is very large and perforated by numerous gill slits.

   These are invisible externally because they are covered by folds of the body wall, which form an outer cavity around the pharynx, called the atrium. The whole arrangement is reminiscent of ascidians.

4. Posterior to the atrial pore is another opening. Can you find it? This is the anus. What proportion of the animal's length is made up of its post-anal tail?

   Note that there is a tail 'fin', and also a median fin fold. These are not the same as the fins of true fishes, because they have

Internal Features

1. Underneath the segmental muscles and running from the tip of the head to the tip of the tail is the notochord. It consists of muscular plates stacked within a sheath made of collagen fibres.

   Fluid-filled spaces within and outside the notochordal cells provide what amounts to a hydrostatic skeleton. The notochord is incompressible but elastic, and is an excellent support for a small animal.

   All vertebrate embryos also have notochords, and the structure is retained even in some adult vertebrates. Note that the notochord extends right into the head of *Branchiostoma*. This is probably an adaptation to a burrowing habit.
2. Above the notochord is a dorsal hollow nerve cord. You can see it in longitudinal and transverse sections - it has black pigment cells distributed along its length.
3. Ventral to the notochord is the large pharynx, whose walls are perforated by elongated gill slits. Transverse sections reveal a complex groove in the floor of the pharynx, which is the endostyle. Its function is the same as that of the ascidian endostyle.
4. Various structures mark the anterior end of the pharynx. They are the velum, with its tentacles, and the ciliated wheel organ. The velar tentacles are sensory, and the pharynx can be closed off by a velar sphincter. The cilia of the wheel organ help to propel food into the pharynx.
5. At the posterior end the pharynx passes into the intestine, and almost at the junction a blind diverticulum leads off the intestine and passes forwards, alongside the pharynx. This structure, called the mid-gut diverticulum, is where digestion occurs. You can see it in transverse sections through the pharyngeal area.
6. The intestine passes straight back to the anus, some distance posterior to the atrial pore.

7. Look also for rows of gonads (either male or female) along the body. The sexes are separate; eggs and sperm are shed into the atrium. Fertilisation occurs externally, and the larvae develop free in the sea.
8. The circulatory system does not include a heart; but its arrangement foreshadows that of all vertebrates. Blood flows forwards in a ventral vessel below the pharynx, upwards between the gill slits, and then posteriorly in the dorsal aorta above the pharynx.

   Veins collect the blood from the tissues and pass it forwards again to a dilation called the sinus venosus, just posterior to the pharynx. This is the site of the heart in fishes. Blood circulation is maintained by contractions in various parts of the system.

   Oxygen is probably taken up through the skin, as well as via the gills. The blood has no haemoglobin and no erythrocytes - they are both vertebrate developments.

VERTEBRATE ORIGINS

What about vertebrate origins? This is not the place to enter into the arguments about precisely how vertebrates might have evolved. Suffice it to say that it is thought that a form resembling the ascidian tadpole was at the foundation of the phylum Chordata.

The characteristics of chordate organisation certainly suggest derivation from an active, motile ancestor. The difficulty is that it is the larval stages, that are active in urochordates and cephalochordates, not the adults.

So, how can larval stages become appropriate ancestors when it is, after all, the sessile adults which breed? This awkward fact can be avoided by invoking a process called neoteny (or paedogenesis), in which the gonads become sexually mature although the animal still has its larval morphology.

Neoteny occurs in several vertebrate groups, such as the Amphibia, and also in the Urochordata and Cephalochordata. An entire class of urochordates, the Larvacea, is composed of neotenous forms, which retain the morphology of the tadpole larva as adults.

The significance of neoteny is that if larval stages are *morphologically* different from the adults, but become sexually mature, then a whole new lineage could arise—the original adult stage would be bypassed completely. Thus, vertebrate evolution from protochordates would have involved the appearance of a tadpole larva, which underwent neoteny. The cephalochordates are believed to represent one offshoot from this sort of stage, and the vertebrates another, possibly later one, in which a sessile adult stage was dispensed with completely, and the active motile nature of the neotenous larvae was retained and became predominant.

Filter-feeding was the original chordate feeding mechanism - hence the perforated pharynx. Its incidental function of gaseous exchange later predominated. The nerve cord, notochord, and tail were all evolved to co-ordinate movement, and these features still prevail in modern fish.

3

Fish: Some Different Designs

In the previous chapter we introduced the various groups surviving today which seem closest to the point of vertebrate ancestry. Now we turn to the group that represents the earliest expression of vertebrate evolution—the fish.

Fish first appeared some 550 million years ago or more, around the junction of Cambrian and Ordovician periods in our geological record. At that time fish had no jaws, which is why this chapter includes a discussion of the organisation of living jawless fish, even though the lamprey is a highly specialised and somewhat enigmatic agnathan descendant.

Later on, jawed fishes appeared, and they have since evolved into a great variety of forms. They are the most numerous vertebrates, and have colonised all possible aquatic habitats. Some even venture onto land for short periods, and one group —the sarcopterygian fish, of whom few now remain—gave rise to all the land vertebrates.

What were the secrets of the success of fishes? Two of them were certainly the evolution of jaws and paired fins; and the extensive adaptive radiation which followed these innovations was a result of exploiting the vast range of aquatic habitats open to animals with versatile feeding and locomotion.

Modern fish have two fundamentally different designs, reflected in the classification above as the two classes Chondrichthyes and Osteichthyes, generally referred to loosely as the cartilaginous and bony fish. We shall discuss only elasmobranchs and teleosts within these groups.

At the outset, some comment is necessary on the evolutionary relationships of cartilaginous and bony fish. It is easy to get the impression that cartilaginous forms are primitive, and that bony fish evolved from them; an impression that is strengthened by the fact that all vertebrate embryos first lay down their skeletons as cartilage and form bone later.

However, teleosts did not evolve from elasmobranchs - they represent two quite separate lines of fish evolution, which have been separate for hundreds of millions of years, since the earliest jawed fishes appeared and perhaps before.

The primitive fish skeleton way back in the days of the fossil aganathans, evolved cartilages, bone, and a notochord. So both cartilage and bone were primitive skeletal materials, and elasmobranchs and teleosts have exploited them in different ways.

By the end of this chapter, you should have a good idea of how these fishes are organised and how they have adapted to particular modes of life. But first, the jawless fish provide a conceptual link with the last chapter, as well as being a logical starting point for a discussion of vertebrate form and function.

Material Required

- Preserved ammocoete larvae; *Branchiostoma* for comparison.
- Adult lamprey *Lampetra fluviatilis,* preserved and/or fresh-frozen or live (preserved material is useful for section cutting).
- Adult eels, *Anguilla,* for comparison; live, fresh-frozen or preserved.
- Slides of bone and cartilage.
- Examples of fish skeletons, e.g. dogfish, *Scyliorhinus,* and trout, *Salmo;* skull of cod, *Gadus.*
- Fresh-frozen *Scyliorhinus* or *Squalus;* whiting, *Merlangius;* mackerel, *Scomber;* ray, *Raja;* plaice, *Pleuronectes.*
- Teleost eggs and embryos; embryos of *Scyliorhinus* and/or a pregnant female *Squalus acanthias.*

JAWLESS FISH: AGRIATHA

The earliest fish had no jaws and no true paired fins, yet they flourished for some 150 million years and gave rise to a range of different forms. Two types of agnathans have survived until today in rather specialised niches. One, the hagfishes or myxinoids, is a group of blind eel-like animals that burrow and live on the sea bottom.

We shall not discuss them here, for they are difficult to obtain for practical observation. The other group, the lampreys, inhabit rivers and can be caught as adults or larvae.

The larvae are particularly. interesting because they have features reminiscent of *Branchiostoma,* and so may be indicative of ancestral vertebrate morphology.

They have been intensively studied for this reason. We shall look at lampreys from the point of view of their chordate and vertebrate characteristics, and then compare them with a bony fish of similar external form (an eel) to emphasise exactly why they are considered primitive by comparison.

The Ammocoete Larva

Most of the life of a lamprey (e.g. *Lampetra fluviatilis*) is spent as a freshwater larval stage called the ammocoete. Eggs are laid in rivers and streams; the larvae hatch, feed, and grow in freshwater; then metamorphose into adults, which may or may not move down to the sea (depending on the species) for a year or two before returning to rivers to spawn.

All lampreys die soon after spawning. Ammocoetes are filter-feeders and live in burrows with their heads protruding. Their mode of life is thus one point of similarity with *Branchiostoma.*

External Features

Note the following:

1. Shape, post-anal tail, and distribution of fins. There are no paired fins but there are median fins—one or two dorsals and a caudal fin. The main propulsive force is produced by undulation of the body, which also serves for burrowing. Blocks of muscle (myotomes) are visible through the skin, giving the body a segmented appearance. Find the cloaca, and note the extent of the post-anal tail.
2. The number of gill openings. Look back to *Branchiostoma;* it has many more openings from the pharynx, but because the whole is enclosed in the atrial folds, only one major outlet is visible externally. Numerous separate gill openings were a feature of many fossil agnathans.
3. The ammocoete head. Look at it preferably under a dissecting microscope. The mouth is covered by a flap called the oral

hood, open ventrally. Inside it are branching oral tentacles, and the mouth is in the middle of them.

4. Turn the animal onto its belly and look at the top of the head. You will see a funnel-shaped opening raised above the body surface. It is the nostril or nasohypophyseal opening, and is characteristic of lampreys and a whole . group of fossil agnathans.

   No other vertebrates have this sort of opening. Note that it is single and on top of the head. Internally, it extends past the olfactory organ to the ventral part of the forebrain, where it is associated with tissue that is the equivalent of the pituitary gland of higher vertebrates.

   Just posterior to the nasohypophyseal opening is a pale non-pigmented area of skin. It lies over the pineal organ, which is light sensitive.

Ammocoetes are best investigated internally by cutting sections of them in various planes with a sharp razor blade. Assuming that you have several animals available, one can be cut in half dorsoventrally from head to tail and one horizontally.

A third can be used for a series of thick transverse sections from anterior to posterior. It is impossible to be absolutely certain of the organisation of the animal without information from all these sources—the same holds for the adult lamprey.

Longitudinal Sections

Try to produce two equal halves of your ammocoete by cutting firmly and symmetrically through the nasohypophyseal opening and gill region, and back towards the tail. Then, using a dissecting microscope, look at the following:

1. The shape of the oral hood, the distribution of oral tentacles, and the position of the mouth itself.
2. The large folds (one on each side) just inside the mouth. They are the velar folds or velum, and are like valves over the entrance to the pharynx, helping in gill ventilation. The cartilages supporting the velum in agnathans may have been those that evolved into the jaws of higher fish. They are the anterior members of a series, otherwise supporting the gills.
3. The gills, behind the velum. They are pouches, with folds of tissue bearing lateral filaments. These are the feeding and respiratory structures of the ammocoete, and so functionally

resemble the perforated pharynx of *Branchiostoma*. However, they are not the same structurally.

Look at them carefully; the gill filaments are more like those of teleosts. You will see the relationship between the external gill openings, and the internal pouches by cutting horizontal and transverse sections.

4. The arrangement of structures dorsal to the gills. Immediately above them is the dorsal aorta (best seen in transverse sections), then the notochord. Note the position of its anterior end; compare with *Branchiostoma*. Dorsal to the notochord are the brain and nerve cord. They are in this position in all chordates and all vertebrates.
5. The nasohypophyseal opening. You should have cut it almost exactly in half. The canal does not extend right down under the brain in ammocoetes, though it does in adult lampreys. Part of it is solid in ammocoetes and opens at metamorphosis.
6. Structures ventral to the pharynx. The main thing to notice is the endostyle, extending from the first gill pouch to the fifth. It is a double structure anteriorly and tripartite posteriorly. The spiral posterior end of its medial chamber is conspicuous.

   The endostyle opens to the pharynx at only one point, about half way along. So although it has a similar function to the *Branchiostoma* endostyle, it is more enclosed and has a more complex structure. Food is collected by ciliary action after it has been trapped in mucous sheets.
7. Structures posterior to the gills. You should be able to see that the oesophagus leaves the pharynx dorsally, passes dorsal to the heart, and to the liver. Follow the intestine to the cloaca. You will also see developing gonads.

Horizontal Sections

Now cut an ammocoete horizontally into two symmetrical dorsal and ventral halves. Cut through the gill series at the level of the gill openings. The main object of this is to see the spatial relationship between them and the gill pouches. Look at the orientation of the gill filaments.

Where are the gill openings in relation to them? Note that in order to reach the outside, most of the water from the pharynx must flow through the gill filaments. Ventilation of the gills is achieved by muscular pumping of velum and branchial skeleton—it is not produced solely by

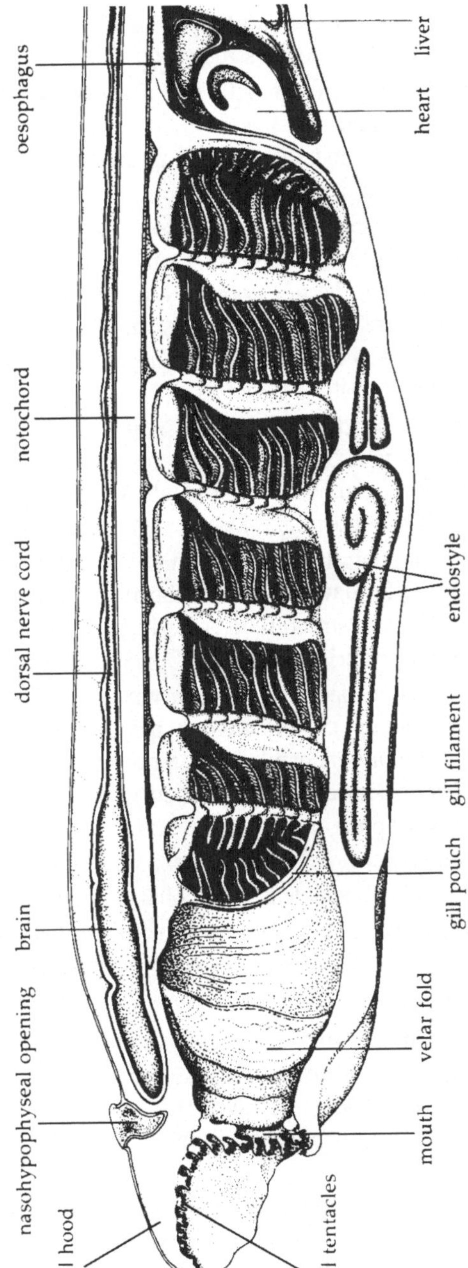

Figure 3.1: Anterior end of an ammocoete (median longitudinal section)

cilia. Ciliary ventilation alone is efficient enough only in animals below a certain size—it suffices in Branchiostoma.

Transverse Sections

It is very instructive to cut thick sections from the mouth back to the region of the intestine. Co-ordinate what you find with your observations on the longitudinal sections. Figures elsewhere in this chapter show prepared sections at the level of pharynx and gut. Suggestions follow for cutting at other levels; make sections of about 2 mm thickness, and cut in series from anterior to posterior.

1. *Mouth*. Cut at the posterior edge of the oral hood. The section shows size and position of mouth, oral tentacles, muscle blocks, and cartilages in the hood.
2. *Velum*. A section at this level allows you to see how the paired velar folds hang across the pharyngeal entrance; and shows a transverse section through the anterior brain and eyes, which are covered with skin in ammocoetes.

   You may or may not include the extreme anterior end of the notochord. Look for a thin cartilaginous case around the brain; this is the cranium.
3. At various levels through the gill series. Again, cut through an external gill opening. Note parts of the brain (e.g. auditory capsules—lampreys have only the internal ear, as do all fish), cranium, notochord, and all other structures labelled in Figure elsewhere in this chatper.

   Towards the back of the pharynx, note the point at which the oesophagus appears. Compare the whole organisation of the ammocoete with that of *Branchiostoma.*

We have gone into some detail with the ammocoete, because it is a pivotal animal in studies of vertebrate functional morphology. It is also easily studied and understood, and so provides a good basis for understanding all other vertebrates. There is no reason why you should not be able to see for yourselves all the structures mentioned here - and probably several that are not.

The Adult Lamprey

A drastic metamorphosis occurs after a larval life of varying length, in which the free-living ammocoete becomes a parasitic adult. The adult looks quite similar, but has completely altered its method of feeding.

External Features

1. Note shape and pigmentation. Most fish are darker above. Why?
2. Freshly killed or live lampreys feel slimy and smooth. Are there any scales?
3. The fins are as in the ammocoete, but females in breeding condition have an anal fin.
4. There are still seven gill openings. Find the nasohypophyseal opening, and note that the eyes are now functional.
5. The mouth region is much altered. There is a circular, fringed sucker containing horny teeth. These are products of the epidermis and are not homologous with the teeth of higher vertebrates. Lampreys hold on to objects (e.g. stones) with their mouths, and also to other fish on which they feed.

Internal features

Unless otherwise stated, assume that these resemble the situation in ammocoetes. Proceed as for the ammocoete, cutting sections of your animals. It is not easy to understand what has happened to the pharynx during metamorphosis without cutting both longitudinal and transverse sections.

1. Behind the mouth, a large mass of muscle can be seen extending right back under the pharynx. These are the lingual muscles which operate the toothed tongue like a piston. It can be pulled in and out, using its teeth to rasp at the flesh of its prey.

   Enzymes and anti-clotting substances are secreted onto the food. The animal meanwhile is attached by its sucker, under which considerable negative pressure can be developed.
2. You cannot immediately see the gill filaments in a median longitudinal section. They have been closed off behind a respiratory tube, and are reached by small internal openings. Find the gill filaments and sort out their relationship with the modified pharynx.

   What is the functional reason for this change? It is that the food and feeding method have changed. Adult lampreys are not filter-feeders; in fact, their food is prevented from reaching the gills (why?).

   Thus, in the adult lamprey, respiration is separated from feeding; it is in other fishes too, although plankton-feeders can trap food on their gill rakers.

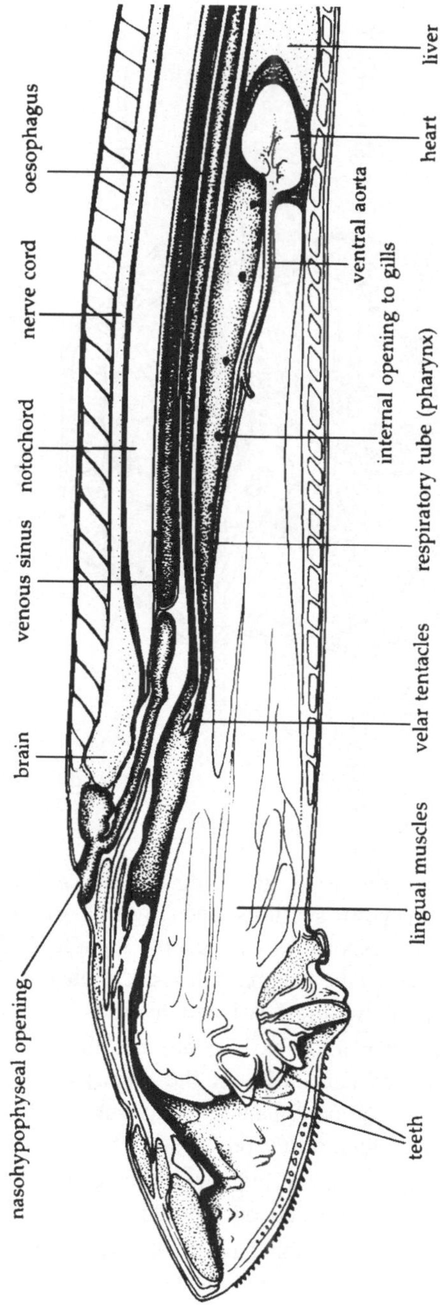

Figure 3.2: Anterior end of an adult lamprey (median longitudinal section).

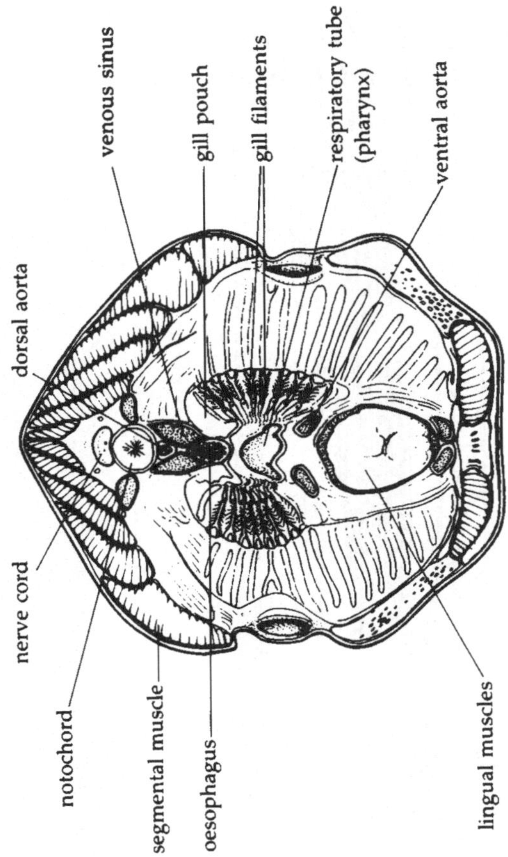

Figure 3.3: Transverse section through pharyngeal region of an adult lamprey.

3. Where does the food go if not to the gill region? Look carefully at your sections and Figures elsewhere in this chapter. The oesophagus has become separated off and is now a tube, dorsal to the original ammocoete pharynx. Posteriorly, it still runs above the heart and liver.
4. The large velar folds have gone, but there are small velar tentacles which can close off the respiratory tube from any food entering the oesophagus. The velum is still important in controlling ventilation currents too.
5. How does the lamprey breathe while feeding? It can in fact pump water both in and out of its external gill openings.
6. Your adult lamprey will have relatively mature gonads. You will be unable to find any ducts leading from these to the

cloaca—there are none. Sperm and ova leave the body cavity via special pores which develop only just before spawning. This is another primitive feature of lampreys.

The Lamprey Compared with the Eel

(Class Agnatha, *Lampetra tluviatilis*
Class Osteichthyes, *Anguilla anguilla*)

The object of this section is to put the lamprey in context. Why is it considered a primitive vertebrate? The reasons can be highlighted by looking at it alongside a more advanced fish of similar form, and it is most frequently confused with eels, which are teleosts.

Superficially they are very similar. Both can be caught in rivers at certain times of year, both have similar locomotion in which the body is undulated, and their shape is adapted to this type of movement.

Lampreys, of course, have a sucker, but this is a specialist feature not a universal characteristic of agnathans, and so is irrelevant to our discussion of their primitive nature.

Table 3.1: The state of the main vertebrate characteristics in the lamprey and the eel.

	Lamprey	*Eel*
Cranium	+ Cartilaginous	+ Bony; cartilaginous
template in embryo		
Vertebrae	– Cartilaginous nubbins	+ Bony in adult
along nerve cord		
Notochord	+	+ Only in embryo
Dorsal nerve	+	+ cord
External gill	+ Seven	+ One *openings*
Gill filaments	+ Seven sets	+ Four sets
Paired fins	–	+
Scales	–	+
Jaws	–	+
Nostrils	+ Single, median	+ Paired, lateral

External Features

1. Note general body form. The eel is more flexible than the lamprey. Its whole body is thrown into waves, which thrust against the water, and so produce forward movement. Note that the posterior part of the body is laterally flattened. Is it in the lamprey? The thrust of the tail fin alone is insignificant

(compare this situation with the role of the tail fin in, say, a shark). Body flexibility is much affected by the nature of the supporting skeleton, which is totally different in these two animals (see below).

2. What is the extent of the tail region? All vertebrates have post-anal tails, so look for the anus in the eel. Compare its position with that in the lamprey.
3. Feel the skin; look at it under the microscope. The eel has tiny scales formed from bone, and embedded in the dermis of the skin. If you cannot see them, look again; try under a phase-contrast objective.

   Lampreys have no scales, an unusual condition for a fish. Dermal bone was commonly present in fossil fish, including agnathans, but no sign of it remains in lampreys. Teleosts, on ' the other hand, retain it as scales and as additional bones in their skeletons.
4. Eels have paired fins as well as median fins. Agnathans never evolved true paired fins. Look at the eel; its median fins are fused together. Where are the paired fins? Are there pectoral and pelvic fins? Why might the paired fins of eels be reduced? Are they of major importance in locomotion?
5. The mouth of the eel has jaws. Agnathans by definition have no jaws.
6. There are two eyes and paired nostrils. No equivalent of the nasohypophyseal opening exists. Find the eel's nostrils—is there just one opening on each side? Water flows through the nostrils and there is no connection with the mouth.
7. Eels do not have a row of gill openings down each side. In teleosts, there is only one opening a side (unusually small in eels), but this does not mean that there is only one set of gill filaments.
8. In the eel you can see a faint line along the side of the body. This is the lateral line, a system of sense organs sunk into a canal, sensitive to water displacements impinging on the animal, and always innervated by branches of cranial nerves. All jawed fishes have a lateral line. Lampreys have the appropriate sense organs, but they are not sunk below the surface in canals and so represent a more primitive condition.

Internal Features

If you try to proceed with the eel as you did with the lamprey, you will find it more difficult to cut sections. Why is this? It is due to a fundamental difference in their skeletons. Probably the best way to proceed is to make a midventral incision at the anus, and work anteriorly from it.

Pin the animal out and concentrate mainly on the branchial region and the extent of the body cavity. Prepared cross-sections of the body will help your comparison with the lamprey.

Try to investigate the following:

1. What is the arrangement of the gill filaments? How many gill arches are there (i.e. sets of gill filaments plus supports—seven in lampreys)? Look at their relationship to the gill opening.

   Eels (and teleosts generally) have an operculum—a bony flap over the gill outlet which assists in pumping water in through the mouth and out over the gills. In eels, skin grows over the operculum, and the gills are enclosed except for a very small outlet near the pectoral fins.
2. Where are the jaws in relation to the gills? They probably evolved from cartilages related to those supporting the gills - possibly the velar cartilages. Look again at the position of the velum in ammocoetes.
3. All vertebrates have a cranium, a bony or cartilaginous box around the brain. In lampreys, it is cartilaginous; in eels, bony. You should have seen it in your lamprey sections. The bone of the eel's cranium will prevent your sectioning its head easily.
4. What is the main supporting structure for the body? In lampreys, you saw a large notochord, with a consistency like cartilage. Eels have an articulated bony vertebral column. Investigate this by cutting thick sections of the tail region.

   The centra of the vertebrae have replaced the notochord. Subdivision of the axial skeleton into many small articulated units provides, or can provide, a degree of flexibility unattainable with the elastic, but stiff, notochord. You may ask why lampreys are classified as vertebrates if they have no vertebrae.

   In fact, the infallible characteristic of vertebrates is not the presence of vertebrae but of a cranium, which lampreys have. (An alternative name for the subphylum is 'Craniata'.) They

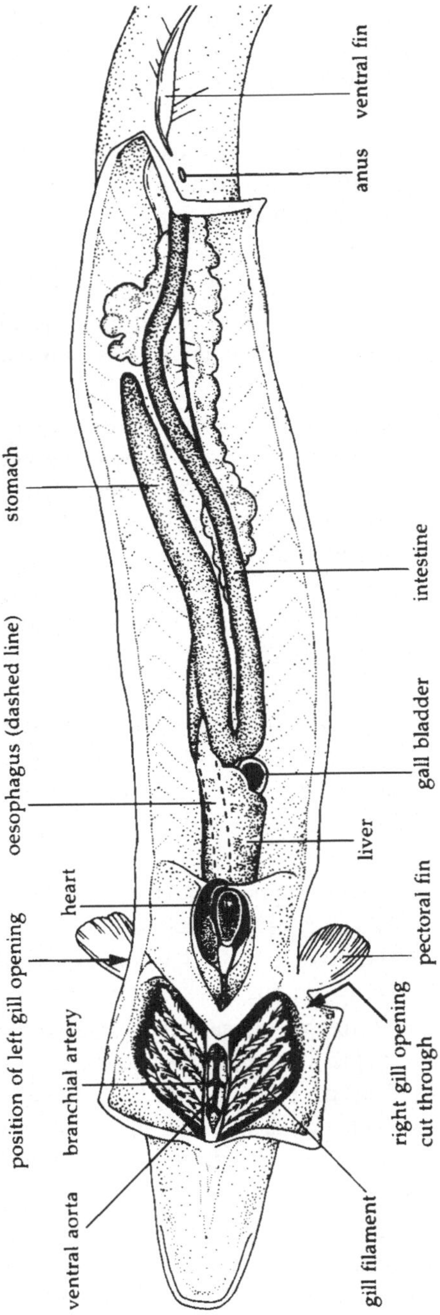

Figure 3.4: Dissection of pharyngeal region and body cavity of the eel.

also have nubbins of cartilage along their nerve cord, in the correct position for vertebrae. In any case, 'vertebrate' is a word now too much a part of common usage to abandon, even though it is not strictly descriptive of lampreys.

Before you go on to the next section, be sure you understand the basic characteristics of chordates and vertebrates. Refer back to this secion and the previous chapter when in doubt later on. The rest of this chapter deals with the two main groups of living fishes. As you work through it, keep referring back to the lamprey to see how these other fishes differ. Also, remember that the eel is a teleost, and so can be used later on as an example of another teleost form.

TWO DESIGNS COMPARED: ELASMOBRANCHS AND TELEOSTS

This section aims to analyse what distinguishes these two groups of fish, and it also introduces the range of forms within each group. Rather than discuss each separately, a comparative approach is adopted throughout.

If you look carefully at the animals, you can see most of the major features that are used to distinguish them in zoological classification. These involve aspects of external form, skeletal anatomy, and various internal features. Together, your observations will also convey information about feeding and locomotory adaptations.

Organ systems will not be discussed as such, because they do not on the whole show the most obvious differences between teleosts and elasmobranchs. Physiological differences, which are very interesting, can only be mentioned in passing, because they are neither easily revealed just by looking at an animal nor easily demonstrated by simple dissection.

A word is needed about the fish chosen for observation. The prime concern was availability, but the animals also illustrate some points about evolution and adaptive radiation within the groups. The ray and the dogfish are good examples of the two main body forms in the elasmobranchs—one adapted for mid-water swimming, one for living on the sea bottom.

The teleosts used include both primitive and advanced forms. Eels (previous section) are classified in a superorder of their own, along with other fish that have similar larval stages. They probably branched off early in teleost evolution.

Trout belong in a superorder thought to have given rise to all the dominant living teleosts (not including the eels). Whiting, mackerel, and plaice are representatives of the most advanced teleosts - the Paracanthopterygii and the Acanthopterygii. The latter, particularly, have the most diverse shapes, forms of locomotion, and methods of feeding.

The Histology of Bone and Cartilage

Both these tissues are products of the embryonic mesoderm in all vertebrates. Most vertebrates have both, but some species have permanently unossified skeletons not because they are 'degenerate' but for sound adaptive reasons.

Examples are the elasmobranchs, sturgeons, coelacanths, and many deep-sea fishes. Land vertebrates on the whole require the greater strength of bone for support, but they still use cartilage in their embryos, and in various places throughout their adult skeletons.

Cartilage and bone are easily distinguished histologically. What you see in cartilage is groups of cells surrounded by an amorphous ground substance, made by the cells. The ground substance is glycoprotein, containing varying amounts of fibrous material such as collagen and elastic fibres.

There are no blood vessels or nerves in the ground substance as there often are in bone. Bone is stronger because the extracellular material is calcified. Mineral resembling hydroxyapatite is laid down on the collagen fibres in the ground substance, which also contains some glycoprotein.

The cells which lay down the fibres and their crystals become enclosed in cavities in the bone, often connected by thin canals. Calcified fibres may become orientated along the stress lines of a bone, which gives it prodigious tensile strength.

The calcium in bone is metabolically active, for bones can act as calcium stores from which calcium can be resorbed if required. The same applies to phosphate. It is possible that this was one reason for the origin of bone.

There are various types of bone, depending upon the arrangement of fibres in it. Dentine is also similar to bone, but the cells that synthesise it do not become enclosed in it. Instead, they control production by extending processes into the dentine and withdrawing their cell bodies as it grows.

The Skeletons of Modem Elasmobranchs and Teleosts

Vertebrate skeletons consist of:

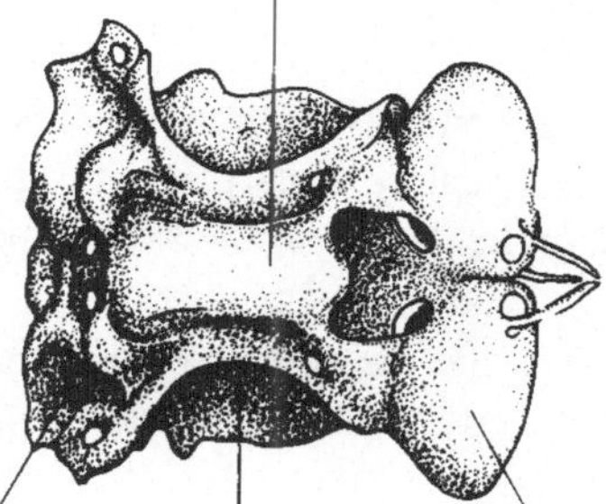

Figure 3.5: Skull of dogfish, scyliorhinus (dorsal view).

(1) a cartilaginous or bony case around the brain, called a cranium;
(2) supports for the gills (gill arches), jaws, and tongue, called the visceral skeleton; and
(3) the supports for the rest of the body and its appendages, the axial and appendicular skeleton. These components are distinguished not just for convenience but also because of their embryological and evolutionary origins.

We shall look at the skeletons of a dogfish (elasmobranch) and trout (teleost). It is not obvious that they are made of different materials, but it is possible to see in them some of the major structural differences between the two groups.

The Skull

Skulls are best understood as consisting of boxes around the fore-, mid- and hind-brain, and their respective sense organs of smell, sight, and hearing. Skull shape is essentially determined by that of the brain it encloses, which makes sense embryologically because the main compartments of the brain develop early, and the cranium forms later around them.

Other factors, such as muscle attachments, can also influence skull shape. The simple situation of a cartilaginous case around brain, eyes, ears, and olfactory organs exists in the dogfish. This is a robust structure which never ossifies, although it does become impregnated with some calcium.

Note that the upper jaw is not fused with the cranium. In teleosts, the skull has become much more complicated. It has a bewildering array of component bones. Although it develops in embryos as a cartilaginous braincase much like that of the dogfish, it is later replaced and added to by bone.

Skull bones can come from two sources: either they arise in connective tissue and replace a cartilaginous template (endochondral bone) or they arise in the dermis of the skin without preceding cartilage (dermal bone).

In teleosts not only has the braincase been replaced by endochondral bone (as it is in most vertebrates, including man), but numerous dermal bones have been laid down around the braincase and some have fused with it. They have arisen in the skin over the roof of the braincase, in the cheek, the sides of the mouth, and in the palate.

A 'skull' in a mammal is also a composite structure of endochondral and dermal bones. In fishes, it is easier to see this dual origin without actually studying embryos, and many of the bones involved can be traced throughout the evolution of the vertebrate skull.

Teeth are also dermal structures, and the lower jaw is a product of both endochondral and dermal bone formation. Think about why embryonic vertebrates make skeletal structures out of cartilage early in development, and then replace and add to them with bone.

There are good functional reasons for it. The skull of the cod is large enough to show most of the component bones clearly. Compare it with the dogfish cranium and jaws. The pattern of dermal bones in teleost skulls is not typical of vertebrates as a whole, because there are extra bony plates, as well such structures as the operculum, which land vertebrates do not have.

It is unnecessary to know the names of all the bones, so we simply point out some that are of interest; you will recognise others when you come to other chapter of this book. Note that endochondral and dermal bones look the same—it is only their origin that is different. Note the following:

1. The position of the true braincase (endochondral bone), indicated by hatching in Figure elsewhere in this book.
2. Some dermal bones formed in the skin over the braincase, and closing it off dorsally: parietals and post-parietals.
3. A dermal bone in the side of the face: the lacrimal.
4. Dermal bones of the upper jaw: premaxillae and maxillae. Which bears teeth?
5. A dermal bone of the lower jaw: the dentary. The premaxilla,

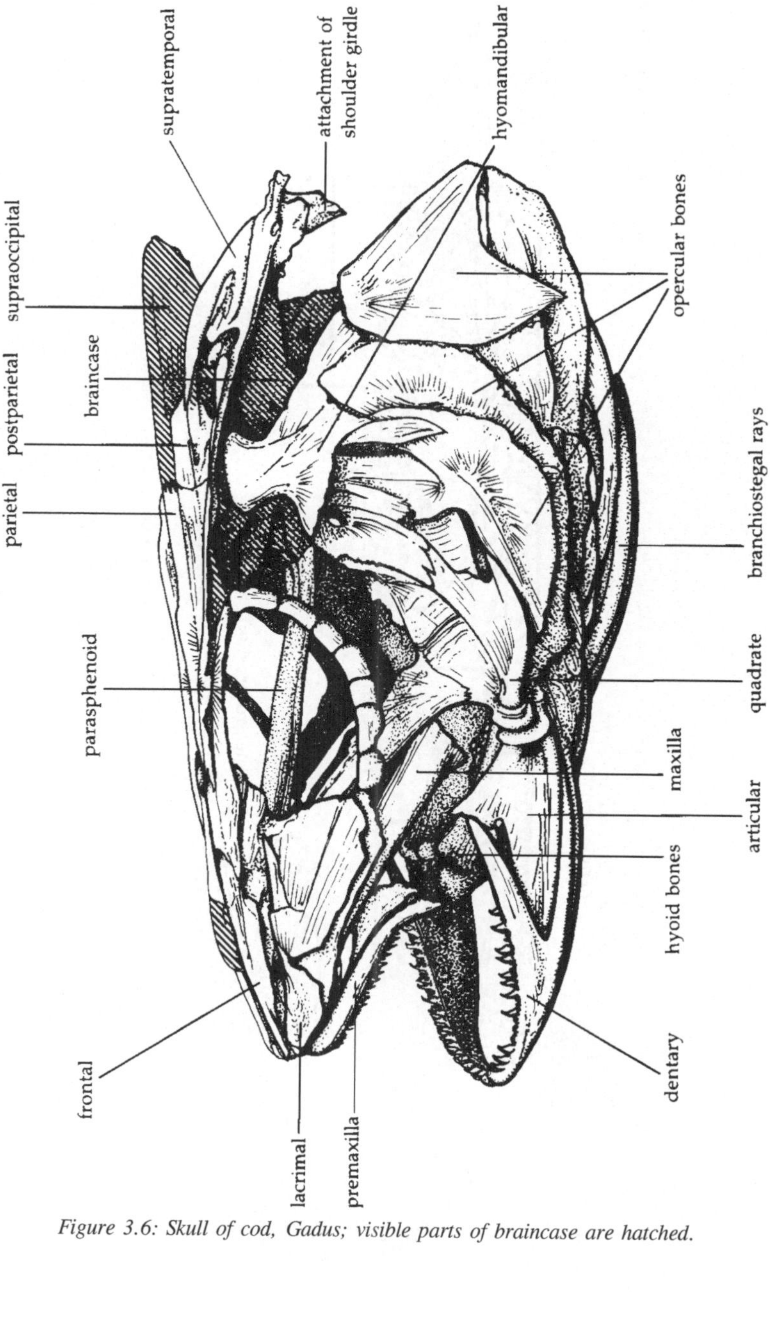

Figure 3.6: Skull of cod, Gadus; visible parts of braincase are hatched.

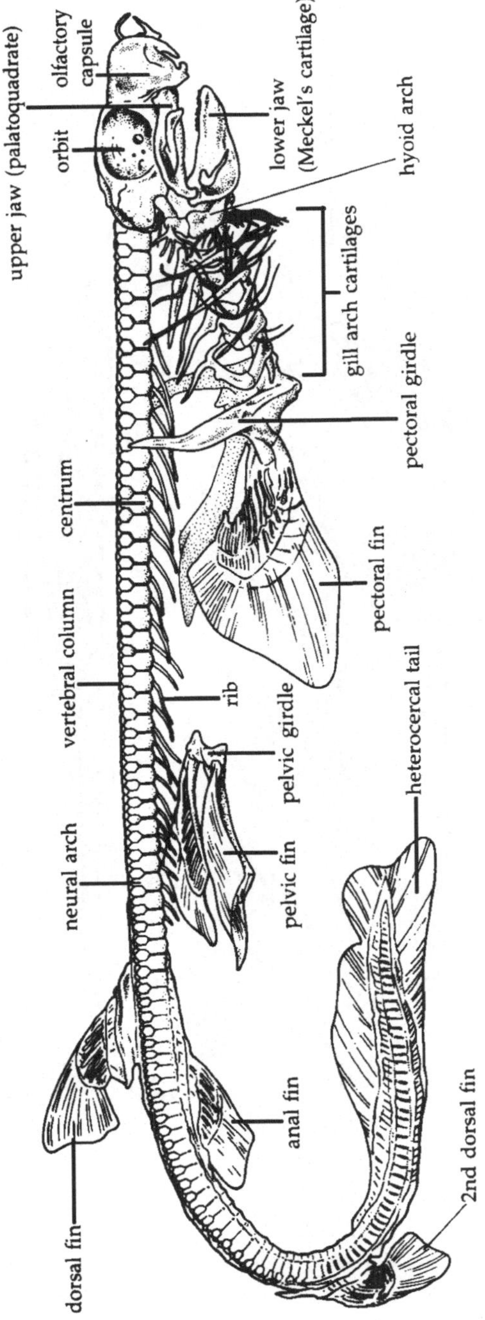

Figure 3.7: Skeleton of dogfish Scyliorhinus (lateral view).

maxilla, and dentary functionally replace the anterior parts of the elasmobranch jaw cartilages, because they bear teeth.

6. The endochondral bones that are the homologues of the dogfish jaws are the quadrate and articular. They are joined together just as they are in elasmobranchs, and become of great significance in the story of the evolution of the mammalian middle ear. Do these fish have a middle ear?
7. The hyoid arch is also represented as the hyomandibular dorsally, and the various hyoid bones. Whereas the hyoid arch is an important strut for the back of the jaw in dogfish, it has a more complex role in teleosts.

   Its lower parts can move backwards and forwards, and the hyomandibular, quadrate, and the whole opercular series can move outwards and inwards.
8. The opercular bones are dermal bones; so are the branchiostegal rays. This whole assemblage of bones serves to ventilate the gills.
9. Now look at the skull as a whole, anci note that the nasal region is very short in teleosts. It is larger in elasmobranchs—their sense of smell is very well developed. In land vertebrates, the tendency is to expand the nasal region, and as it were push the frontal and parietal bones back towards the occiput.

The effect of adding on dermal bones to the simple braincase and jaws is to interpose a more superficial skeletal layer between them and the exterior, and to take over or augment certain of their original functions. As you learn more about other vertebrates, you will be able to trace this tendency throughout the different vertebrate groups.

The Visceral Skeleton

The gill region of elasmobranchs is expanded in comparison to that of teleosts, and is therefore easier to see. The dogfish skeleton side on shows that the gill series follows immediately behind the jaws. Not only that, but the jaws look like enlarged members of the same series of cartilages as those supporting the gills—they are just more massive and do not carry gill filaments.

Evidence from both the embryology of fishes and the fossil record supports the idea of an origin of jaws from the anterior members of the gill cartilages. Jaws were a great innovation, allowing the capture of larger food and providing a means of holding on.

Each gill support has four components, the two central ones bearing the gill filaments on their posterior edges. The gill arch immediately behind the angle of the jaw is the hyoid arch.

In dogfish, the jaw does not articulate directly with the skull, but is supported against the skull by the hyoid arch, a method of support known as hyostylic jaw suspension. The hyomandibular still has this role in teleosts, but the endochondral jaw bones also have another anterior connection with the skull.

Compare the whole array of gill supports in the dogfish with that in teleosts. What are the major differences?

The Appendicular Skeleton

Support for the paired appendages of vertebrates is provided by the pectoral and pelvic girdles, of which the former is composed of both dermal and endochondral bones, and the latter is solely endochondral.

The pectoral girdle is attached onto the back of the skull in teleosts, whereas in the dogfish it is well separated from the head and there are no equivalent connecting bones. Is there a flexible neck in fishes?\

Consider the requirements of streamlining, and also the ability of a fish to move in three dimensions. Fish pectoral girdles have several components, sometimes fused in the midline (elasmobranchs). There is no connection with the vertebral column.

The fin supports are parallel arrays of cartilaginous or bony radials, which always articulate with the endochondral part of the girdle. The radials are in the skin at the base of the fin, and there are also collagenous or bony fin rays in the body of the fin itself.

The number of radials and rays varies widely. In elasmobranchs it can readily be demonstrated that the rays give the fin stiffness, as well as allowing some flexibility. The pectoral fins, with their narrow bases, are the most manoeuvrable.

In teleosts, on the other hand, the rays may be stiff but carry thin webs of tissue between them, and the whole fin can be opened and closed like a fan by erecting the fin rays.

They articulate at their bases with the radials and carry their own extrinsic muscles for movement. Teleost fin rays are either segmented and branched, or unsegmented, stiff spines. The latter occur at the leading edge of various fins in the Paracanthopterygii and Acanthopterygii.

The manoeuvrability of the fins in teleosts has unquestionably been one of the major reasons for their success, since it allows precise control of swimming movements. When you look at fresh fish specimens,

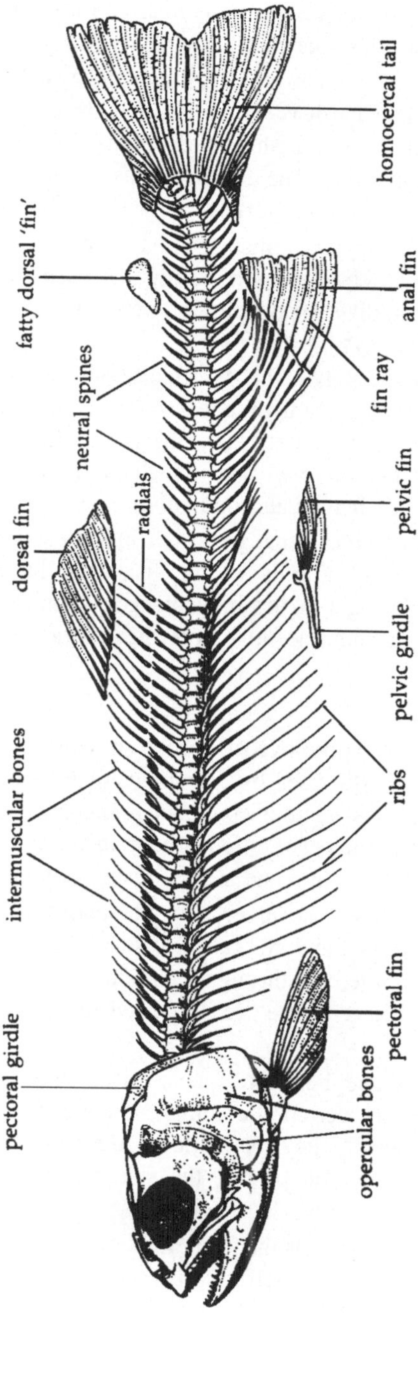

Figure 3.8: Skeleton of trout, Salmo (lateral view).

raise and lower the rays of the pectoral fins, and note their structure. No elasmobranch has fins like this.

Also look at a live fish in an aquarium and watch carefully the movements of its fins when it is swimming quickly, slowly, and when it is stationary in the water. Fish pelvic girdles are simpler, usually consisting of two components. The degree to which they join or articulate with each other in the midline varies.

In elasmobranchs they are joined by a bar of cartilage. There is no connection with the vertebral column in 'any fish. Articulating with the pelvic girdle are the radials supporting the pelvic fins, which, like the pectoral fins, contain rays.

The position of the pelvic fins is often about half way down the body, but during the evolution of teleosts they shifted progressively further forwards. In advanced teleosts, the pelvic fins are below (or slightly anterior to) the pectoral fins, which have themselves altered position to lie laterally behind the operculum.

These apparently aimless changes result in both sets of paired fins lying near the centre of gravity of the fish, and have to do with stabilising the fish during braking movements. When you look at the fishes described in the next section, note the position of their paired fins.

The Axial Skeleton

As we have seen, the primitive supporting structure for the vertebrate body is the notochord, still used by living agnathans and all vertebrate embryos. Several fishes have an unconstricted notochord with additional elements which protect the nerve cord above it and blood vessels below; they are equivalent to the neural and haemal arches of higher vertebrates.

In most living fishes, however, the notochord is more or less replaced by the centra of the vertebrae. Sections of the notochord often remain between vertebrae, and through the middle of the centrum itself. Some examples of fish vertebrae are illustrated in Figure elsewhere in this chapter.

They vary in shape between species, but show little regional differentiation within the vertebral column. Note the shape of the centra and their articular facets. They must allow lateral flexibility in a fish. Other parts of the vertebrae protect the spinal cord, articulate with ribs, or provide sites for muscle attachment.

The vertebral column joins the skull at the back or occipital region; this is part of the braincase itself. In fish, there is a single articular facet between vertebral column and skull. Note the rigidity of the spine

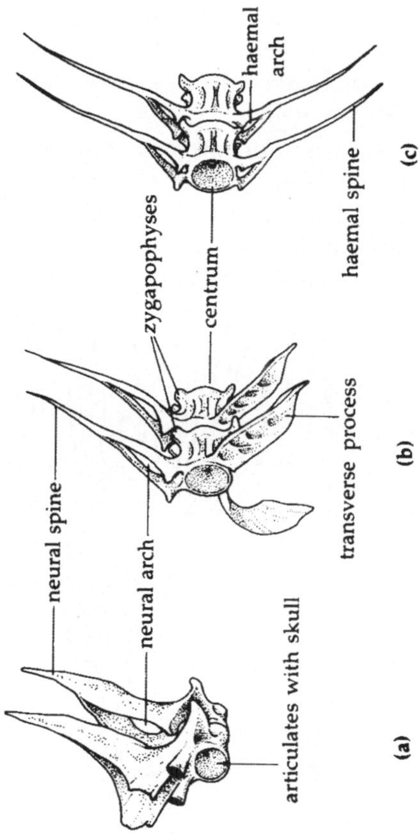

Figure 3.9: Cod vertebrae from (a) behind the skull, (b) trunk region, (c) tail.

behind the head. Also decide what the numerous bones are that must be removed or avoided when you eat something like a trout. Ribs, and neural and haemal spines are all present. Which region of the body contains ribs?

Median Fins and Tail

Fish have dorsal, anal, and caudal fins besides their paired fins. Their number and extent vary, but their internal structure resembles that already described for the paired fins.

The tail is of great interest because it provides the main propulsive force in fish swimming, and certain features of tail structure are diagnostic of some of the major groups in fish taxonomy. The two types of tail that you will see here are called heterocercal (elasmobranchs) and homocercal (teleosts).

In a heterocercal tail, the vertebral column bends dorsally as it enters the tail itself. The tail fin is asymmetrical, the ventral lobe being larger. The dorsal epichordal lobe may be very small. In movement, the dorsal part of the tail stiffened by the backbone is the leading edge, with the flexible ventral part trailing.

All elasmobranchs and some primitive bony fish (not teleosts) have heterocercal tails. The exact shape of the tail in different sharks is quite variable, and mirrors the precise swimming requirements of each species, for slight adjustments in size and flexibility of the tail's lobes will influence the precise direction of the force produced by the moving

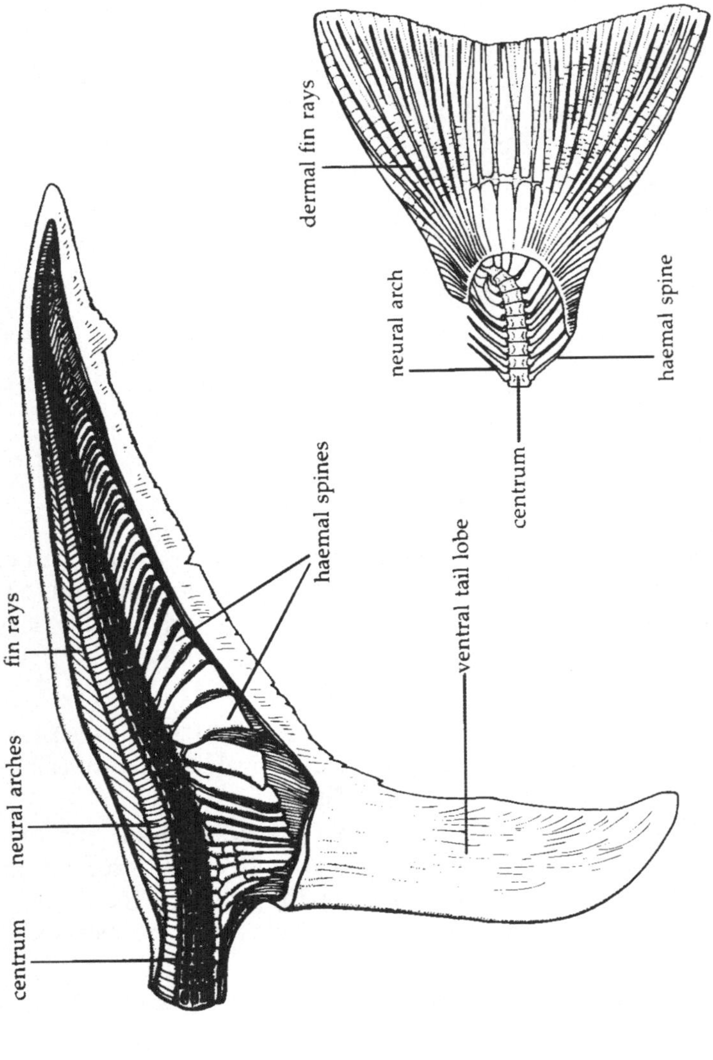

Figure 3.10: Homocercal tail of Salmo.

tail. Teleost tails are outwardly symmetrical, or homocercal. The vertebral column appears to pass straight back, but on close inspection it kinks up at the very end.

This signifies that teleosts evolved from animals with heterocercal tails, and it means, of course, that the ventral part of the tail fin is actually larger; but because the overall shape is symmetrical, these tails are different from true heterocercal tails.

The thrust they deliver is symmetrical. There is great variation in tail size, shape (though it generally remains symmetrical), and importance in locomotion. In some teleosts, various fins may replace the tail functionally as the main propulsive organs.

All of this variability is a reflection of the exuberant adaptive radiation of teleost fishes, due largely to the evolution of manoeuvrable fins and neutral buoyancy (of which more later).

We shall now look at two pairs of marine fish, each pair with similar modes of life, but one an elasmobranch and one a teleost. We are interested in how the fish are adapted to their environmednt, which is most obvious in their external features, because it is the outside of the animal that meets the environment first.

The Dogfish and the Whiting
(Class Chondrichthyes, *Scyliorhinus caniculus*
Class Osteichthyes, *Merlangius merlangus*)

These fish live near the bottom or in mid-water in coastal areas, and feed on crustaceans, molluscs, and other fish. They are not high-speed swimmers.

External Features

1. Look carefully at body shape. Both fish are streamlined, the whiting more so. The dogfish is elongated, with a dorsoventrally flattened anterior end, a more or less rounded body, and a long flexible caudal region.

   The whiting is shorter and more fusiform in shape. Is its head flattened like the dogfish head? Find the vent (anus) so that you can define the limits of trunk and tail regions. Note the different proportions.
2. Look at the skin of the whiting under the microscope. Note pigment cells and shading. What about pigmentation in the dogfish?
3. Feel the body surface of both fish. The dogfish is rough because of the placoid scales or denticles in its skin. What is the

structure of these and how do they resemble mammalian teeth? Take some skin off and look under the microscope at the scales embedded in it.

If you let the skin dry a little, the scales will stand out from it. Now remove some whiting scales. How do they differ from those of the dogfish? You should be able to see why whiting scales are described as 'cycloid'. They consist of thin bony material. Scale structure is one of the major differences between chondrichthyan and osteichthyan fish.

4. The teeth of elasmobranchs are derived from denticles and have a similar structure; teleost teeth are not like their scales. Look at some dogfish teeth and compare them with some body scales.

   Is there any difference? Note the arrangement of the teeth, which are carried on a sheet of connective tissue and constantly replaced. How are the teeth of the whiting arranged? Are there teeth on the palate? Many vertebrates have palatal teeth.

5. How large is the nasal region of the head in relation to the region behind the eyes? Dogfish have large olfactory organs and associated lobes in the brain.

   Their heads are also covered in sense organs of the lateral line system and the ampullae of Lorenzini. Teleosts also have lateral line canals on their heads, and in both groups they pass above and below the eyes, and also right along the body. The main lateral line canal is externally visible on these fish. The ampullae of Lorenzini are peculiar to elasmobranchs, and are highly sensitive to minute electrical currents. You can see where the ampullae are by looking for pores in the skin, particularly on the underside of the snout and around the edge of the mouth.

   If you press on the skin, a transparent jelly is extruded. It comes from a canal below the pore, which leads to a sensory cell. Dogfish use their ampullae to detect hidden food, such as small fish or worms.

6. Look at the eyes, spiracles, and gill slits. How are these arranged on the head? Only the dogfish has a spiracle, which is a modified gill slit and lies between the dorsal part of the hyoid arch and the back of the jaws.

   What is its function? How many gill slits are there in the

dogfish? Notice that they are separated from each other. The whiting has one opening on each side, covered by the operculum. When you have finished looking at the external features of these fishes, you can look at the exact arrangements of the gill filaments.

7. The mouth and nostrils also differ. Note their ventral position in the dogfish. The nostrils do not communicate directly with the mouth in either elasmobranchs or teleosts, although land vertebrates and the fish that gave rise to them did evolve such connections.

   Dogfish have their incurrent openings at the base of a nasal flap. If you lift the flap, you can see into the nostril, where the sensory olfactory folds lie on the floor of the chamber. The edge of the flap fits into a groove on the opposite side of the nostril, and so excurrent water passes out backwards under the flap, near the mouth.

   Are the nostrils in a similar position in the whiting? How many nasal openings are there? Look very carefully—they are small. Which is incurrent and which excurrent? Explore them with a seeker.

8. One of the striking features of teleosts is their mobile jaws. The two cartilages (palatoquadrate and Meckel's) in the elasmobranch jaw are not very mobile.

   During teleost evolution on the other hand, the tooth-bearing premaxillae and maxillae became detached from the cheek bones and so can swing forwards and out. If you look at jaw mechanisms in a trout, whiting, and plaice, you will see three slightly different situations.

   In trout (relatively primitive), the premaxilla is small and immobile, but the maxilla is movable because it is joined to the cheek and lower jaw by folds of skin.

   Both bones bear teeth. In the whiting (more advanced), the premaxilla is long and bears the teeth; it excludes the maxilla from the front of the mouth. Both bones are held in place by skin and ligaments, and both can be rotated forwards and down.

   Plaice (advanced) have mouths that can be protruded in a spectacular way—the premaxilla and maxilla pivot far forwards and out. This is probably an essential movement for them in catching food on the bottom (see later). Manoeuvrable mouths are an essential accompaniment to the highly adaptable feeding mechanisms of teleosts.

9. The appearance of paired fins was an important step in vertebrate evolution. Their position is quite different in these two fish, for the whiting is an advanced teleost, and has anterior pelvic fins. In fact, they are even slightly anterior to the pectoral fins.

   Compare this position not only with that in the dogfish but also with the position in the trout skeleton. Look at some other teleosts too, such as mackerel or herring. Note the relative position of the pectoral fins in whiting and dogfish. Next, manipulate the fins; compare flexibility and manoeuvrability.

   You can see the rays in teleosts; look at their structure. Are there any fin spines? Dogfish fins are stiffer because the collagenous rays are closely spaced and have no webs of thin tissue between them. The pectoral fins are the only really manoeuvrable fins (excluding the tail), whereas in teleosts all the fins may be erectile and manoeuvrable.

   Teleosts are capable of far more delicate control of their movement and posture in the water. Elasmobranchs have simply adapted to a life that requires less precise movements, and are very successful as predators and scavengers.

10. How are the median fins arranged? How many dorsal and anal fins are there in each fish? Note their structure. These fins are mainly concerned with control of rolling and yawing but in some teleosts they have other functions, including propulsion.

11. The tail, as already noted, is heterocercal in elasmobranchs and homocercal in teleosts. Can you see the difference? In the dogfish, the backbone extends to the tip of the tail, and kinks up slightly as it enters the tail proper. The dorsal part of the tail is stiffer. The whiting tail is symmetrical - look at its structure.

12. Could you now distinguish between these two fish, and give some of their major diagnostic characteristics? Try the same exercise with some other teleosts that are mid-water swimmers. Mackerel, for example, are highspeed swimmers; you can

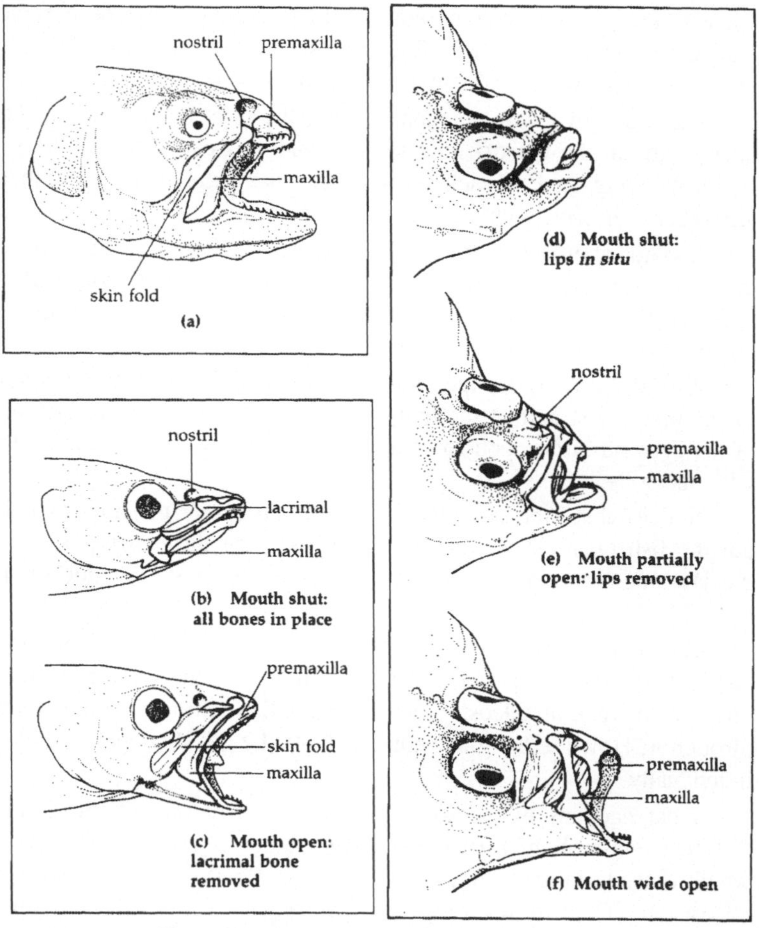

Figure 3.11: Jaws, closed and open, of (a) trout, (b, c) whiting, and (d, e, f) plaice.

tell this from their shape. Other fast swimmers such as the tuna and porbeagle shark *(Lamna)* have the same shape, which includes what is called a high asvect ratio tail. This means that the ratio of length to average width is high; such tails are hydrodynamically efficient.

Internal Features

The intention here is to pick on areas of obvious difference between elasmobranchs and teleosts. We shall concentrate on three: (1) the arrangement of the gills; (2) buoyancy mechanisms; and (3) reproduction.

1. Start by looking into the mouth of an intact whiting. Prop its mouth

open if you can, and imagine yourself to be an entering food particle. Notice the arrangement of gills, the 'sieve' formed by arches and rakers through which water will pass and food will not.

There are two ways of approaching the gills by dissection. The operculum can be cut off on one side, and you can then see the gill filaments lying against each other. How many are there? Are there gill rakers on each arch?

Another approach is to make a midventral incision at the level of the pelvic fins, and continue it back towards the vent. If you want to preserve the viscera intact, pass to one side of the vent in order to avoid cutting the rectum and other structures.

With the fish on its side, you can remove the skin from the whole of the uppermost half of the body cavity. If you also remove one side of the pectoral girdle, you can expose the heart, and see its relationship with the gills.

Notice where the oesophagus begins. To reveal the dogfish gills, put the fish on its back, and cut down one side through the angle of the jaw and the middle of the gill series to the posterior side of the last gill slit.

Then cut across the floor of the pharynx to the other side and open out. Leave intact the gills on one side. How does the gill arrangement differ from that of teleosts? Note the dogfish spiracle—water enters through it. How are the gills ventilated? Do the gill slits open and close individually?

What happens in the whiting? The structure of the gills is also different; elasmobranch filaments have a tough septum between them, which extends laterally beyond their ends. No such septum exists in teleost gills. Confirm this difference yourself. 2. Teleosts have evolved neutral buoyancy, achieved by a structure called the swim or air bladder, which grows out from the gut.

Elasmobranchs never have swim bladders, though some are neutrally buoyant or nearly so. How does this happen? They store a substance that is less dense than water - find out where, and what it is. Dogfish are not neutrally buoyant and sink when they stop swimming.

Whiting have well-developed swim bladders that are easy to see, particularly in fresh specimens. Look for an elongated white sac up against the dorsal wall of the body cavity and extending throughout its length.

It will be covered by a very thick black layer of peritoneum, which can be gently stripped off. The thick ventral wall of the bladder is

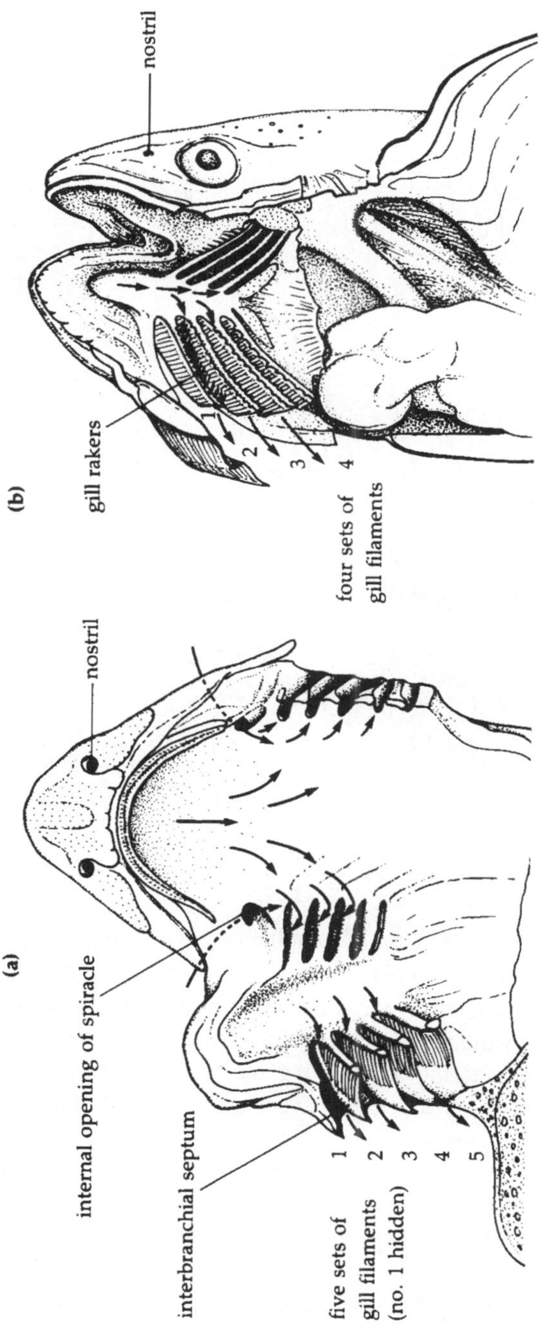

Figure 3.12: Branchial regions of (a) dogfish and (b) whiting, from ventral side.

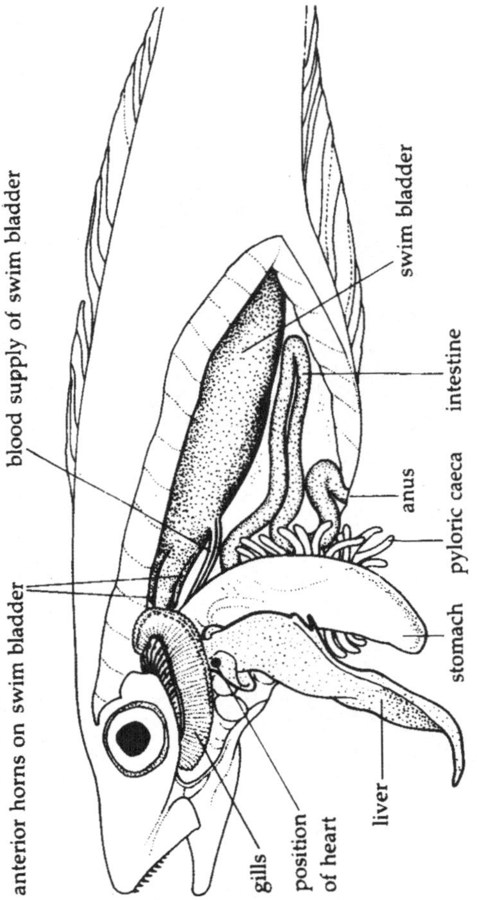

Figure 3.13: Dissection of whiting to show position of swim bladder.

impermeable to gases because of guanine crystals incorporated into its structure—hence its whiteness.

There are two anterior horns (cornua) on the whiting air bladder, which project forwards beside its anterior end. Look carefully, and note the blood supply entering and leaving the bladder ventrally near the anterior end. Cut the bladder open ventrally, avoiding the immediate area of the blood vessels.

This reveals a mass of tissue like a reddish-brown rosette between the bases of the cornua. It is composed of blood vessels, and is called the gas gland. Its function is central to the whole physiology of the air bladder.

Lactic acid, produced in the gland, lowers the pH of the blood and decreases the affinity of haemoglobin for oxygen, which then enters the bladder from the blood. Oxygen is often the predominant gas in fish air bladders, and the regulation of its partial pressure there is what controls buoyancy.

3. Although the overall structure of the reproductive system is similar in elasmobranchs and teleosts, their reproductive strategies are markedly different. You can investigate this by looking at mature male and female animals in their breeding season, and at eggs and embryos.

Male elasmobranchs have claspers; male teleosts do not. They are used for copulation, for fertilisation is internal in all elasmobranchs whereas it is usually external in teleosts. One clasper is inserted into a female by a male dogfish at mating, and sperm is then transmitted through it, down a groove, and into the female genital opening.

Investigate the component cartilages of a clasper, and note the groove. Female elasmobranchs have the option of retaining their eggs inside the body, or of releasing them well protected and well supplied with food. Scy*liorhinus* follows the latter course, and produces its eggs inside the wellknown 'mermaid's purses'.

If you can obtain a mature female, investigate the reproductive system by looking for the structures illustrated in Figure elsewhere in this chapter. Note the very large yolky eggs, prominent shell glands, and the completed mermaid's purses in the two oviducts; each purse contains an egg.

The spiny dogfish, *Squalus acanthias,* goes further towards true viviparity, and retains its embryos for long periods in the oviducts. By the time they are released, they can swim and feed. The lining of the oviduct is highly vascularised and essential to the maintenance of the embryos, but there is no direct placental connection.

Squalus is thus ovoviviparous. Finally, dissect a gravid female teleost (trout, whiting, or plaice), and look at some teleost embryos. Most teleosts release large numbers of small eggs into the water, which are fertilised and develop externally.

Although the eggs are yolky in comparison to a mammalian egg, they have much less yolk than a dogfish egg. Viviparous teleosts are a small minority, so as a group teleosts invest in many eggs so that a few may survive, whereas elasmobranchs produce fewer eggs.

Why is this an efficient strategy for them? How do some teleosts ensure greater protection for their eggs without resorting to viviparity or ovoviviparity?

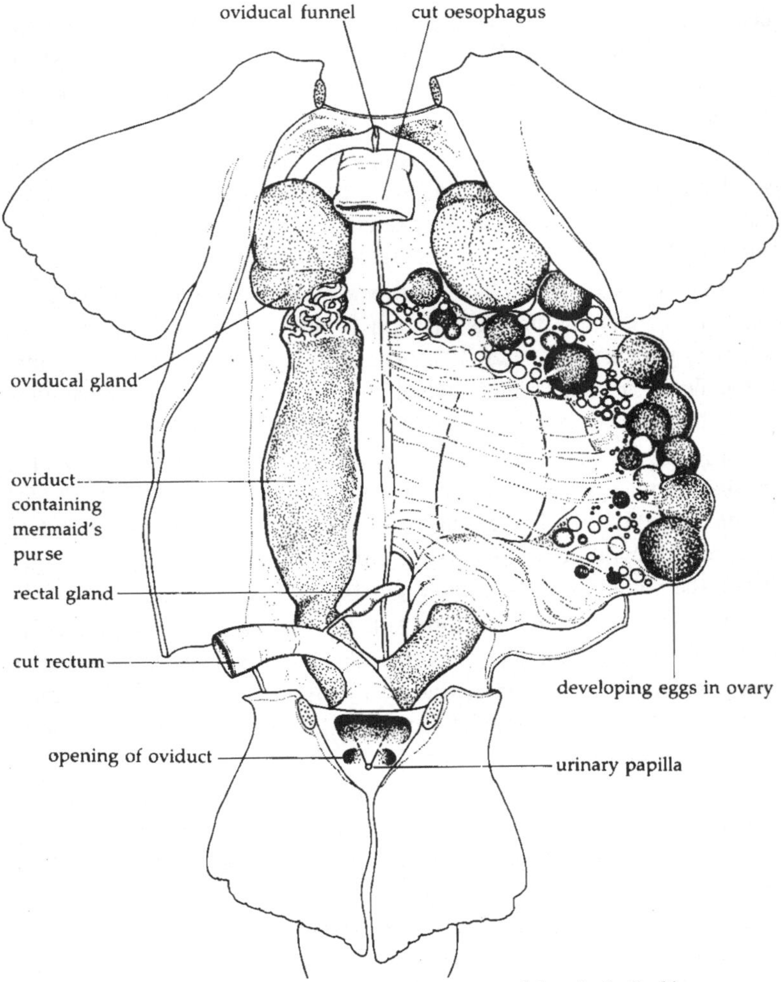

Figure 3.14: Dissection of reproductive system of female Scyliorhinus.

The Cuckoo Ray and the Plaice
(Class Chondrichthyes, *Raja naevus*
Class Osteichthyes, *Pleuronectes platessa)*

Both these fishes are adapted for living on the bottom of the sea. This should be immediately obvious because their bodies are flattened. Are there fish which are flattened, but not bottom-living? If so, what is different about their flatness?

External features

1. The ray is flattened dorsoventrally. Compare its shape not

only with the plaice but also with the dogfish. In plaice, flattening develops anew in every generation in a manner that is very bizarre and quite different from rays.

Note that the body is asymmetrical—the upper surface is not the true dorsal surface; the animal is lying on its side (which?). Thus, the plaice is laterally flattened.

2. Note the colour of the upper surface. Plaice are excellently camouflaged, and can alter their colour to fit in with their background. Rays are also darker above. The pigmented 'ocelli' on this ray are diagnostic of this particular species.

3. Feel the body surface of the ray. Its dermal denticles are not uniformly distributed as in the dogfish. One reason for this is the necessity for flexibility in the large pectoral fins.

   The large spines are presumably defensive, and there are batteries of spines lying in grooves towards the outer edges of the pectoral fins in this species. Spines are modified denticles; look at some under the microscope.

   Take some scales off the plaice; note the smooth body surface except for the row of bony knobs behind the eyes. Are the scales cycloid scales like those of the whiting? Look also at the teeth. Ray teeth are simpler than dogfish teeth, having only one 'cusp'.

   Find out about their respective diets and see if you can suggest a good reason for this. Plaice teeth are few, and are better developed on the side facing the ground.

4. The dorsal surface of the ray bears eyes and spiracles, and projects forwards into a snout, which has its own strong ligaments and muscles, and can be raised. Are the eyes flush with the body surface? Consider the implications of eye position in an animal that lies on the bottom.

   Why are the spiracles very important in ray respiration? Note that they are externally far removed from the gill slits. Compare with the dogfish spiracle. Now look at the plaice head and the position of its eyes.

   Even though the animal lies on its side, both eyes are on the upper surface; the lower surface is blind. What happens is that the left eye migrates over towards the right side during larval development.

   A newly hatched plaice is symmetrical. Because one eye

migrates, striking internal asymmetries develop; for instance, in the nerves supplying the migrating eye. Plaice do not have spiracles. How do they ventilate their gills when lying on the bottom?

5. The mouth of the ray is ventral. Is it in the plaice? In general, chondrichthyan fish do not have terminal mouths. Rays often pounce on top of their prey and enfold it in their pectoral fins, so a ventral mouth is an advantage.

   The plaice has an asymmetrical mouth. Open it out and notice the way in which it can be protruded. When open, it is skewed towards the left side; that is, towards the most likely position of food. Note that it is part pigmented and part white.

6. Where are the nostrils and gill openings? Both are on the ventral surface in rays. It is helpful to imagine a dogfish flattened dorsoventrally in order to see how the situation in rays has arisen. Ray nostrils are similar in structure to those of dogfish, as are their gill openings.

   In plaice, there are two nostrils, each with two openings. Can you find them? Note that they are not as asymmetrically placed as the eyes. The gill openings are structurally similar to those of whiting, but one is above and one below, and the opercula are coloured accordingly. They are a striking indication of the orientation of the animal.

7. Ray pectoral fins are huge and extend forwards along the side of the head. The lateral extension of the body is mainly due to the enlarged pectoral fins and their musculature. Find out how rays move, and what the role of the pectoral fins is. The pectoral girdle in these animals is joined to the vertebral column for additional support. Do the pectoral fins perform the same function in plaice? What about dogfish? When you look for them in the plaice, note that there is only one pectoral fin and one pelvic on each side.

   This again emphasises that the animal lies on its side, not its belly. Are the two pectoral fins the same size? Check the pelvic fins. Now consider how the plaice moves; look back at the ray and make sure you understand the differences.

   Also look at fin structure again, and note the erectile fins with bony rays on the plaice. The pelvic fins are close together near the midline, at the base of the tail region in the ray; in plaice they are well forward below the pectoral fins. Plaice are advanced teleosts.

8. Median fins are reduced in rays, but well developed in plaice. This indicates a major difference in function. Near the tip of the tail in this ray species, there are two dorsal fins attached by webs of skin to the body surface. The tail fin is very reduced, but the tail is basically heterocercal.

   What does all this tell you about tail function in rays? Compare with the dogfish tail. The plaice has dorsal, anal, and tail fins, all with bony rays. The dorsal fin extends from just behind the head right back to the tail, and the anal fin likewise extends from pelvic fins to tail.

   The tail is well developed and homocercal. Most of the plaice body is taken up with muscle, used to flex the body when it moves arid when it buries itself in the substratum. The body cavity is very small, as you can easily discover by finding the vent and carefully cutting away from it on one side, until you have exposed the whole cavity.

9. The lateral line is clearly visible in these fish, and helps in understanding their orientation. Plaice have a lateral line canal on each side. In rays the main canals pass along either side of the midline, at the junction between pectoral fins and body. You can just see them externally as a faint line, but if you strip off some skin in this area close to the head, the gelatinous content of the canals is then revealed. The ampullae of Lorenzini are also very conspicuous on the snout and underside of the head, particularly if the white underskin is dried slightly. Pores and canals then stand out as dark lines. Note their arrangement on the head and near the mouth.

Internal Features

Differences in gill structure between elasmobranchs and teleosts can be studied as easily in rays and plaice as in dogfish and whiting, so refer back to the earlier account if you are interested in this. Plaice do not have a swim bladder, for it is lost in adult flatfish.

This is not unexpected, since they live on the bottom; but other teleosts (e.g. mackerel) dispense with swim bladders too. As far as reproductive strategies are concerned, this species of ray produces yolky eggs, and secretes a horned case around each egg—as *Scyliorhinus* does. Plaice lay large numbers of small eggs. A gravid female has the entire posterior two thirds of the body cavity absolutely packed with eggs in her two ovaries. They are fertilised externally and develop free in the sea. Young plaice are planktonic, and become bottom-living when they are about 40 days old.

The animals described in this chapter provide an introduction to some of the main adaptive features of the various groups of fishes. The lampreys are an interesting example of the jawless state, whereas the elasmobranchs and teleosts are the two major groups of modern fish.

Neither of the latter two groups includes amongst its members any of the relatives of the fish that were ancestral to land vertebrates. Whereas the teleosts have been immensely successful quite recently in terms of geological time, the sarcopterygian fishes (now represented by the coelacanths and lungfishes) were much more common 400 million years ago than they are now.

But during their ancient adaptive radiation, these fish left descendants which evolved into the Amphibia, and they are the subject of the next chapter.

4

Amphibians: Moving and Breathing on Land

Amphibians are common, but relatively inconspicuous inhabitants of ponds and moist places in the world today. Occasionally we see them *en masse* at mating time, or hear their numerous voices in the tropical night. They are the descendants of the first land *vertebrates*, which *ventured* ashore sometime in the Devonian period nearly 400 million years ago.

Very little is known of the connections between modern amphibians and the diverse and numerous animals that evolved during the Carboniferous, for there are few amphibian fossils later than the Permian. Two main groups survive today—the Urodela and Anura, which express two rather different ways of moving on land, and form the subject of this chapter.

A third order, the Apoda, is composed of legless, burrowing amphibians. It is interesting that having evolved paired legs, various groups of vertebrates then dispensed with them again.

The Apoda (or caecilians) are perhaps the least known of these groups, because they not only live in the tropics but also burrow and are nocturnal, and so are seldom seen by most people. What are the problems facing land vertebrates?

They concern support, desiccation, respiration, reproduction, and sensory perception. In othez words, the structure and biology of vertebrates was very broadly affected when they colonised land. This chapter looks at some adaptations of the common living amphibians to life on land -

not those that require physiological experiments for demonstration but those that are manifested in the skin, the functional morphology of the skeleton, and the circulatory system. To begin, there is a discussion of the structure of the skull of a fossil amphibian.

This is included as an aid to understanding and interpreting vertebrate skulls in general. The same names constantly crop up in vertebrate anatomy, and as the skull reflects so much of importance about a vertebrate, you will often need to look at skulls in the rest of this book. A common plan is a great help when making comparisons.

Materials required

- Live frogs and newts for observation.
- Skeletons of a large anuran and urodele, e.g. the bull frog, *Rana catesbiana,* and the hell-bender *Cryptobranchus*.
- Some freshly killed and/or preserved frogs for dissection.
- Newts or salamanders for demonstration dissection. Interesting comparisons could be made with neotenic salamanders such as the axolotl, *Ambystoma mexicanum,* which retains gills in the adult, and is often kept as a laboratory animal.

THE TETRAPOD SKULL

('Tetranod' simply means 'four-footed'. and is an umbrella term used to refer to all the groups of land vertebrates.)

Amphibia, and hence all land vertebrates, probably evolved from a group of fishes called the Rhipidistia. This is an entirely fossil group, included with the coelacanths and lungfishes under the general umbrella term of Sarcopterygii or 'lobe-finned' fishes.

The only close living relatives of amphibians among the fish are the coelacanths, *Latimeria,* and the lungfish which are, alas, never likely to appear regularly in university classrooms.

However, if we look back at the fossil record, evidence of numerous sarcopterygians may be found. It is among these forms that it is possible to find animals resembling early amphibians. Some of the resemblances are so detailed that a close relationship is certain.

One of the chief areas of similarity is the skull, and the basic organisation of certain rhipidistian skulls underlies that of all tetrapods. We illustrate here, not a rhipidistian skull (for rhipidistians were still fish) but one belonging to a Carboniferous amphibian, *Greererpeton*.

More specimens exist of this animal than of any other Carboniferous amphibian, so it is the earliest amphibian to be represented by a sizeable number of articulated skeletons. It has many characters which are now recognised as being primitive for the Amphibia as a whole, and it belongs to a group which may be related to the modern orders of Amphibia, particularly the Anura.

The structure of the skull of *Greererpeton* not only resembles that of certain sarcopterygian fish but also provides a basis for comparison with the skulls of all later land vertebrates. Thus, the features of the skull discussed below should be kept in mind throughout the rest of the book.

In the last chapter we discussed the make-up of the fish skull, and said that there were two types of bones, endochondral and dermal. Endochondral bones of the braincase are indicated by hatching in Figure elsewhere in this chapter, as they were in Figure elsewhere in this chpater.

In the diagrams of the skull of *Greererpeton,* most of the visible bones are of dermal origin. The braincase itself is to a large extent concealed beneath the dermal bones, which have been applied to it from the skin over the brain, and in cheeks and palate.

Think of the skull as consisting of three basic parts—the endochondral braincase plus its two complexes of dermal bones in skull roof and palate. It is unnecessary to remember the names of all the bones now; you will get to know many of them through repetition in the rest of the book.

For now, try to obtain a working knowledge of the general layout of the skull. Some features to look for are:

1. A series of paired bones over the top of the head and snout - nasals, frontals, and parietals. The grooves passing across these bones and between the eyes in an hourglass pattern are canals of the lateral line system, indicating that *Greererpeton* spent much of its time in water. Note that canals also occur elsewhere on the skull.
2. Bones bordering the sides and top of the eye sockets (orbits) —prefrontals, postfrontals, and postorbitals:
3. A row of bones extending back from behind the postorbitals to the occiput—supratemporals and tabulars. A third bone, the intertemporal, is often present here in early amphibians. *Greererpeton* lacks it, or may have it only on one side as in Figure elsewhere in this chapter;
4. The bones of the occiput, or back of the skull, where the vertebral column is attached. Here you can see some

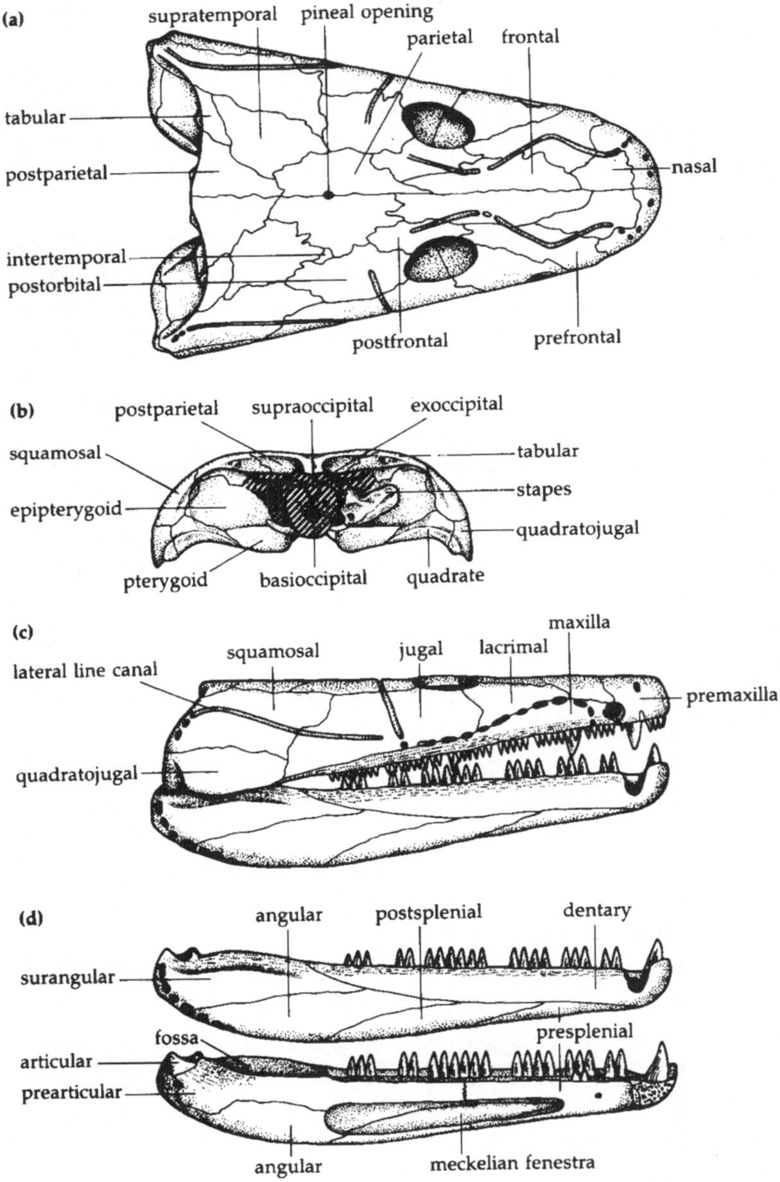

Figure 4.1: Skull of Greererpeton: (a) dorsal view, (b) occipital view, (c) side view, (d) lower jaw, and (e) palatal view. (Figure Contd.)

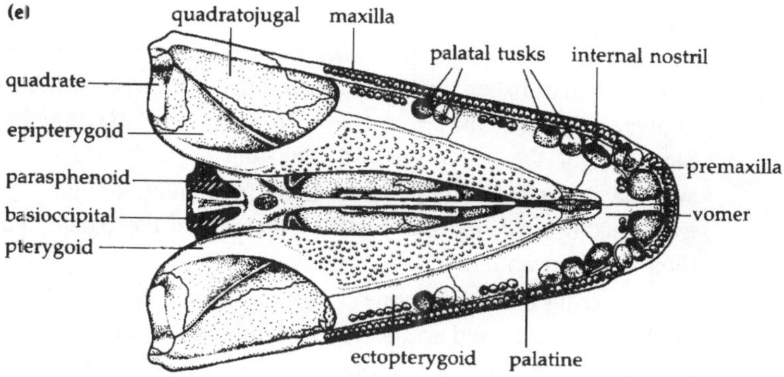

(Contd.) Figure 4.1: Skull of Greererpeton: (a) dorsal view, (b) occipital view, (c) side view, (d) lower jaw, and (e) palatal view.

endochondral bones (e.g. the basioccipital).

5. Bones covering the side of the head and bordering the lower half of the orbits—lacrimals, jugals, and squamosals.
6. Bones bordering the jaws and bearing teeth - premaxillae and maxillae above.
7. Below, the lower jaw contains several bones. Most of the teeth are borne by the dentary, but coronoid bones also bear teeth. Coronoids are not shown in Figure elsewhere in this chapter.

   The articular is a remnant of Meckel's cartilage of fishes. It is an endochondral bone, and provides the articulation with the quadrate in all tetrapods except mammals.

   On the inner side of the lower jaw you can see a cavity or fossa; this houses the insertions of the jaw adductor (closing) muscles.

   The fossa extends forwards, anbd is visible again along the ventral side of the jaw as a window in the bone. It emphasises the way in which dermal bones have been laid down around the original cartilaginous lower jaw; in fact, Meckel's cartilage would probably have occupied this space in life.
8. The palate also bears teeth: *Greererpeton* had large palatal tusks and batteries of denticles. Dermal bone covers much of the palate too, except for the central area, and two large openings for the jaw adductor muscles behind. Two other paired openings are the internal nostrils and recesses for the large anterior tusks on the dentary.

Internal nostrils are a new innovation - none of the animals so far discussed in this book has them. They evolved first in sarcopterygian fishes, which also had lungs. Once air breathing evolved, the nostrils became not just areas of olfaction but passages for the air *en route* to the lungs.

All the tetrapod skulls you look at from now on may be expected to have internal nostrils opening on the palate, but their position and size vary.

9. The covering of dermal bone is complete over the dorsal side of the braincase, and in the sides of the skull. As you study the skulls of reptiles, birds, and mammals, look out for losses among these bones, and the appearance of openings in the skull. Note which dermal bones always remain, and which are lost in each group. In modern Amphibia, too, there has been extensive loss of bone in the skull.
10. There is one little opening in the skull table, between the parietal bones. This lies over the position of the pineal gland. In other chapter of this book you will see that lizards have an opening here too. It is a useful landmark in the skulls of amphibians and reptiles, for it pinpoints the position of the parietal bones.
11. One of the differences between early amphibian skulls and those of sarcopterygian fish is the relative size of the nasal region in relation to the area behind the eyes. Think how you would measure this difference and quantify it. Sarcopterygians had short nasal regions; *Greererpeton* had a lengthened nasal region. What about the teleost skull?
12. Why was the cod skull not used as an example of the basic vertebrate skull design instead of this extinct amphibian? The fact is that although you will recognise from other chapter of this book many of the names given here, yet teleost skulls are difficult to compare to those of amphibians, since teleosts evolved quite separately from (and much later than) the sarcopterygian ancestors of amphibians.

    Consequently, zoologists are not always certain of the exact homologies of the bones in teleost skulls, and their difficulties are compounded by the tendency of teleosts to increase the numbers of dermal bones present.

    In contrast, *Greererpeton* can be related without such doubts both to the sarcopterygian fish and to subsequent Amphibia. The general plan of its skull is also not unlike that of early reptiles, and hence all other tetrapods.

THE AMPHIBIAN SKIN

Modern amphibians have soft moist skin without scales (except for some of the Apoda). There is a very good reason for this - namely, that gas exchange occurs through the skin. But there is also a cost attached to having a moist skin on land because water is constantly lost by evaporation, causing desiccation and affecting temperature regulation.

These problems do not arise in aquatic animals. Amphibians are generally found in damp places, many are nocturnal, and those that do live in deserts make burrows. A section through the skin of a frog shows its glandular nature.

Mucous secretions keep the skin moist, capillaries bring blood to the skin surface for gas exchange (particularly CO_2, which diffuses out from the blood), and granular glands produce various substances that make amphibians unpalatable to predators. Some amphibian poisons are among the most potent known.

Note that the epidermis forms layers of cells that secrete keratin, and are replaced from a dividing basal layer. The keratinised cells on the outside are shed periodically *en masse,* not singly as in fishes. Skin with keratinised outer layers is characteristic of land vertebrates.

Keratin is water repellent, and protects the animal from desiccation. For obvious reasons, it is generally not very thick in amphibians, but in reptiles it forms scales, in birds feathers, and in mammals hair.

In larval amphibians, local thickenings of keratin form the teeth. Many amphibians are brightly coloured. The colour is produced by the interaction of light with pigments in the skin.

If you look at some frog skin stretched on a slide under the microscope, you will see mainly the large, branched cells (*chromatophores*) containing the black pigment melanin; they are in the dermis of the skin, as are other pigments, such as carotenoids, and refractile substances, such as purines.

In combination they often produce shades of green and yellow. *Rana temporaria* skin, viewed at a magnification of x 45 using incident light, reveals refractile guanine crystals grouped around large granular glands on parts of the dorsal surface of the body. The openings of these and the mucous glands can also be seen.

Light shone on fresh skin will cause the melanin to concentrate in the centre of the melanophores - an effect which you can easily observe yourself. Compare the distribution of melanophores on the dorsal and belly skin.

Do this using transmitted light, and then convert to incident light to show up the refractile purines concentrated in the paler areas of skin. Colour is used by amphibians for camouflage, sexual advertisement, and in some for advertising to predators the folly of eating their owner.

Some South American frogs are bright yellow and black; they sit around in broad daylight looking very conspicuous, but they can afford to do so because they are exceedingly poisonous. Tree frogs are also brightly coloured, though not poisonous, and they can modify the colour of their skins, as can many frogs.

You can observe colour change in *Rana temporaria* by putting it successively on pale and dark backgrounds, and allowing it time to adapt to each.

SKULLS AND SKELETONS

It is perhaps most instructive to look at amphibian morphology by comparing the typical urodele form with that of the anuran throughout, rather than discussing each separately. Urodeles are closest in form to the original amphibians.

They swim and walk on land by sinuous movements of the body, and in the water their tails also provide propulsion. Certain aspects of their locomotion, even on land, are reminiscent of fish locomotion. Urodeles that spend most of their time in water have relatively unosiified skeletons.

Anurans, on the other hand, have well-ossified skeletons, and are highly modified for a particular type of jumping and swimming, in which thrust is delivered by both hind legs simultaneously. The tail is reduced; so is the relative length of the body.

The jump is not just a way of moving about, but also an effective method of escaping predators. The examples chosen to show skeletal structure are *Rana catesbiana* and *Cryptobranchus,* because both are large animals and hence their, various bones are easier to see.

Skulls

1. The skulls of *R. catesbiana* and *Cryptobranchus* are superficially quite similar. Note the wide, flattened shape in both. All adult amphibians are carnivorous, and their wide mouths allow them to engulf large prey. The teeth are small and numerous, similar to each other, and made entirely of dentine. They are borne on the premaxilla and maxilla above, and on the dentary

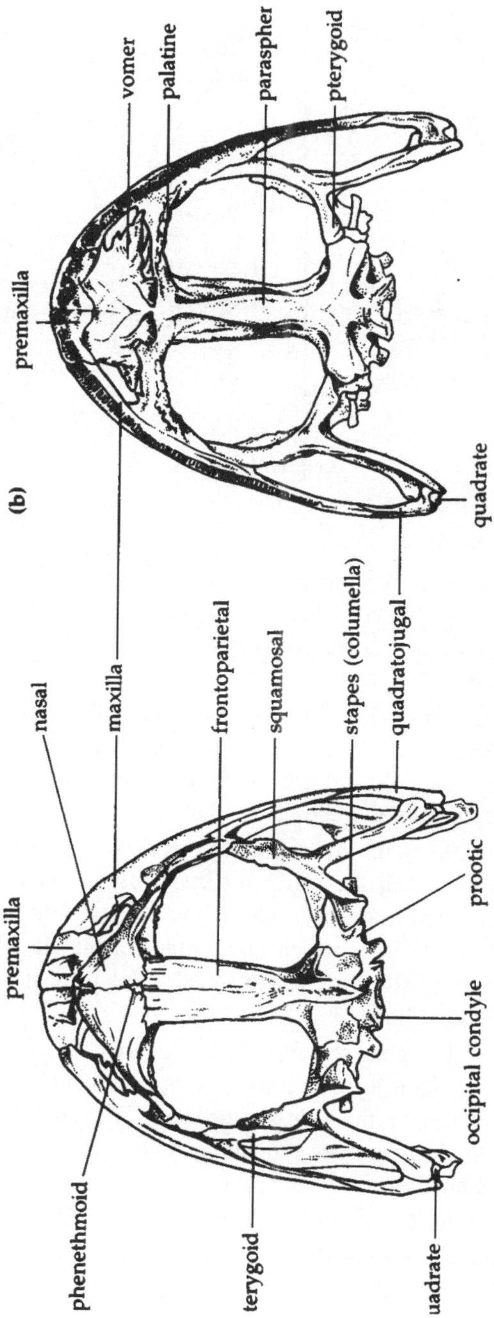

Figure 4.2: Skujll of bull frog, rana catesbiana: (a) dorsal and (b) ventral views.

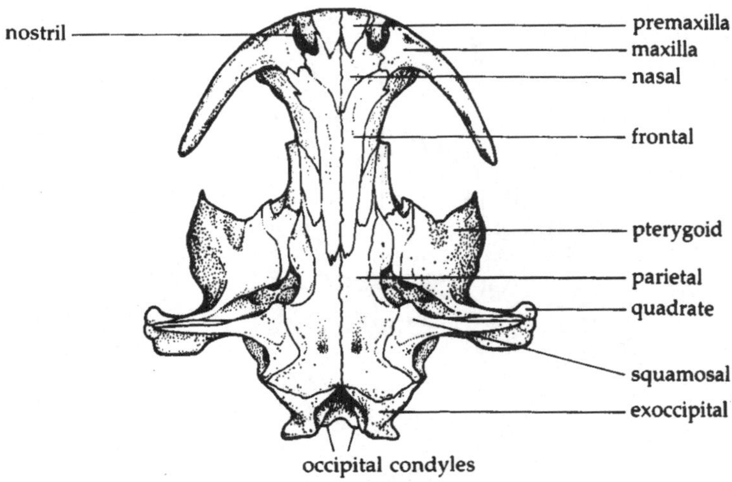

Figure 4.3: Skull of hell-bender, cryptobranchus, dorsal view.

below. Some amphibians have palatal teeth too.

2. The nasal region is generally short but broad. Prey is caught mainly by sight not smell, but smell and taste are important senses and have correspondingly large co-ordinating areas in the brain.
3. In rnrrelatinn with (71 the eves are nften large in *Rana* particularly, the skull seems to have been emarginated and modified largely to accommodate the eyes, whereas in *Cryptobranchus* the eyes are small.
4. What are the main losses and fusions of bones, if we compare these skulls with the skull of *Greererpeton?* Concentrate on the *Rana* skull. Dorsally, frontal and parietal fuse into a single bone on each side, which abuts onto the nasals. Part of the braincase itself may be exposed here and is called the sphenethmoid bone.

   Much of the snout region is in life filled with cartilage, so in a prepared skull it looks empty. Drastic reduction has occurred in the bones of the side of the skull. Bones have not only been lost, but the ones remaining become like struts or bars, rather than flat plates (e.g. the squamosal).

   Note that in R. *catesbiana,* there are no lacrimals, prefrontals, postfrontals, postorbitals, supratemporals, or tabulars. The jugals are also absent; instead, the maxillae extend right back to meet the quadratojugals directly. Even the quadratojugals may be missing in some anurans and many urodeles.

In the palate, pterygoids and palatines have become bars of bone, so that the region of the palate beneath the eyes is not covered by bone. The eyes can be retracted into these spaces. Note the large parasphenoid.

The modern anuran skull is adapted to fulfil its functions with the minimum amount of bone; ossification occurs where stresses occur and protection of soft parts is essential. Elsewhere losses and reductions have taken place, the skull is built for lightness with strength, and several areas are cartilaginous.

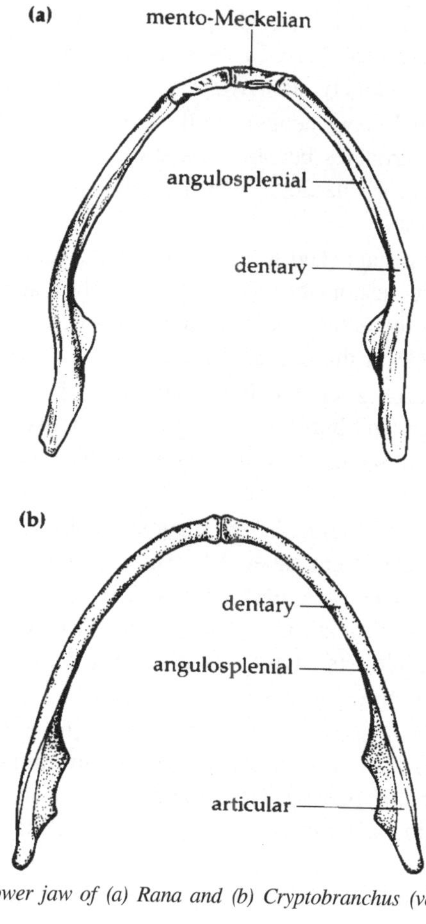

Figure 4.4: Lower jaw of (a) Rana and (b) Cryptobranchus (ventrral views)

5. In the lower jaw, the equivalent of the whole lower jaw cartilage (Meckel's cartilage) of vertebrate embryos remains. You can see part of it at the front, where it becomes ossified as the mento-Meckelian bone.

   The rest of it is covered by the dentary and by another dermal bone—the angulosplenial. The jaw articulation is formed between the posterior part of Meckel's cartilage, called the articular, and the quadrate in the skull. It is interesting that both these bones can be cartilaginous in frogs.

   However, the quadrate and articular are the same bones that form the jaw articulation in fish, and also reptiles.

6. Parts of four of the gill arches are still present in adult *Cryptobranchus* although no gills are visible externally. This is a good example of a widespread phenomenon among the urodeles, namely neoteny.

   We talked about neoteny in the context of the protochordates. Several urodeles become sexually mature while still Showing such larval characteristics as gills, spiracles, rudimentary limbs, etc.

7. What has happened to the bones of the hyoid arch? These, in fish, are responsible for supporting the back of the jaw and moving the entire opercular apparatus (look at the hyomandibular bone in the cod skull).

   In *Greererpeton,* the opercular bones have disappeared and the hyomandibular is a large strut between braincase and cheek—it seems to have supported the braincase, which had only a fragile attachment to the skull roof.

   In modern Anura, the hyomandibular forms the stapes in the middle ear. Remember that fish only have an inner ear. On land, vertebrates have to receive sound signals that are travelling through air. One of their adaptations for doing this is a middle ear cavity straddled by a bone or bones.

   The ear drum, a taut membrane that can vibrate, is another; look for it on a live frog. It is becoming clear from studying *Greererpeton* and other Carboniferous amphibians that the tympanum appeared late in amphibian evolution, and that the stapes in early forms could not have conducted airborne sound.

Note here an important example of change of function in evolution - a bone which, in fish, was involved in jaw support and gill ventilation, has become involved in braincase support in early amphibians, and hearing in later amphibians. Urodeles have no tympanum and often no stapes.

They apparently pick up sound from the ground via their shoulder girdles. The ventral part of the hyoid arch forms the hyoid apparatus in anurans (together with parts of other branchial cartilages).

It is very important in raising and lowering the floor of the mouth during lung ventilation and in tongue movements. Other remnants of the branchial cartilages are found supporting the larynx.

Vertebral Column

1. The vertebral column is long and unspecialised in urodeles, and much shortened in anurans. Consider what forces the

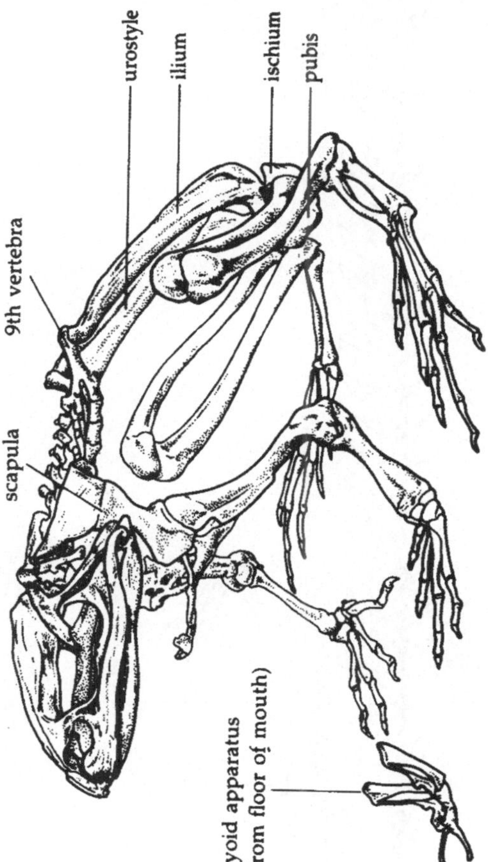

Figure 4.5: Skeleton of Rana catesbiana.

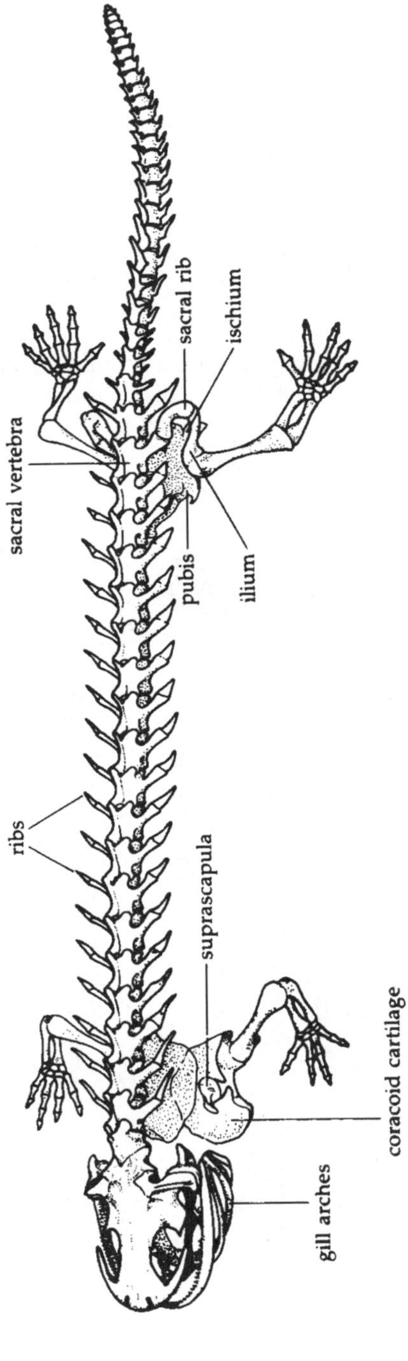

Figure 4.6: Skeleton of Cryptobranchus.

backbone of a land vertebrate is required to bear. It carries all the weight of the body—land vertebrates cannot rely on the buoyancy effect of water.

So it must not sag, and it must resist twisting as limbs are moved during walking. On the other hand, horizontal bending is an important part of urodele locomotion. What adaptations are there in response to these requirements?

2. One major one is the articular facets (zygapophyses) on the vertebrae. Note their position and orientation. Fish vertebrae may have zygapophyses but they rarely form strong articulations.

   Are there zygapophyses on the vertebrae of mammals that have returned to an aquatic mode of life, like whales? What about ichthyosaur vertebrae? Also note that frogs have ball and socket articulations between their centra.

   What shape are the centra of fish vertebrae? Note further that frog vertebrae do not have ribs attached to them, but those of *Cryptobranchus* do, albeit short ones. Both urodeles and anurans have vertebral transverse processes, which are often not well developed in fish.

   These bear muscles important in body support and movement. Other adaptations to do with the transmission of weight to the limbs are discussed below.

3. Note two other features at this point. One is that whereas teleost fish have dermal bones which connect their heads to their shoulder girdles (and no neck region), urodeles and anurans

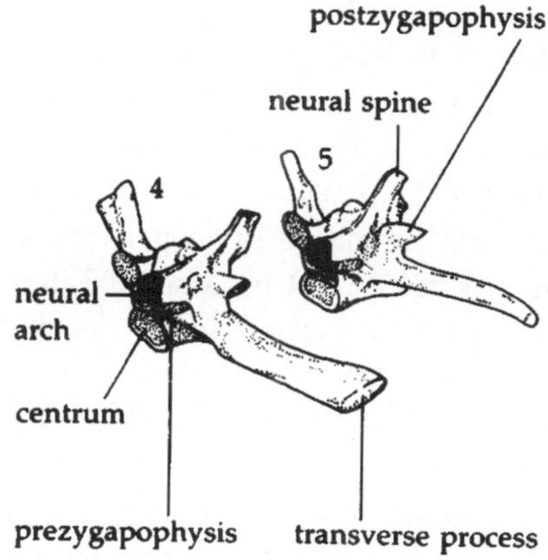

Figure 4.7: Trunk vertebrae of Rana.

have free heads. Land vertebrates generally have mobile heads and a more or less extensive neck region. supported by cervical vertebrae.

The head cannot be moved from side to side in amphibians, but it can in reptiles where the first two neck vertebrae are modified to form the atlas and axis (see later). The other feature to note is the number of trunk vertebrae.

Frogs have only nine. The ninth vertebra articulates with the pelvic girdle. Behind it is the urostyle, composed of fused tail vertebrae (but, of course, anurans have no externally visible tail).

This drastic shortening of the anuran body is correlated with their jumping method of locomotion, which could produce whiplash movements if the vertebral column was long. Note the lack of regional differentiation of vertebrae in amphibians.

The appearance of distinct cervical and sacral vertebrae marks the first stage in the adaptation of the vertebral column to land life. At its most complex (in mammals), vertebrae from different parts of the column vary greatly in their morphology.

The above description applies to *R. catesbiana* and *Cryptobranchus*. Other amphibians may not be quite the same. There are numerous minor variations (e.g. in skull bones) between different amphibians.

LIMBS AND LOCOMOTION

The prime question here is how land vertebrates overcome the problems of supporting their weight in air and transporting it about over the ground.

So the first task is to look at how amphibian limb girdles differ from those of fish, and then to see how the limbs themselves differ from fins. Then, we can look at the specific adaptations of urodeles and anurans in relation to their particular ways of moving.

1. If the vertebral column is to support the weight of the body above the ground, it must be connected in some way with the limbs. How is this achieved? In fish, neither the pectoral nor pelvic girdle is generally attached to the vertebral column (can you think of an exception to this statement?).

   Fish locomotion does not require such an attachment. But in all land vertebrates both girdles are attached; one indirectly by muscles or via sternum and ribs, and one directly. If you have skeletons in front of you, look carefully at the relationship between girdles and backbone. Muscles attach the scapula to the stout transverse processes on the vertebrae (and to the ribs, if any), thus effectively slinging the front part of the body from the dorsal part of the pectoral girdle.

In contrast, in the pelvis, one vertebra articulates directly with the ilium. Notice later on in the book how more advanced land vertebrates tend to incorporate more vertebrae into this important joint.

They are called sacral vertebrae; amphibians always have only one. What do you think might infjuence the number of sacral vertebrae?

2. What are the components of the limb girdles? We concentrate here on those of *Rana*. Again, as in the skull, there tend to be reductions in the bones as compared with fish. The main bones in the shoulder girdle are the scapula, clavicle and coracoid.

   The scapula and coracoid are endochondral bones, and carry the articulation with the forelimbs. Dermal elements are the ones that are reduced, and they tend to be throughout the tetrapods (note, however, that mammals retain only, scapulae and clavicles; they have no coracoids).

   Anurans retain a cleithrum, but urodeles do not—and the supracleithrum and interclavicle are absent. The pectoral girdle

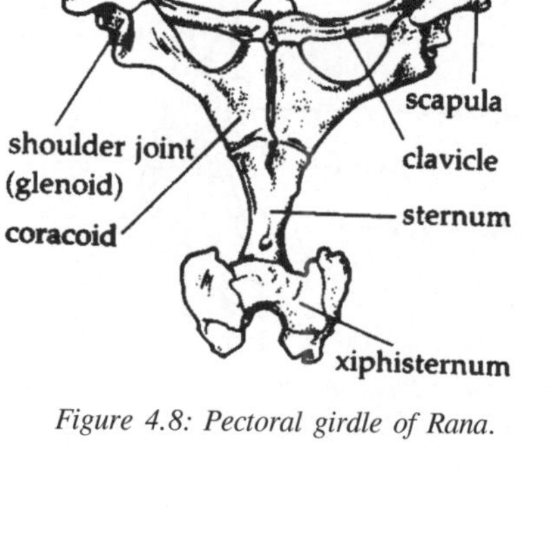

Figure 4.8: Pectoral girdle of Rana.

of *Cryptobranchus,* an aquatic form, is largely cartilaginous.

3. In the pelvic girdle, there is greater constancy in the arrangement of bones throughout the tetrapods than there is in the pectoral girdle. This reflects a more conservative functional role (see

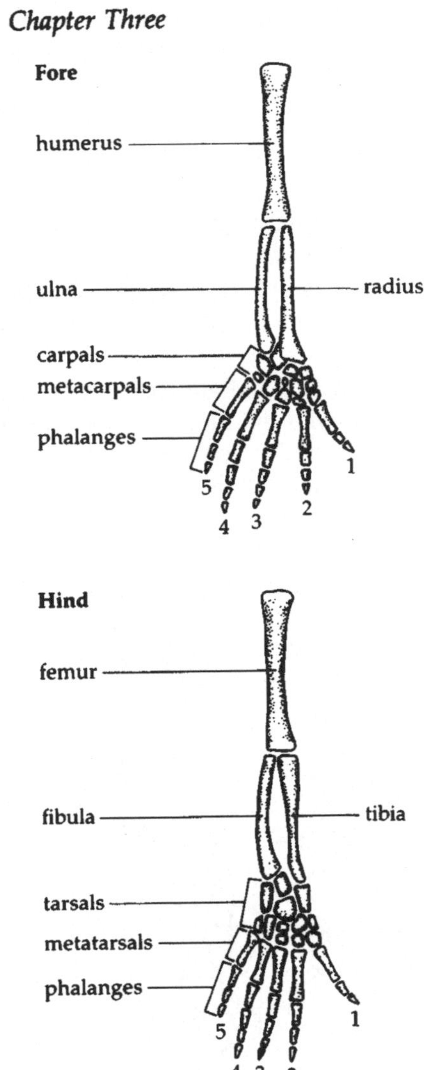

Figure 4.9: Plans of bones in fore- and hindlimb of a generalised primitive tetrapod.

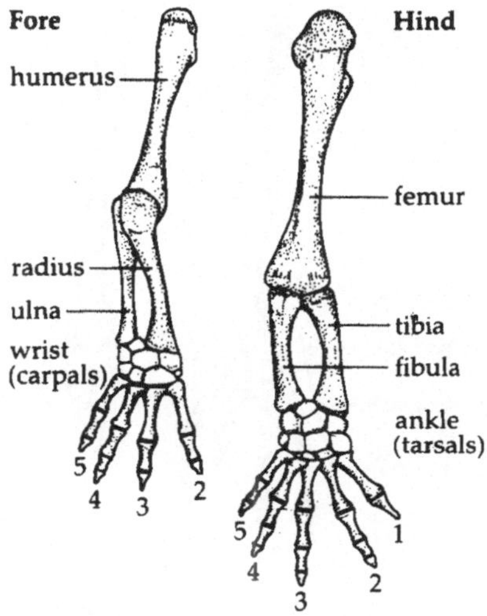

Figure 4.10: Fore- and hindlimb of Cryptobranchus.

comments in other chatper of this book on the mammalian skeleton).

There are three bones on each side of the girdle—a dorsal ilium, an anterior ventral pubis, and a posterior ventral ischium. The three meet at the articulation with the hindlimb, and the socket for the head of the femur is called the acetabulum.

4. The bones of fore- and hindlimbs are built to a common plan in all tetrapods. One bone articulates with the girdle, and in turn articulates with two distal bones.

   At wrist and ankle, several small bones then follow, originally in three rows, and the five most distal of them then articulate with the digits, of which there were originally five. These features characterise what is referred to as the pentadactyl limb—a basic attribute of all land vertebrates.

   The axial arrangement of bones in the tetrapod limb is quite different from the fin structure of teleosts, and is an appropriate adaptation for converting the limbs into systems of levers for support and propulsion.

   Of course, not all living land vertebrates have pentadactyl limbs, but the fossil record suggests that this was the primitive number of digits, and embryology adds support to the fossil evidence.

   Fossil sarcopterygian fish already had the '1 + 2' axial

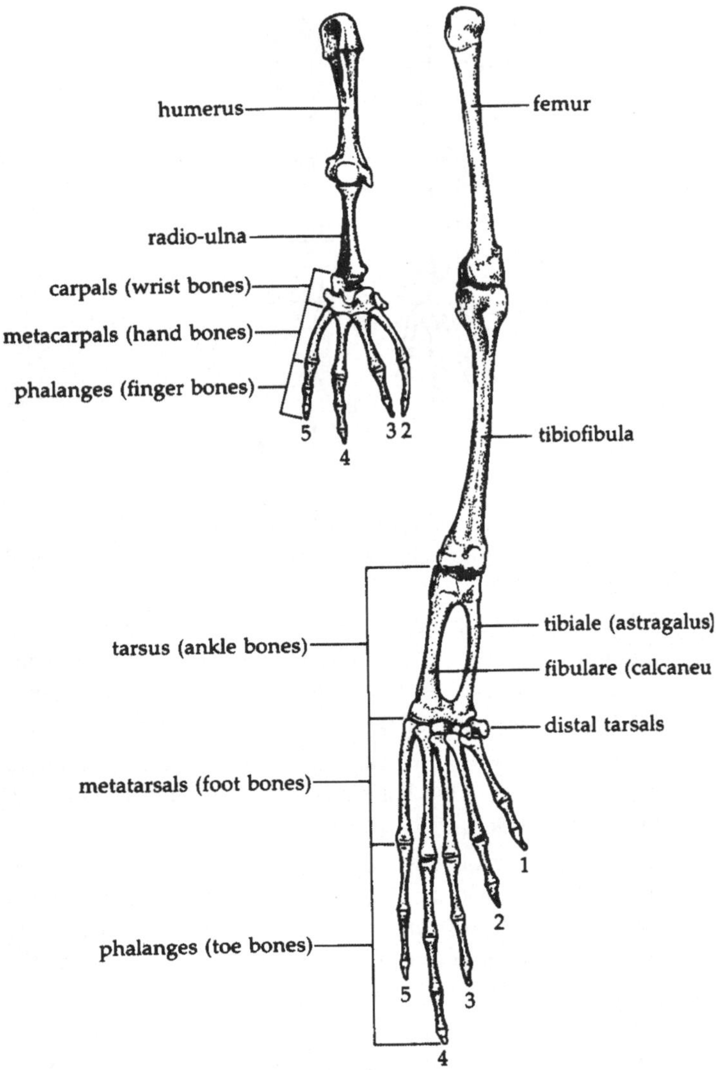

Figure 4.11: Fore and hindlimb of Rana.

arrangement of bones in their lobe fins. Figure elsewhere in this chapter shows plans of the layout of bones in the fore and hindlimbs of a primitive tetrapod.

Compare them with the actual situation in *Cryptobranchus* and R. *catesbiana*. As you look at vertebrates that run, jump, dig, or fly, notice what happens to their limb bones.

5. What is the posture of the limbs? The body is supported above the ground because the limbs hold it up, but they are not held straight down from the body. Instead, they are bent at various points.

   Note the angles of the bones in the limbs. Flexibility at elbow, knee, wrist, and ankle is essential - not so much in the digits themselves in these animals. In general, the joint at shoulder and hip allows rotation in tetrapods.

   Elbow and ankle joints are also capable of rotation as well as flexion and extension, whereas the wrist and knee are hinge joints and tend to be more restricted in their movements.

   Note, in *Cryptobranchus,* how the humerus and femur are held almost horizontally out from the body. This is the sort of posture that early tetrapods had. It is also characteristic of many small quadrupedal vertebrates.

   It is a stable posture but the body has to be prevented from sagging between the limbs, and the muscles running between body and limbs are correspondingly large, particularly ventrally. Consequently the expectation is that the ventral part of the limb girdles will also be large to accommodate these muscles. You can check to see whether this is so.

6. Now look at the limb bones themselves, and observe carefully their proportions. First, look at *Cryptobranchus*. Its fore- and hindlimbs are about the same size. This is as would be expected from the fact that salamanders walk quadrupedally, with all four limbs providing thrust.

   If you look at the *Rana* skeleton, you will see that the proportions of the limbs are quite different - the hindlimbs are much longer. You will discover with other examples of the same phenomenon later in the book, that relatively long hindlegs are a sure sign that they deliver most of the thrust during locomotion.

   Frog hindlimbs are long, and yet strong and light. If the forelimbs were very long too, then you might conclude that *they* also were used in frog locomotion to deliver thrust. Why is it possible to conclude this?

   The reason is that if an animal has long legs, then it can deliver the thrust necessary over a longer period of time, because it remains in contact with the ground for longer as it

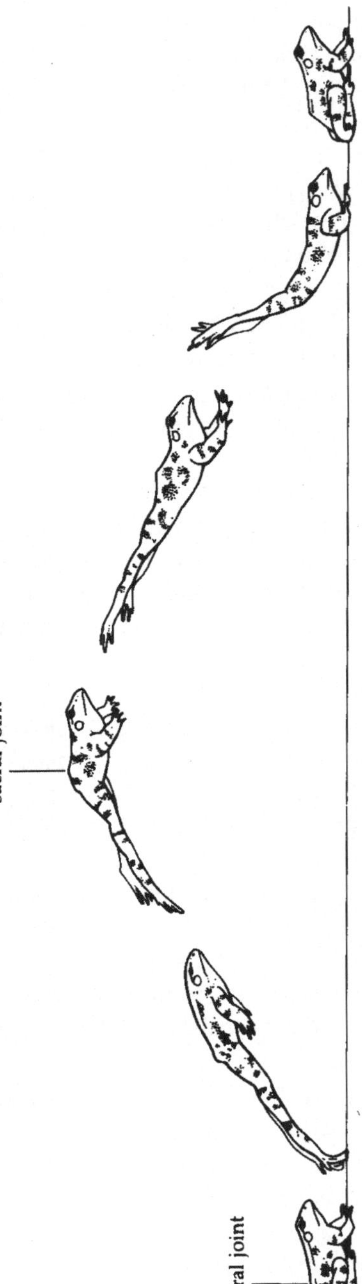

Figure 4.12: Rana: sequence of movements during a jump.

extends its limb on push-off. This makes for a more economic use of energy. The stride or jump length is also increased. As you will see from the drawings of a frog jumping, the hindfeet are still on the ground when the body is projected up well above the ground by the leverage of the legs.

7. How is the length of the hindleg produced? What bones are lengthened? Note that the tibia and fibula are fused; a single bone with a given crosssectional area is stronger than two with the same total area. Count the joints in the frog's leg. Which would correspond in position to your ankle? What are the two long bones distal to the ankle?

   They are tarsal bones that have become very elongated. They belong to the proximal row of tarsal bones, and are the tibiale or astragalus, and the fibulare or calcaneum. The long tarsus adds yet more length to the leg; so do the long toes.

   Note that a powerful thrust with the hindlegs is not only important in the jump but also during swimming, and the large webbed feet help to puh against the water.

8. Have you noticed that the ilium in the pelvis is also long in the frog skeleton? Look at the position of the acetabulum; then look at where the ilium articulates with the vertebral column.

   The long ilium can pivot on the sacrum during the jump, and effectively adds yet more length to the system of levers propelling the frog into the air. The position of the sacral joint is indicated in Figure elsewhere in this chapter.

9. What is the role of the forelegs in the jump? They land first at the end of the jump, and so must withstand the impact of the body with the ground. They are short and robustly built, with the feet angled inwards.

   Look again at the short stiff backbone, and compare the whole set-up of the frog body with that of *Cryptobranchus, now* that you know more about what happens during a jump. The contrast between the shapes of these two animals highlights their very different methods of locomotion. We discuss urodele movement in more detail in the next section.

MUSCLES AND LOCOMOTION

Whereas fish use their extensive axial muscles (those of neck, trunk, and tail) for propulsion, it is the limbs of land vertebrates that take over most of the propulsive effort. The overall volume of axial muscles is reduced in tetrapods even if one includes the limb muscles, which were probably originally derived from axial sources. A newt or salamander walks by levering itself over the ground, supported on a triad of limbs or on one diagonal pair followed by the other.

Thus, the right forelimb leaves the ground first, followed nearly simultaneously by the left hindlimb, and they move forward in a recovery stroke, while the left fore- and right hindlimb are propelling the animal forwards by applying force to the ground.

This pattern of quadrupedal locomotion whereby limbs are moved in diagonal pairs is characteristic of many tetrapods. Frogs and toads also use this pattern when they walk—toads use the walk more than frogs. The frog jump is a bipedal movement, involving simultaneous extension of both hindlimbs.

The forelimbs are held back beside the body until it has reached the highest point of the jump, and are then brought out and forwards to absorb the impact of landing. How are these movements produced? In urodeles, both vertebral and limb muscles are involved, the vertebral muscles being particularly important in bending the trunk so as to lengthen the stride.

In frogs, the intrinsic muscles of the hindlimbs are primarily responsible for the propulsive force. We shall compare and contrast the muscles of the hindlimbs of a newt and a frog, for it is there that we may expect to see the most obvious functional differences.

If possible, look at the muscles of freshly killed animals (you could have one or two for demonstration purposes), for it is then easier to manipulate them and work out their actions; preserved material is inevitably stiffer and more brittle.

It is also possible to investigate muscle action by electrical stimulation of muscles in a freshly killed and pithed frog. Muscles and their activities have an elaborate terminology associated with them, which you need to know about in order to understand this section and several others in later chapters.

The names of muscles usually refer to one of three things - their shape or position, the bones that they move, or the action that they perform. For example, the longissimus dorsi is a long muscle lying along the back; the iliolumbaris runs from ilium to lumbar region; and the flexor digitorum flexes (i.e. bends) the digits.

Unfortunately, not all names have such an obvious rationale—the gluteus muscle, for example. Muscles are also described in terms of

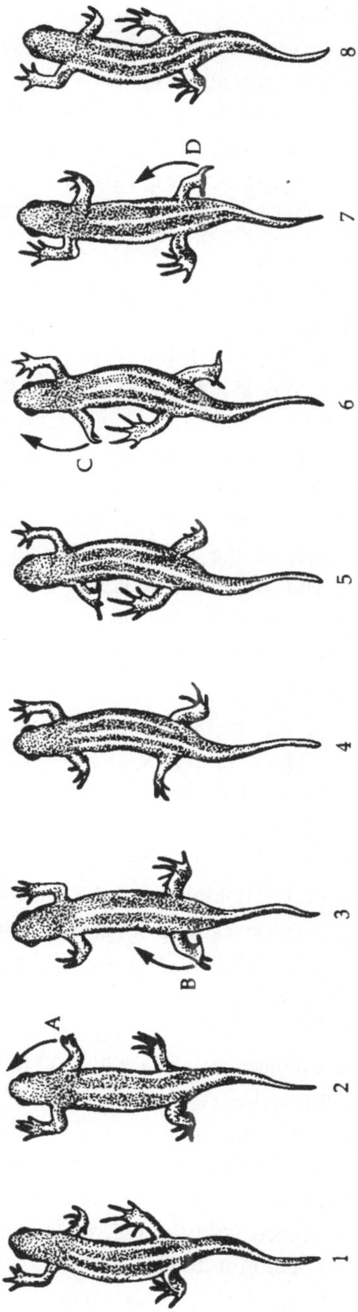

Figure 4.13: The newt, Triturus, walking, Arrows and letters indicate the sequence in which legs are moved.

their 'origin' and 'insertion'. The origin refers to the end closest to the body itself, or which is fixed when the muscle contracts. The 'insertion' is the end attached to the structure that is moved.

Thus, a depressor mandibulae muscle causes the mandible (lower jaw) to be lowered; it originates on the back of the skull and inserts on the back of the mandible, which is the structure that is moved. Other words that refer to muscle movements will be explained in context.

The Frog, *Rana temporaria*

1. If you have a freshly killed frog, pick it up by holding it just behind the shoulders. Allow the hindlegs to hang downwards. The two articulations of the ilia with the sacral vertebra stand out as knobs at the point of flexure of the ilia on the backbone.

   The urostyle also stands out as a ridge of bone under the skin, continuing posteriorly in the midline between the ilia. It is easy to demonstrate, with the frog in this position, that the ilium can rotate on the sacrum, and that the articulation of urostyle and sacrum is also movable.

   Notice in what plane the movement occurs. This degree of flexibility would be impossible if either articulation involved more than one vertebra.

2. Place the frog on its belly and remove the skin from the dorsal surface up to the level of the forelimbs. The ilia and urostyle can be seen as white lines.

   Remove connective tissue carefully to expose bones and muscles further. The articulation between each ilium and the sacral vertebra is enclosed in a little joint capsule.

3. The longissimus dorsi muscle passes down the back from shoulder to urostyle. Cut it at sacral level on one side and deflect it anteriorly. Underneath it can be seen the transverse processes of the trunk vertebrae, and their interconnections with the iliolumbaris muscle, which extends forwards to the fourth vertebra.

   This muscle originates on the dorsal side of the sacro-iliac joint, and when it contracts, the vertebral column is pulled dorsally. Rotation occurs about the sacro-iliac joint until the backbone is aligned with the ilia, or even slightly beyond this point (i.e. producing a hollow back).

4. Other muscles involved in movement of the pelvic girdle and

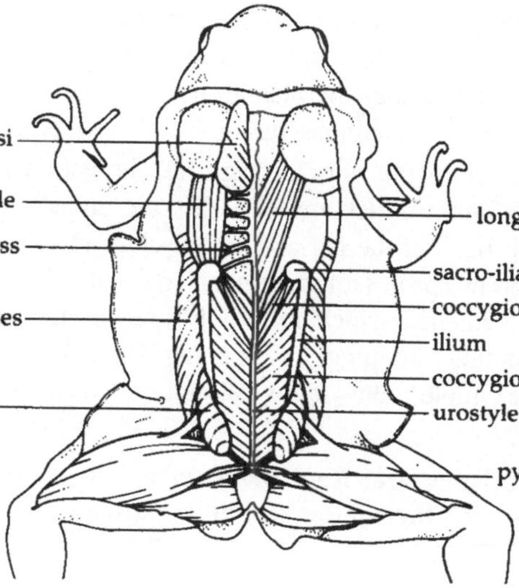

Figure 4.14: Dissection of back and sacral muscles of Rana Temporaria.

urostyle are the coccygeo-iliacus and coccygeo-sacralis muscles. These muscles also cause straightening of the back.

When the frog jumps, it unfolds itself from a squatting position until its foot, leg, thigh, and trunk are almost in a straight line. Its back becomes hollow just before landing, and this together with the subsequent refolding of the pelvic and hindlimb joints, helps to absorb the considerable inertial force of the jump.

The muscles mentioned so far, together with the pyriformis, all control the movement of trunk on pelvis and urostyle.

5. In the hindlimb itself, the main extensor muscles (i.e. those that extend or straighten out the leg) can be seen by simply removing the skin from one leg and investigating with a probe from dorsal and ventral sides.

   The individual muscles of the thigh are less easy to distinguish from each other than the muscles in the lower leg and foot.

6. Muscles that extend the hip are the semimembranosus and gracilis major. Muscles extending the knee are the cruralis and gluteus. On the other hand, the sartorius flexes both hip and knee. Note the origins and insertions of these muscles if you are dissecting an animal yourself.

7. The strong push-off by the lower leg during a jump is controlled

by the gastrocnemius muscle, whose large plantaris tendon runs over the ankle joint and along the underside of the foot, where it becomes the plantar aponeurosis (an aponeurosis is a flat sheet of tendinous tissue).

Where does the muscle originate? Its action is to extend the ankle joint. Which muscles flex the ankle? Note the overall proportions of the leg and its muscles, and their relative sizes. Different species of frog may have slightly different muscle arrangements, which reflect differences in movement during swimming, jumping, or catching food. The sacro-iliac joint, for example, may allow sliding rather than rotation, as in *Xenopus*.

Table 4.1: Equivalent terminologies of the major hindlimb muscles.

Newt	*Frog*
Dorsal muscles	
(i.e. seen from dorsal side)	
Puboischiofemoralis internus (pif.in)	Iliacus externus (ila.ex)
Iliotibialis (il.tib)	Tensor fasciae latae (t.f.1)
Iliofibularis (il.fib)	Iliofibularis (il.fib)
Ilioextensorius (il.ex)	Cruralis + gluteus (c + gl)
Extensor digitorum communis (ex.dig.com)	Tibialis anticus longus (tib.an.long)
Extensor fibularis (ex.fib)	Peroneus (p)
Ventral muscles	
Puboischiofemoralis externus (pif. ex)	Adductor magnus (a.m.)
Puboischiotibialis (pu.is.tib)	Sartorius + semitendinosus (sa) (combined in higher Anura)
Pubotibialis (pu.tib)	Part of adductor magnus
Ischioflexorius (is.fl)	Semimembranosus + part of gracilis (sm + gr)
Flexor primordialis communis (fl. prim.com)	Partly equivalent to gastrocnemius (ga)

The newt, *Triturus cristatus*

The hindlimb of *Triturus* is relatively much shorter and the muscles are less easy to distinguish than those of *Rana*. It will help to use a

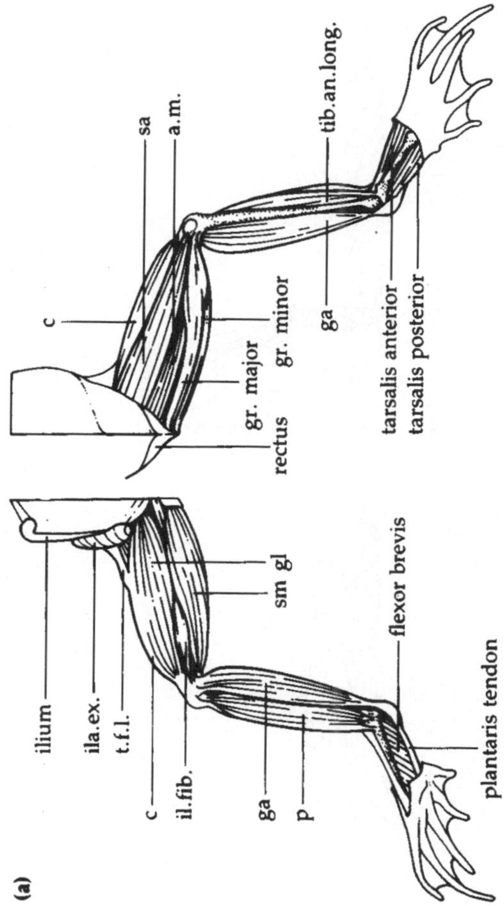

Figure 4.15: Hindlimb muscles of Rana temporaria: (a) dorsal and (b) ventral views.

low-power microscope (e.g. with a magnification of × 7-10).

1. Skin the animal so that the whole of one hindleg is exposed down to the base of the toes, and also the area immediately around the pelvis on that side, and for about a centimetre along the tail. This will expose intrinsic limb muscles, and also those originating on the pelvis and tail.

2. Work out where the various muscles are by using Figure elsewhere in this chapter as a guide. This is where microscopic examination will help. Very little further dissection is required - but careful observation is essential in order to see the precise location of tendons, bones, and muscle insertions.

3. The nomenclature of amphibian muscles is confusing because of a tendency to use a mixture of names, some of which were originally

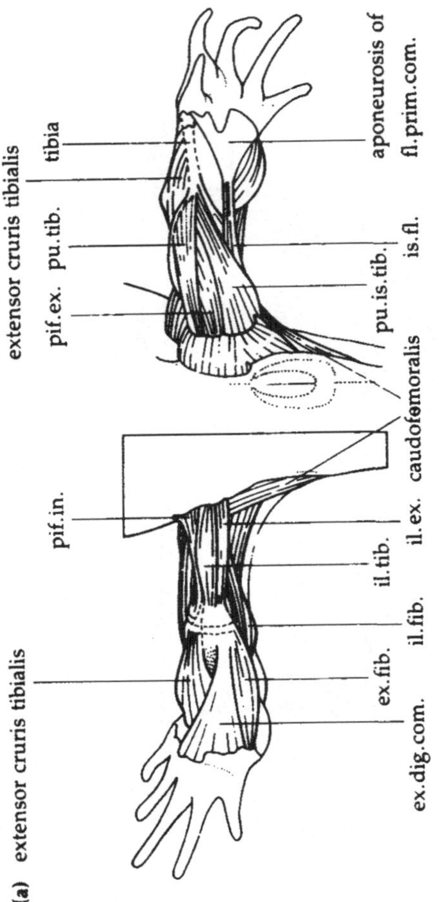

Figure 4.16: Hindlimb muslce of Triturus cristratus: (a) dorsal and (b) ventral views.

used in mammalian anatomy. The original explicit Latin terminology is cumbersome, but at least tells you something about each muscle. Table elsewhere in this chapter relates the two terminologies for some of the major 'muscles in the hindlimb.

The list is incomplete because some homologies are unclear or complex, and the problem is compounded by the fact that urodele leg muscles are unspecialised, whereas in the frog they are highly specialised. Note that homologous muscles may not have quite the same effect in the two animals, because of the very different proportions of the hindlimbs.

4. The movements of the newt hindlimbs are very different from those described for the frog. A newt moves fast by holding its limbs back against the body, and undulating body and tail laterally, belly to the ground.

When walking, its legs hold the body off the ground and move through a propulsive and recovery stroke. Lateral bending of the body, produced by the dorsal epaxial muscles of the back, adds length to the stride.

5. In the propulsive stroke, the sole of the foot touches the ground and points in the direction of motion. It is symmetrical, with toes splayed out, and grips the ground firmly as the flexor primordialis communis contracts.

Newts cannot walk up on their toes - they are said to be plantigrade because the whole sole of the foot is applied to the ground. The femur moves in a horizontal plane back towards the tail. The muscles responsible for this retraction are mainly the caudofemoralis, the iliofemoralis, and the puboischiofemoralis externus.

The knee and ankle are flexed during most of this, and the tibia crosses over in front of the fibula as the femur is pulled back. Tibia and fibula are unfused in urodeles.

6. The recovery stroke starts when the foot is lifted off the ground. The femur is then moved forwards by the puboischiofemoralis internus. When it has swung to about a right angle with the body axis, the knee is flexed, and the limb continues forwards held in a position like that adopted by the human arm when it is doing the crawl in swimming.

At the end of the recovery stroke, the foot is extended again by the extensor digitorum communis. It is also turned forwards by the flexor primordialis communis, and in this position it makes contact with the ground to begin another propulsive stroke.

This very simplified account of urodele hindlimb movement during locomotion applies also to the forelimbs, except that they are not lifted so high off the substrate. This is the basic tetrapod method of locomotion, and the structural adaptation to it shown by the limbs can be regarded as a sort of ground plan upon which all the subsequent modifications of vertebrate locomotion are built.

The frog's jump is one example of the potential variations that can be played upon this theme. Several others are mentioned later in the book.

BLOOD CIRCULATION AND LUNGS

There is one important circulatory question that relates particularly to amphibians, because they were the first land vertebrates. What happend when lungs took over the oxygenation of blood from the gills?

Lungs seem to have appeared early in fish evolution, and are probably homologous to swim bladders. Both are endodermal outgrowths from the anterior gut.

Enclosure within the body protects the respiratory surfaces from desiccation and damage, but requires the development of ventilation systems to bring fresh air to them. These vary in different vertebrates.

Frogs, for example, which do not have thoracic ribs for chest ventilation, use instead a pumping mechanism that involves filling the mouth cavity with air and then driving it into the lungs by closing the nostrils and raising the floor of the mouth.

The blood supply to the lungs comes from one of the original branchial, or gill, arterial arches. In fish, six aortic arches appear in embryos, between the developing gill slits.

Adult elasmobranchs have five of these, the first (most anterior) having mostly disappeared. Adult teleosts have four aortic arches, the second usually disappearing as well during development. Lungfishes have the same four arches, and the lungs are supplied from the most posterior of the four.

This is equivalent to the sixth of the original embryonic series. The lungs of all land vertebrates are supplied with blood from this source. In this section, we shall look at two aspects of amphibian circulation. The main one is the disposition of the aortic arches; the other is the structure of the heart.

Urodeles and anurans have an interesting difference in their arterial circulation, because urodeles often have four functional aortic arches (and are therefore superficially more like fish), whereas anurans only have three like all other living tetrapods. Which of the original six arches are present and what are their functions in amphibians?

Figure elsewhere in this chapter shows in diagrammatic form what the arrangement is in urodeles and anurans, with a teleost fish and a lungfish for comparison. The four arches in urodeles are the third to sixth, whereas in anurans the fifth arch does not develop.

The third arch always carries blood to the head, and is called the carotid arch; the fourth carries blood to the body, and is called the systemic arch; and the sixth always carries blood to the lungs, and so is the pulmonary arch.

The fifth arch, even though present in urodeles, is often only functional in larval stages (or where gills persist in adults), and in *Triturus* adults is represented only by a line of pigment. All the arterial arches emerge from the heart together in a common large tube called the conus arteriosus, which leaves the ventricle on the ventral side - the same position as in fish.

The dissection involved in demonstrating the amphibian arterial system is straightforward, but requires care. For this reason, use precision dissecting instruments and a good dissecting microscope, and avoid wasting animals if you are inadequately equipped.

This section concentrates on Rana *temporaria,* which is much easier to dissect than *Triturus.* If you use other amphibians than these, expect differences between this text and your own observations, because there is considerable variation in gas-exchange mechanisms and hence in the vascular system in different species—even, to some extent, between individuals within a species.

Arterial Arches of the Frog

1. Lay the frog on its back and pin it out through each foot. Make a midventral incision in the skin, and cut anteriorly to the throat and posteriorly to the cloaca. Cut along each limb and pin the skin out away from the body on each side.

2. Note the anterior abdominal vein, which is a large blood vessel lying in the midventral line; it runs to the liver. If your animal is freshly killed, you will have to ligature this vein. Make two little longitudinal incisions through the body wall, one on either side of the vein, close to where it enters the liver.

Insert the thread and tie two ligatures, with the anterior one close to the liver. Cut the vein between them; then extend your incisions back alongside it and expose the abdominal contents.

3. Extend one of your incisions forwards towards the heart. Be very careful not to pierce it. Hold the body wall up with forceps and keep your scissor blades un.

When vnii reach the nectnral girdle. cut around beside its posterior edges on each side, avoiding the cutaneous veins. You can now turn back the entire body wall of the trunk and pin it on each side.

4. You will have to remove the ventral part of the pectoral girdle in order to see the arterial arches. Hold up the xiphisternum and look beneath it as you cut carefully forwards.

The heart will drop away from it; then cut through the two coracoids and clavicles, close to their junction with the humerus and scapula, and lift them out.

5. The heart and arterial arches will now be exposed. It remains only to clear away connective tissue and pericardium, and to work out

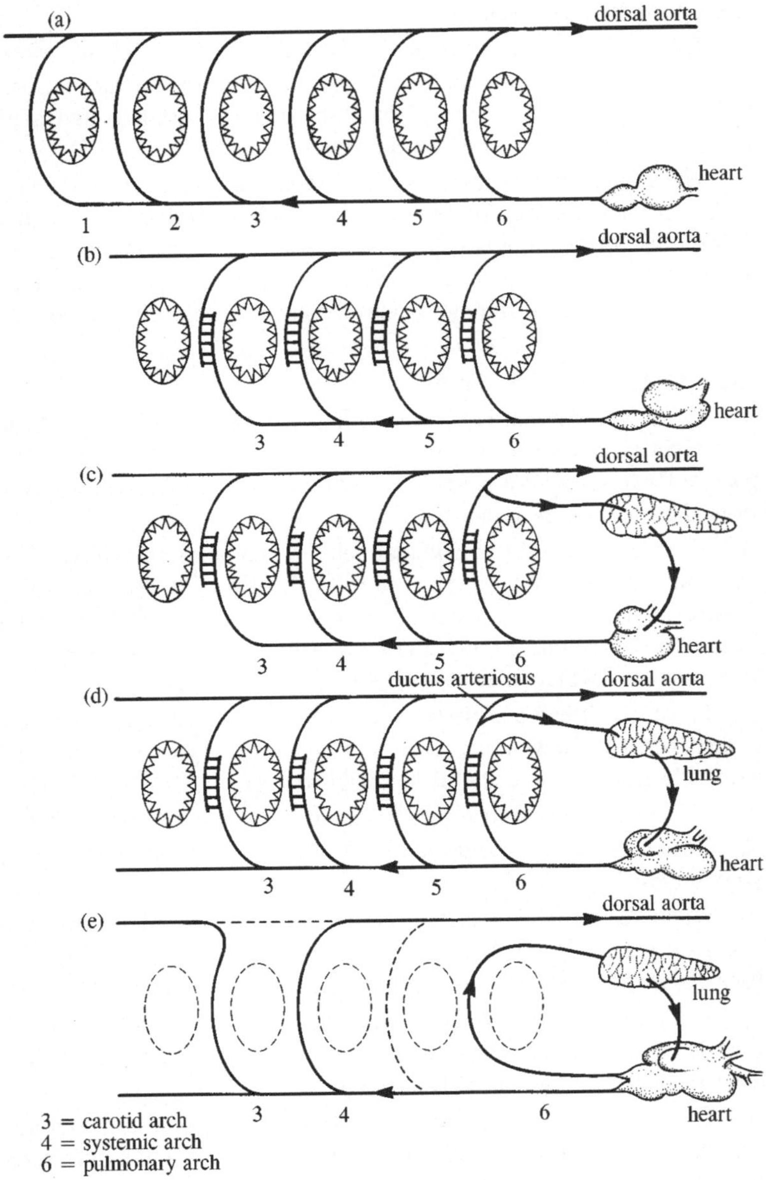

Figure 4.17: Diagram of the arrangement of aortic arches in (a) vertebrate embryo, (b) teleost, (c) lungfish, (d) larval urodele, and (e) anuran.

where the blood vessels go. You may find that the connective tissue is populated with melanophores, in which case it is easier to distinguish from underlying blood vessels, and to remove it selectively. A dissecting microscope and good illumination are a help too.

6. Clear away the pericardium from around the conus arteriosus and the origins of the aortic arches. The conus is a Y-shaped structure emerging from the ventricle.

7. Locate the lungs, and note their relationship to the heart. They are thinwalled pinkish structures, full of air bubbles in frogs. Note the melanophores on them too.

Concentrate now on one side of the animal. Find the pulmonary blood vessels and decide which is arterial and which venous. Trace the

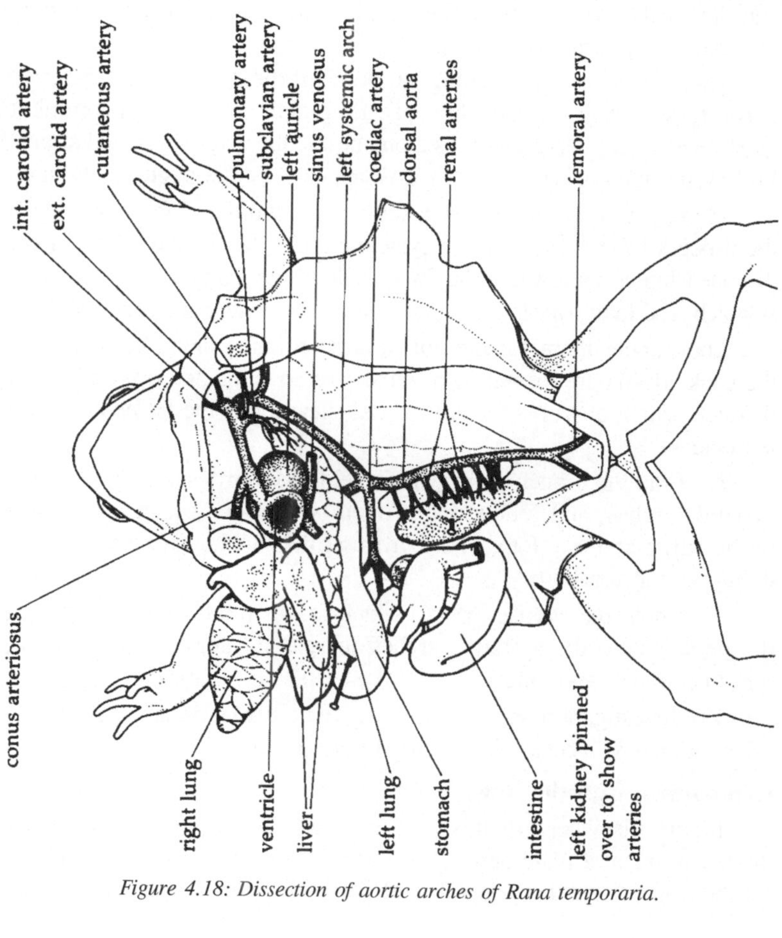

Figure 4.18: Dissection of aortic arches of Rana temporaria.

pulmonary artery back to where it separates from the other aortic arches. What part of the heart does the pulmonary vein enter?

8. In the process of all this, you will have noticed a large blood vessel passing out laterally to the skin from near the left auricle. It runs ventral to the lung, and so lies on top of it when you dissect from the ventral side.

This is the subdavian vein, which receives a large cutaneous branch. You can follow its course until it joins the jugular veins, and enters the superior vena cava. Care is required, or you will pierce the left auricle.

9. There is also a cutaneous artery. It branches off the pulmonary arch and travels laterally to the skin. Uncover its origin too.

10. Next, find where the carotid artery branches off. It is the most anterior of the three aortic arches. Make sure you can distinguish both external and internal branches.

There is also a thickening at or near the base of the external carotid, which is called the carotid gland. Note the prominent glossopharyngeal nerve that runs along beside the external carotid artery. Follow the internal carotid until it disappears by the angle of the jaw.

11. If you have cleared the arteries successfully so far, you will in the process have seen the large systemic arch (the middle of the three) disappearing down towards the dorsal side of the animal. Push the lung, stomach, and liver over to the opposite side from where you are dissecting.

Look under them for the dorsal aorta running along the centre of the back. If you are dissecting a female, remove the anterior end of the oviduct, which obscures the aorta. Also clear away the fat body and its mesentery.

12. Find the branch point where the dorsal aorta splits into the two systemic arches, and follow one of them around until it meets the rest of the aortic arches. Note, in the process, the subclavian artery leaving to supply the forelimb.

Also note the coeliac artery, which leaves the dorsal aorta just at the point where the systemic arches merge. It supplies the stomach, intestine, liver, and spleen.

13. Investigation more posteriorly will reveal renal arteries and other branches. These will not be discussed here.

Comparison with the Newt

Figure elsewhere in this chapter shows the right arterial arches dissected out in a male newt. The procedure is essentially the same as for the frog, except that you will find skin and connective tissue generally more difficult to remove. A helpful technique if you have trouble distinguishing smaller arteries is to inject a dye such as methylene blue into the ventricle, from where it will enter the arteries.

Note the following:

1. The conus arteriosus and general layout of major arteries is the same as in frogs.
2. The fifth arterial arch would lie between the systemic and pulmonary arches. This is where it may be found in some adult urodeles, but in adult *Triturus* it persists only as a line of pigment.
3. There is a connection between the systemic and pulmonary arches called the ductus arteriosus. Look at the diagrams in

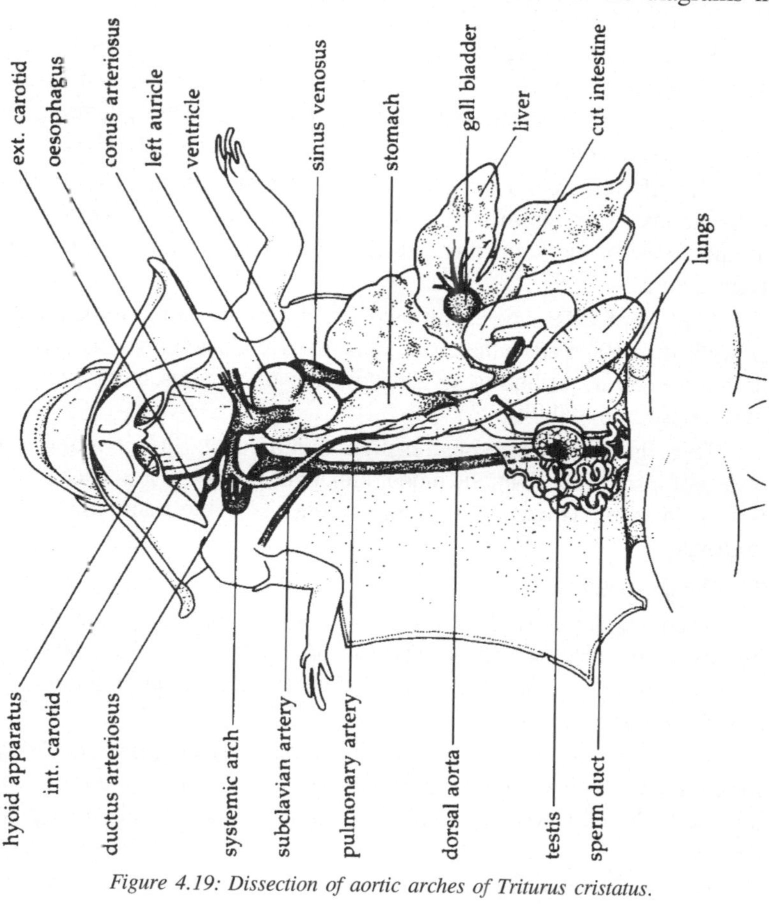

Figure 4.19: Dissection of aortic arches of Triturus cristatus.

Figure elsewhere in this chapter to see what this corresponds to.

In some urodeles this sends small arteries to the skin, and could allow shunting of the blood directly around the body, bypassing the lungs, which are often relatively unimportant as oxygenating organs.

Many urodeles hardly use their lungs, since gas exchange occurs almost entirely through the skin. Some are lungless, such as the plethodontid salamanders of North America.

4. *Triturus* has no cutaneous artery coming off the pulmonary arch. But this does not mean that its skin is not used for gas exchange, since it is supplied from other sources such as the dorsal aorta.
5. The point at which the systemic arches merge is much further forward in *Triturus,* and as a result, the-subclavian artery branches from the dorsal aorta, not from each systemic arch as in *Rana*.

The differences you can see between the major arteries of urodeles and anurans, as exemplified by a common European frog and newt, give an indication of the versatility that amphibians show when it comes to respiration.

The use of gills, lungs, skin, and sometimes the lining of the mouth as well, is widespread in the group, and an individual animal may adjust its physiology according to its development or circumstances between these various possibilities.

Thus, in frogs, cutaneous respiration is particularly important as a means of losing CO_2 from the blood, although some O_2 is also exchanged across the skin. However, the lungs seem to be the main site of O_2 exchange.

The Frog Heart

Accommodating to the presence of lungs is not simply a matter of modifying the arterial arches. The site of oxygenation of the blood is now at a different point in the circulation. In fish, blood circulation is a one-way through system.

The heart only pumps deoxygenated blood returning from the body forwards to the gills. Blood runs forwards ventrally, passes up through the gills (where it is oxygenated), and then goes back dorsally to supply the body.

In amphibians, oxygenated blood does not circulate directly around the body from the lungs, it returns to the heart. So the heart has to pump both oxygenated and deoxygenated blood. How is mixture of the two to be prevented?

Crocodiles, birds, and mammals have what is described as a double circulation, in which deoxygenated blood returns to the right auricle from the body, and is kept separate as it enters the ventricle because a septum divides the ventricle into right and left halves.

The right ventricle pumps deoxygenated blood to the lungs. Oxygenated blood enters the left auricle via the pulmonary vein, and is pumped around the body and head by the left ventricle, which is larger. In amphibians, the ventricle is a single chamber, and only the two auricles are separate.

However, although mixing of oxygenated and deoxygenated blood would be expected to occur, it is actually minimal. Measurements have shown that blood with most oxygen enters the carotid arch first, and so reaches the brain. The systemic arch receives some deoxygenated blood, and the pulmonary arch receives mainly deoxygenated blood.

The fact that very little mixing of the two occurs seems to be due to a combined effect of the spongy subdivisions of the ventricle, and the spiral fold in the conus arteriosus. Note that oxygenated blood returning from the skin enters the systemic circulation and is not routed directly into the left auricle along with blood from the lungs.

It is easy to remove the frog heart and look at its gross morphology. To look at it in detail requires a microscope and fine dissecting instruments, because it is tooa small to dissect properly with the naked eye, let alone to see its internal structure.

The instructions and observations below refer to a frog heart measuring 6-7 mm from anterior to posterior, dissected under a binocular microscope at × 7-20 zoom magnification.

1. Cut out the heart, severing the arteries and veins at least a centimetre away from it, so as to work out connections more easily. Probine with a seeker is helpful in doing this. Note the conus arteriosus and sinus venosus, and find where the pulmonary veins enter the left auricle.

   The sinus venosus enters the right auricle, and becomes part of it in higher vertebrates. This arrangement of the major vessels around the heart is similar in all tetrapods. 2. To look at the heart's internal structure, lay it on its dorsal side, so that the conus is uppermost.

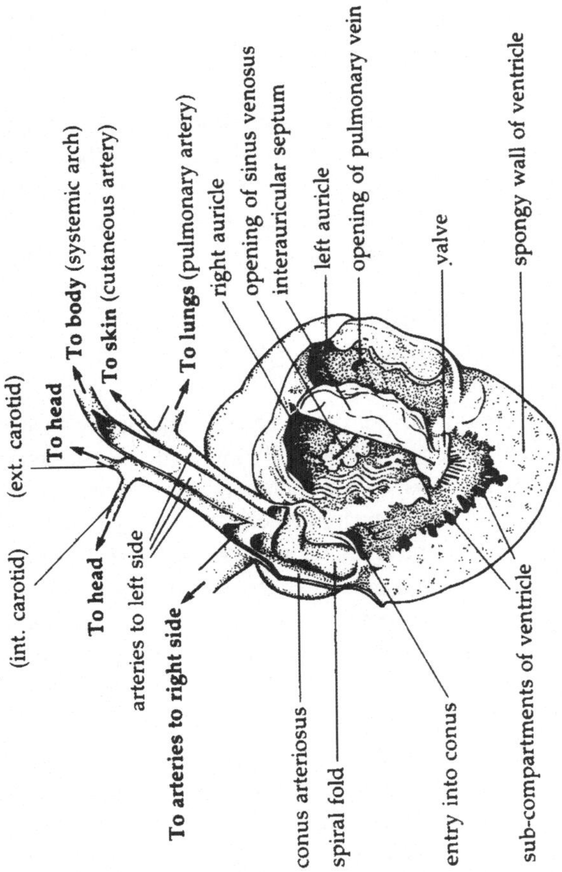

Figure 4.20: The heart of Rana temporaria with ventral side cut away to show internal structure.

Using the microscope, carefully cut away the ventral side of the ventricle, and extend the cut up the conus to expose its internal structure from ventricle to aortic arches.

Push the conus over to one side, and cut away the ventral side of the auricles as well. You should end up with the inside of the heart exposed from the ventral side as in Figure elsewhere in this chapter. Note the following:

(a) The thick, muscular wall of the ventricle, and its subdivision internally by spongy trabeculae into many small channels and spaces. This structure prevents free mixing of incoming blood.

(b) The auricles have much thinner walls, but they too are criss-crossed by muscle fibres.

(c) The auricles appear to be a single structure externally, but when you look inside, there is an interauricular septum - thin, but complete—which separates them into a larger right auricle and smaller left one.

(d) Where the auricles enter the ventricle, there is a large valve. The interauricular septum extends down onto it, and underneath it is supported on tendinous strands of tissue.

(e) The entry points of sinus venosus into right auricle and pulmonary veins into left auricle should be visible, though they are concealed by folds of tissue in the empty, collapsed auricles. Again, a seeker will help you to find them.

(f) The conus arteriosus has a spiral fold in it. Look at its position and note its relation to the major arteries. It is responsible for controlling the passage of blood out of the ventricle, so that deoxygenated and oxygenated blood remain almost separate in practice.

(g) When you have investigated the frog heart, look at the heart of a bird or mammal, and work out what structural changes have occurred in comparison to the amphibian level of organisation.

Amphibians provide a conceptual link with fish because of their gills and partial dependence on water, however far they may actually have come from their fishy ancestors in evolutionary terms.

We see in their circulation the sort of adaptation that occurred with the introduction of lungs (and skin) into the system as sites of gas exchange, and the decreasing importance of gills.

Their hearts further reflect a requirement to transfer oxygenated blood efficiently from the lungs to the body, particularly the brain; as a result there are partial physical barriers to mixing of bloodstreams and a surprisingly effective separation in practice. This is followed in later vertebrate evolution by complete separation, and the double circulation of birds and mammals.

5

Reptiles: Three Modern Orders

Living reptiles are the remnants of a once *widespread* and varied group, whose members were the *dominant* land vertebrates during the Mesozoic era. Although *modern reptiles* show a diversity of form and function, yet it is a pale reflection of the *profusion* of animals that existed 150 or so million years ago.

For instance, then there were not only fossil representatives of the three subclasses listed above—such as the *archosaurian dinosaurs* and *pterosaurs*—but also three other subclasses of reptiles now all extinct.

One of these extinct subclasses, the *Synapsida*, gave rise to the mammals. This chapter looks at those reptiles that flourish today, some of them relatively unchanged since those early days of reptilian adaptive radiation.

Representatives of three main orders of living reptiles - the *Chelonia*, Squamata, and *Crocodilia*—are discussed below, with emphasis in each case on their own particular specialities. A fourth order, the Rhynchocephalia, has only one living genus, the tuatara or *Sphenodon*.

It exists now only on certain islands off the coast of New Zealand, and is sometimes classified with the lizards in the order Squamata. It will not be discussed here.

We begin with some information on skin, for the skin has played an important role in the *adaptation* of reptiles to life on land.

Material Required

- Slides of lizard or snake skin.
- *Tortoise shell* and *skeleton*, live *tortoises* or turtles for

demonstration, e.g. *Testudo graeca*.

- Live lizards for demonstration of scales, locomotion, etc. Skeleton of a lizard; good ones to use are *Iguana* or *Varanus*.
- Live snakes for demonstration, e.g. the grass snake, *Natrix,* or the garter snake, *Thamnophis*.
- Snake skeleton, skulls, e.g. of python and/or a viper.
- Alligator skull, e.g. *Alligator mississippiensis,* or any available crocodilian material.
- Film of animals in their natural habitats moving and feeding, etc.

THE SKIN OF REPTILES

Land life brings with it problems of water balance. Reptiles have been much more diverse and successful (in terms of *numbers* of *genera*) in *colonising* land than have *amphibians*. The main reptilian adaptations to life on land are a waterproof egg that can survive in dry habitats, and the development of a modified *kidney*.

However, reptilian success has also been due to their relatively waterproof skins. Reptile skin is much less permeable than amphibian skin; it is dry, and hence is not adapted for gas exchange. What makes it *impermeable*?

The skin of a frog, described in the previous chapter, has a layer of keratin formed by the epidermis. In reptiles, this is much thicker where it forms scales, and thins out between the scales, so that expansion and movement of the skin is possible—as in the distended neck of a snake *swallowing* prey.

It is the presence of thick layers of *keratin* which reduces the *permeability* of *reptile skin*. There are also very few glands present, and hence few openings in the epidermis through which *moisture* can escape. However, water is lost through reptile skin, and at a much higher rate in some species than others.

The tortoise shell is a highly developed manifestation of the tendency of reptile skin to produce thickenings of keratin and bone. Its structure will be discussed below. *Lizard*, *snake*, and *crocodile* skin also contains scales, which are underlain by bone in crocodiles and many lizards

In all reptiles that have them, the bony plates (or osteoderms) are dermal structures, and hence have the same origin as other bony products of the *vertebrate dermis*, such as fish *scales*. What are some other vertebrate bones formed in the dermis? Note that *amphibians* and *reptiles* are not alone among land vertebrates in having keratin on the outside of their bodies.

Birds and mammals also produce keratin in the skin epidermis: in birds it forms feathers; in mammals hair (not to mention horn, hoofs, claws, etc.). Some *mammals* (e.g. *armadillos*) have bony dermal plates too. If you look at the scales of a reptile, you will see that they are not all the same size.

A closer look at several animals reveals a constancy of pattern; for example, lizards often have larger scales on the tops of their heads, and most snakes have broad, rectangular *belly scales* (see later). The reasons for the patterns are not always clear, though there is a relationship with the basic *segmentation* of the body.

The belly scales of snakes often have a role in *locomotion*, with muscles attached to them in such a way that they can be moved in relation to the ground. It is interesting that legless lizards do not have these enlarged *belly scales*, and some snakes appear not to use them for locomotion.

Wear and tear on the skin *necessitate* its constant renewal. As in *amphibians*, *reptiles periodically* shed their skin in large pieces simultaneously all over the body.

A new outer layer is produced by the activities of the basal cell layer of the epidermis. Look at a *sloughed* skin if you get the chance—it is thin, and obviously represents only the outermost part of the epidermis.

Many prepared slides of lizard skin show what look like two epidermal layers; the inner one is the new skin forming under the old. What do other vertebrates do about replacing their skins? All of them face the same problems of wear. Reptile skin has *numerous* other interesting properties and roles.

It contains pigment cells, *sensory structures*, and some glands; it forms various appendages, such as the *rattlesnake's rattle*. The dermis contains *blood vessels* which are a crucial part of the heat-exchange system in lizards.

All of these things are essential functions of the skin; it is above all the main interface between animal and environment, and, as such must have had a considerable part to play during the *colonisation* of land by reptiles.

TORTOISES AND TURTLES

Members of the order Chelonia have become adapted to living within a shell. This is their protection from *predation*, and it has drastically influenced their form, as well as affecting such bodily functions as respiration.

However, the shell has obviously proved a successful *adaptation*, because *chelonians* evolved it about 200 million years ago and have survived with little *modification* ever since.

They are still successful in terrestrial, marine, and freshwater habitats today. The shell itself, and the main skeletal adaptations associated with it in a land tortoise, form the subject of this section.

External Features: the Shell

There are two parts to the shell, a carapace above and a plastron below, with openings for limbs, head, and tail. Plastron and carapace join laterally, between fore- and *hindlimbs*, and each is composed of an assemblage of horny scales *overlying* bony plates.

If you look carefully at the exact arrangement of scales (or scutes) and plates, you will see that the divisions between scutes are not coincident with those between the underlying plates. This will add strength to the *shell*.

You can also see growth lines on the scutes, which grow out from the centre as new keratin is laid down below and around it. It is a risky business calculating the age of a chelonian from these lines, for *numerous* environmental factors can affect the rate of growth.

The carapace generally has a central dorsal row of scutes and plates, a lateral row on each side, and a row of smaller units around the edge. The *plastron* consists of two rows of scutes and plates, parallel to each other and joining in the *midventral* line.

One central bony plate occurs just anterior to the pectoral girdle. This is the typical structure of the shell in many chelonians. The skin on the rest of the body, on *neck*, *head*, and *limbs* is covered with small scales much like those of *lizards*, and these are not underlain with bony plates.

The shell represents a considerable proportion of the body weight, as much as 30 per cent in some terrestrial forms. In marine chelonians it tends to become reduced, so that leathery turtles (*Dermochelys*), for example, have numerous tiny bony plates, completely covered over with *smooth*, *leathery skin*.

There are no *horny scutes*. Their reduced shells mean that they are lighter for their size than a land tortoise, and their smooth skins help to streamline them as they *swim*. Being enclosed in a rigid, heavy box poses problems of *mobility*. Where are the points of movement in a

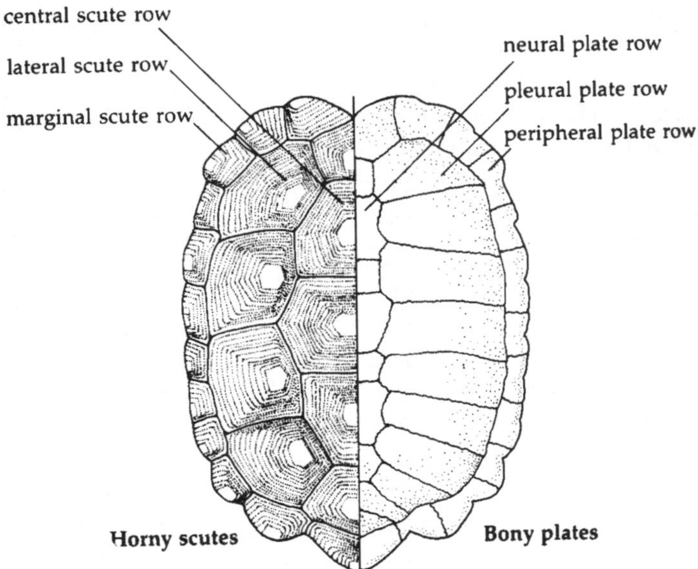

Figure 5.1: The arrangements of scutes and plates in the tortoise carapace.

tortoise's body? Some *chelonians* have areas of flexibility in their shells, particularly hinges in the plastron.

But movement mostly occurs at *knee*, *elbow*, and *neck*, and at the articulations between the limbs and their *girdles*. Notice that the continuity of the shell between the two limbs on each side means that their movement backwards and forwards is somewhat restricted.

Tortoises move in a slow and stately manner, their legs held out laterally and bent downwards at elbow and knee. They may not go places very fast, but they are very stable, and their armour protects them almost completely because both legs and head can be withdrawn into the shell.

Some chelonians cannot withdraw in this manner. Which are they, and how do they defend themselves against *predators*?

Internal Features: Modifications of the Skeleton

Figure elsewhere in this chapter shows a cut-away view of a tortoise skeleton surrounded by its shell. Note the following general and specialised features:

1. The head, on its long neck, is the most freely mobile part of a tortoise's body. Notice the shape and extent of the space

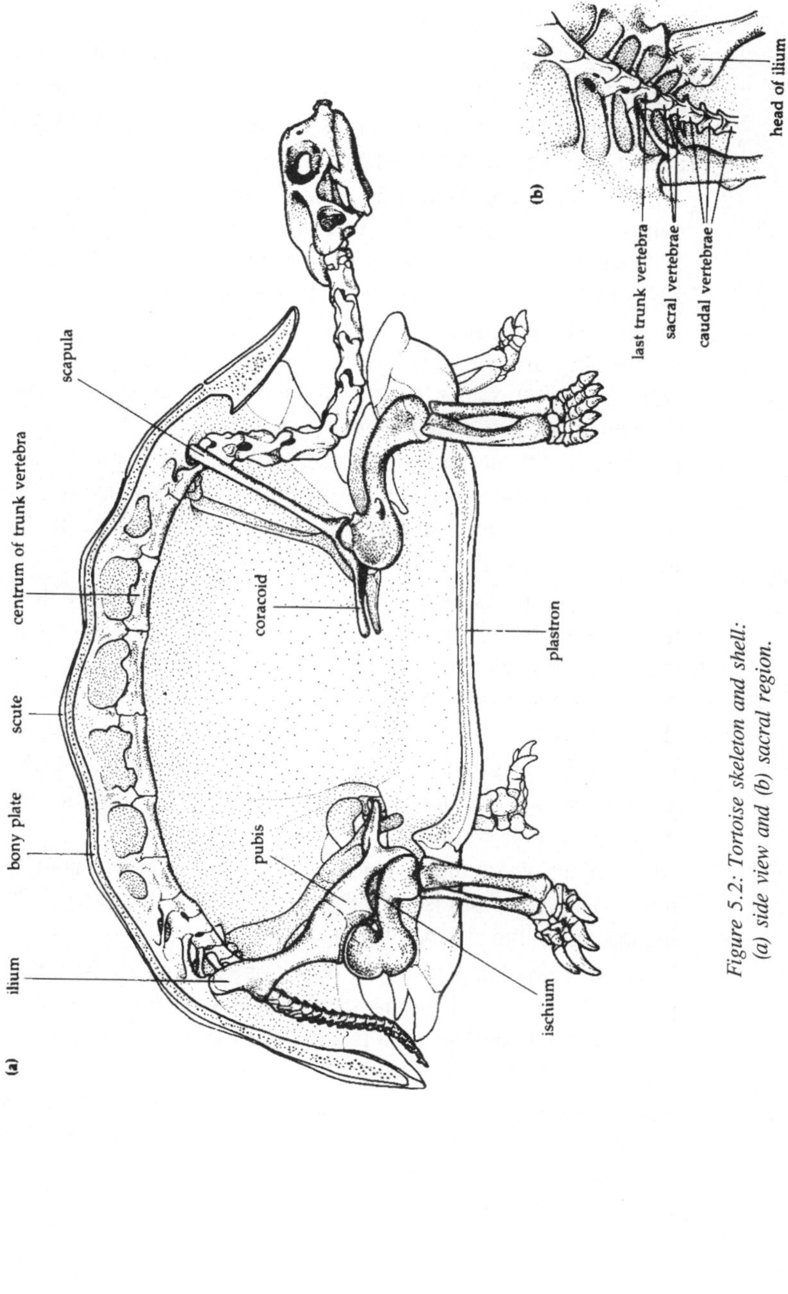

Figure 5.2: Tortoise skeleton and shell: (a) side view and (b) sacral region.

between carapace and plastron where the neck *protrudes*. It is free to move in all directions, which is essential when feeding, *particularly* because of *constraints* imposed by the rigid body.

The neck must also be highly flexible to allow withdrawal into the shell, and bending occurs at specific points. Do those chelonians that withdraw their heads always do so with the neck folded in the same plane?

2. Tortoise skulls are interesting for a variety of reasons. One is that they bear no teeth. The front of the upper and lower jaws is covered by a *horny beak*, with sharp horny ridges along the edges of the jaws. Even carnivorous chelonians have no teeth.

   At the back of the skull, extensive excavations in the bones are visible (they are not *homologous* with the *temporal* openings in other *reptilian skulls* described later). These are for the attachment of jaw and *neck muscles*.

3. Eight cervical vertebrae form the neck in this tortoise, and their *articulations* provide the *flexibility* referred to above. Note that no amphibian has this degree of flexibility of the neck region, nor do many other reptiles.

   zHowever, reptiles as a whole tend to be able to move their heads more freely than *amphibians*—just as amphibians can move theirs more freely than fish, because unlike fish they have no connection between the back of the skull and the shoulder *girdle*.

   Reptiles have gone in for further specialisation of the articulations between their neck vertebrae, and for modification of the joint between head and neck.

4. At the point where the neck joins the trunk region, remarkable things happen to tortoise vertebrae and ribs. Both are partially incorporated into the bony part of the shell.

   How does this happen during development, and is the upper part of the bony shell perhaps entirely formed from expanded vertebrae and ribs? In the embryo, the *carapace* forms in an area of thick tissue on the dorsal surface.

   The developing ribs become attached to this as it grows and expands out laterally. There is no sternum in chelonians, so the distal ends of the ribs are free to be extended outwards around the limb girdles.

This is an extraordinary situation—no other vertebrate has its limb girdles inside the *ribcage*.

5. The *neural spines* of the vertebrae also become incorporated in the *carapace*. Note that the centra of the vertebrae are visible, but cannot move in relation to one another.

   Note also that there is little room for large back muscles, which are much reduced, as are the trunk muscles as a whole.

6. The body of *chelonians* is very short for a reptile; in fact, it is short compared with vertebrates generally. Frogs are the only other vertebrates with such a low number of trunk vertebrae.

   This tortoise has ten plus two sacral vertebrae joined to the ilium. Look back to other chapter of this book to see how many frogs have. What are some possible functional reasons for the short *trunks* of chelonians? What about frogs?

7. Note that whereas frogs have only one sacral vertebra, chelonians have two. This is a basic difference between amphibians and reptiles: no amphibian has more than one sacral *vertebra*, and reptiles always have at least two.

8. Now look at the limb girdles. The pectoral girdle consists of *scapula* and *coracoid*, the other bones (e.g. *clavicle* and *interclavicle*) having become involved in the *plastron*.

   The pectoral girdle is attached via ligaments to the shell and can rotate, so increasing the stride length of the *forelimb*. The pelvic girdle consists of ilium, ischium, and pubis as usual, with a broad symphysis in the *midline*.

9. Both humerus and femur are at right angles to the body axis. They are robust, curved bones which move horizontally fore and aft during walking. Both can rotate about their own longitudinal axes as the animal moves its limbs.

   Note the proportions of the limbs—the forelimbs are relatively shorter and more robust in this tortoise. What does this suggest about the stresses of locomotion in tortoises? Toes are short and clawed; the number of phalanges is small.

   Compare the bones and proportions of this terrestrial tortoise with those of the limb of a swimming turtle if you have one available. What modifications for swimming can you see?

The characteristics mentioned here are those most obviously associated with life in a shell. There are other *repercussions*; for example, how do chelonians breathe? Most reptiles use their ribs to produce respiratory movements, but *chelonian ribs* are incorporated into the shell.

Experiments on a snapping turtle, *Chelydra,* have shown that when a turtle breathes in, muscles under the flexible skin at the base of the legs contract. Their movement stretches some transverse abdominal muscles that lie under the viscera. This decreases the pressure around the lungs, and they expand.

When the turtle breathes out, the transverse muscles contract, compressing the *viscera* and lungs, and forcing air out. Tortoises have a similar *mechanism*, but it differs *anteriorly* where movements of the pectoral girdle and *forelimbs* are important.

All of this shows the extensive effect of this particular form of body armour. The chelonians are the only armoured vertebrates that we shall discuss in this book, but look for some other examples if you get the chance.

There are various armoured mammals alive today, and several groups of fossil reptiles and mammals with plates and scutes of some kind. When you get to the next section of this chapter, on lizards, make comparisons with the tortoise *skeleton*.

Look for differences and similarities, and then summarise all the features of the tortoise body which you think are related to the presence of the shell. This design, involving armour at the expense of agility, proved adaptable to life in many habitats, and 'chelonians are still

LIZARDS AND SNAKES

Lizards and snakes are the commonest living reptiles in terms of numbers of species, and probably numbers of individuals also. We shall use lizards as a sort of model reptile to compare with other land vertebrates, and with other reptilian forms discussed in this chapter.

The rationale for this comes from the fact that the earliest reptiles had a lizard-like form even though they are not classified in the same group as modern lizards, which are more advanced and evolved later. Tortoises and turtles, snakes and crocodilians are all modifications of this type of *reptilian morphology*.

Some General Features of Lizards

Figure elsewhere in this chapter shows the external features of a common European lizard, *Lacerta viridis*. Note the proportions of the animal. Most lizards are *small*, *nimble*, *quadrupedal* reptiles with moderately *elongated* bodies, and tails often as long again as the trunk

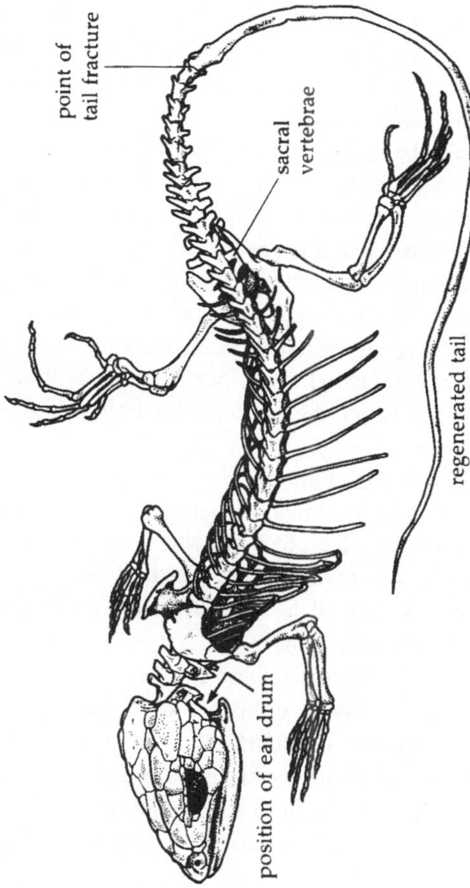

Figure 5.3: A lizard, Lacerta viridis.

and head. They have scaly skins, as already described, and may be a variety of colours. Each of their limbs has five digits, and they can walk fast by pushing themselves up on their toes (which is called a *digitigrade* stance) or even, in some cases, *running* along on their *hindlegs*.

Nevertheless, their proximal limb bones are held in such a way that the legs point out sideways and the feet contact the ground some distance to either side of the *vertebral column*. The length of the stride, as in *salamanders*, is increased by lateral *undulations* of the body, but a digitigrade stance will also increase stride length—an option not open to salamanders.

At rest, lizards lower their bodies so that they touch the ground. Some lizards show reduced legs and *elongated bodies*, and some groups are entirely legless—particularly *burrowing forms*. The skeleton of *Lacerta viridis* shows the exact proportions more clearly. The head is rather long and narrow, flattened dorsoventrally and broadening out towards the back. The skull of *Lacerta viridis* is atypical in that it has numerous extraneous osteoderms applied to it.

These are of a similar nature to the plates in tortoise shells; they are characteristic of lacertid skulls, but they obscure its basic layout. For example, in *Lacerta, you* can see only three paired openings in the skull—the nostrils, orbits; and the spaces left by the *eardrums* just behind the jaw articulation; but some other openings in the *temporal* region behind the eyes are also characteristic of reptiles.

They are covered over by osteoderms in lacertids. The details of lizard skull structure are discussed in the next section. Behind the head is a short neck region, to which the head is joined by a single occipital condyle.

Unlike the double condyle of amphibians, the reptilian one is single. Lizards have a more mobile head than amphibians, which cannot move their heads from side to side. Two features which allow this in reptiles are modification of the first two cervical vertebrae into an *atlas-axis* complex, and the development of a more distinct neck region.

If you define neck vertebrae as those between the head and shoulders, in which any ribs do not contact the sternum, then *L. viridis* has eight cervical vertebrae. Most lizards have this number. The trunk region of *L. viridis* contains twenty-one vertebrae, all with ribs.

The anterior ribs connect with the sternum to form a basket around heart and lungs, which is joined onto the coracoid bone of the pectoral girdle. Look back to the frog and salamander to see what arrangement they have.

This rib basket in lizards foreshadows the mammalian thorax, although it is not possible to produce a consistent definition of a thoracic region in lizards because there are ribs on all the trunk vertebrae. Lizards use their ribs for *lung ventilation*—the first vertebrates so far in this book to do so.

The ribs can alter the volume of the body cavity through movements controlled by *intercostal muscles*, and so force air in and out of the lungs. Lizards can also raise their ribs laterally to expand their bodies when *basking* in the sun, and so can *alter* their shape to present a greater surface area for *absorbing heat*.

Look at the posture of the limbs in *L. viridis*. The *hindlimbs* are longer than the forelimbs and provide most of the thrust in locomotion. The *forelimbs* mostly steer and orientate the animal.

Note the angles of femur and *humerus*, and the relative lengths of the toes. Although the feet touch the ground some distance out from the long axis of the body, as in *salamanders*, *lizards* are considerably more *nimble*.

The main reasons for this have to do with changes in the limb muscles, the articulations between bones, and the ankle region particularly. These changes are mentioned in the appropriate sections of the *Varanus* description below. When looking at the tortoise skeleton, you saw that reptiles have at least two sacral vertebrae joined onto the *ilium*. Two are present in *Lacerta*.

The incorporation of more vertebrae into the sacrum suggests increasing *commitment* to support and locomotion of the body on land. The sacral vertebrae also tend to become *immovably* connected with each other.

There is no functional advantage in keeping movable centra, because the role of the sacrum is to provide a strong attachment between pelvis and vertebral column, and to transmit forces efficiently between them.

When you study birds and *mammals*, notice how many sacral vertebrae there are in the animals you look at, and the extent of fusion between them. Relate this to the posture and method of locomotion of each animal. Lizards have long tails: most reptiles do.

This specimen of *L. viridis* has a *regenerated tail*. Note that individual vertebrae are not regenerated; instead, a solid core of cartilage is produced. Most of the *caudal vertebrae* of lizards have fracture planes across their *centra*, which allow loss of the tail without serious injury to the animal.

Snakes and monitor lizards do not have these fracture planes. The first few caudal vertebrae of *Lacerta* are stout with broad transverse processes. These carry the powerful caudofemoralis muscles, which, as in the newt *Triturus,* are important in pulling the leg back during walking.

The above description has dealt with the most noticeable superficial aspects of lizard skeletons. We can now look at some things in more detail. Rather than use a small lizard like *Lacerta* for this, we shall use the big monitor lizard, *Varanus*. Monitors are common Old World lizards, more advanced than lacertids and big enough for the details of their structure to be clearly visible.

The Skull of *Varanus*

1. Monitor lizards are generally *elongated* animals. Their skulls

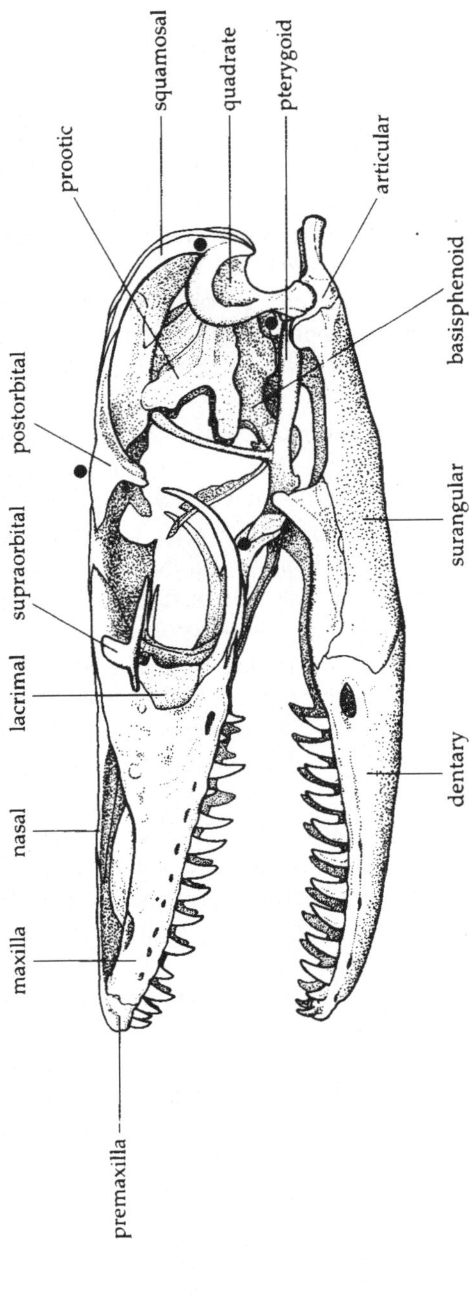

Figure 5.4: Skull and lower jaws of Varanus.

are no exception: note the long snout, armed with large pointed teeth set into the inner side of the jaw. Monitors are predaceous lizards, the larger ones sometimes killing quite large mammals (e.g. antelope).

2. Start by looking at the skull 'table', or dorsal side. Check back to the *Greererpeton* skull for the basic pattern of tetrapod skull bones; then compare it with *Varanus,* and you will see several losses and modifications.

   At the back is a single parietal bone; it is composed of two fused bones, and has a pineal opening in its centre—in a homologous position to that in *Greererpeton.* The pineal (or parietal) foramen marks the position of the pineal gland, and allows light to reach it.

   The parietal bone has two bony wings extending back to meet the squamosal and supratemporal. This assemblage forms a strut between the skull table and the two quadrates. Note that there are no postparietals or tabulars (cf. *Greererpeton*).

3. In front of the parietal are the frontals, and a long splint of bone representing fused nasals. A posterior process from the fused premaxillae at the tip of the snout extends back to meet the nasals.

   The two spaces on either side of the nasals are the large openings of the nostrils. Note that the internal openings of the nostrils are near the front of the mouth in all reptiles except crocodilians.

   When you get to the section on the alligator skull, you will see what happens to the internal nostrils in them. Along their posterior border are two prefrontals, which also border part of the eye.

4. What bones form the long snout? You have seen that the nasals are long, so is the splint from the premaxilla; but the main bones of the snout are the maxillae. They bear most of the teeth and form the whole side of the face back to the eyes. What bone carries the remaining teeth?

5. Look at the bones bordering the eye. There are four: the prefrontal we have mentioned, a small lacrimal, a crescent-shaped jugal, and the postorbital.

   The lacrimal is so named because it carries the tear duct from the eye to the nasal passages. The bone projecting across the

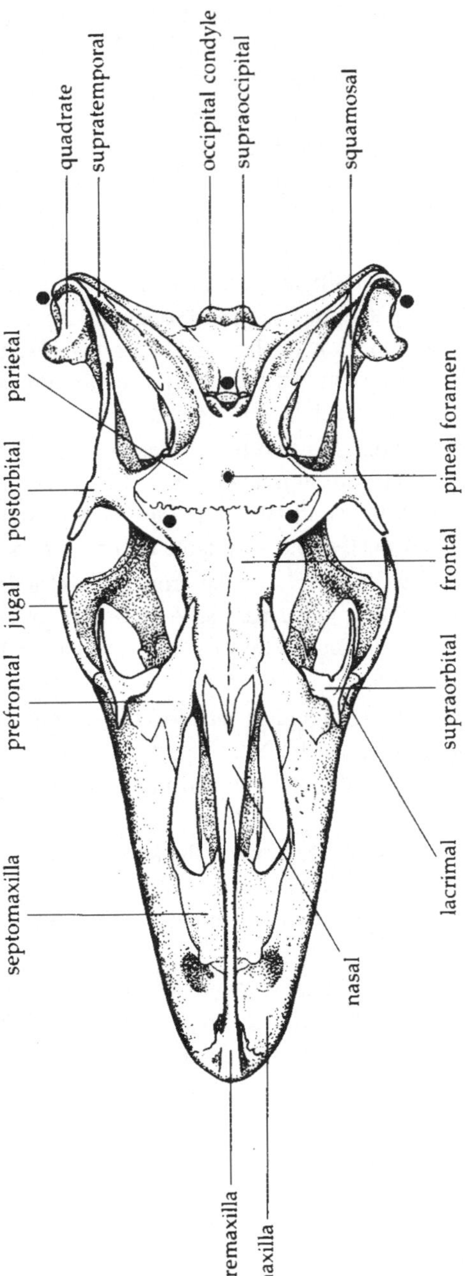

Figure 5.5: Skull of Varanus, dorsal view.

orbit is called the supraorbital bone; there is no homologue of it in *Greererpeton.*

Not all reptiles have one (look at the tortoise, alligator, and snake), and it is not really part of the skull proper, for it lies in the upper eyelid.

6. Behind the orbit, the side of the skull is very open. The *Greererpeton* skull is closed over here with dermal bones; so is the *Lacerta* skull with its osteoderms.

   But most lizards have much less bone in this, the temporal region of the skull. Reptiles, from the beginning of their evolution, tended to reduce the bones in this area of their skulls.

   The functional reason was apparently to allow room for the expansion of larger and more complex jaw muscles between the braincase and outer dermal shell of bone. Lizards are derived from reptiles with two openings in the temporal region, a condition called, 'diapsid'.

   Snakes and crocodilians are also diapsid reptiles. Chelonians, on the other hand, do not have these temporal openings, and are said to be 'anapsid'.

7. Which are the two temporal openings in *Varanus?* Look behind the parietal bone. Find the postorbital—it sends a long spur posteriorly. This meets another fine spur, which is the squamosal bone.

   These two bones, postorbital and squamosal, always border the upper temporal opening in diapsid reptiles, and lie between it and the lower opening. So the upper temporal opening is high up, behind the parietal and just above the occipital region on each side.

8. What about the lower temporal opening? This is very large in *Varanus,* and has no lower border. All lizards have lost this lower arcade of bone—only *Sphenodon,* the tuatara, has one. The bone that has disappeared is the quadratojugal, and the jugal curves up around the eye and does not extend back to meet the quadrate. So, there is a large space here, providing room for the big jaw adductor muscles required by a predator such as *Varanus*.

   These muscles run from the lower jaw up to the parietal and occipital region of the skull.

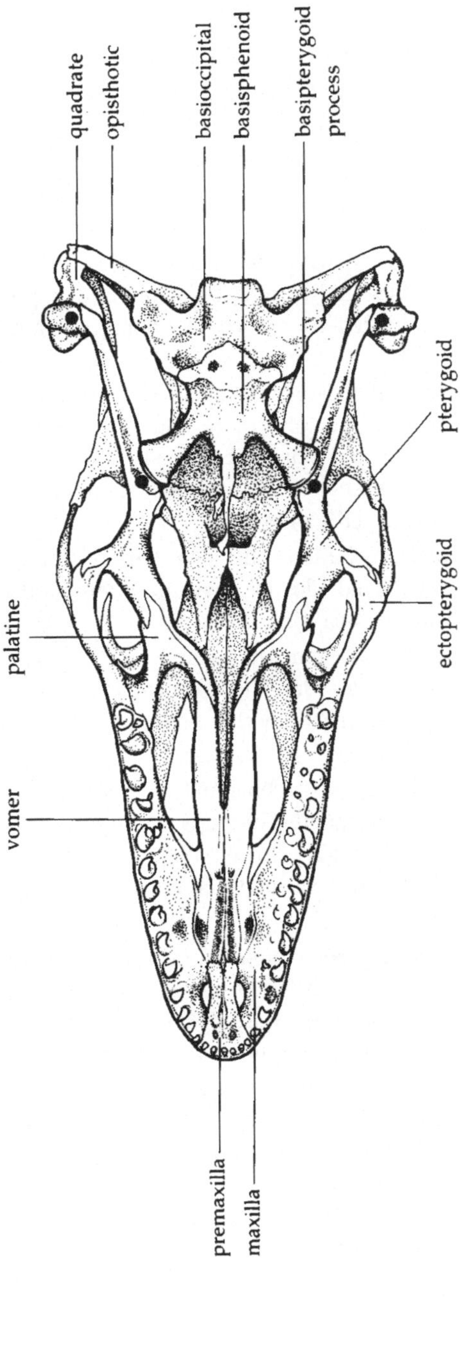

Figure 5.6: Skull of Varanus, palatal view.

9. Note the quadrate, a robust bone which articulates with the lower jaw. It is not fixed in position, but can move at its dorsal end, and ventrally on both the lower jaw and the pterygoid. This movable condition of the quadrate, called streptostyly, is a common feature of lizards, many of which have what are called 'kinetic' skulls.
10. 'Kinesis' actually refers to the ability of the upper jaw and snout to move on the rest of the skull. This is achieved because the pterygoids can move against the braincase at the basipterygoid processes. Note the long bars formed by the pterygoids; their movement is transmitted forwards to the whole snout.

    Look at given Figures elsewhere in this chapter, in which points of movement are indicated by dots. The snout can be raised as a whole because the front part of the braincase is not ossified,' and so is flexible.

    Not only that, but also the rear part of the skull allows movement either between frontals and parietal, or between the parietal and occiput.

    In *Varanus,* movement can occur in both these places.

    If you watch carefully some film of a lizard feeding, you may see the animal raising its snout as it gets its mouth around the food. All of this foreshadows the extraordinary processes involved in snake feeding.
11. What are the bones visible through the open temporal region? Look at side and palatal views of the *Varanus* skull. Find the main lateral components of the braincase, the pro-otic and basisphenoid.

    In front of the pro-otic, the braincase is not well ossified in lizards, except in burrowing forms. Look at the dermal palatal bones (e.g. palatines and vomers). There are no palatal teeth. Find the connections that are flexible in this part of the skull too (indicated in the figures).
12. On the occiput, at the back of the skull, note the large processes passing laterally to meet the quadrates. Another pair of openings—the post-temporal openings - is formed here. Note the single occipital condyle, commented on before.
13. The lower jaw of *Varanus* has eight component bones. Of these, the articular is the only endochondral bone in the lower

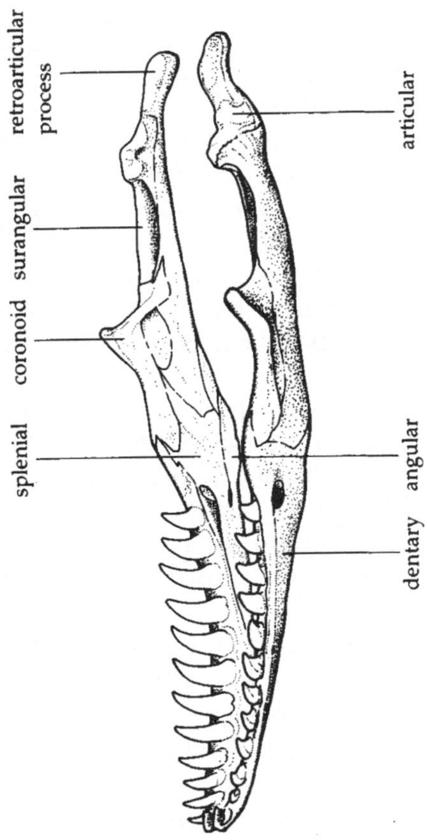

Figure 5.7: Lower jaws of Varanus.

jaw. What is the name of its homologous cartilage in fish? Could you also see it in *Greererpeton*?

At the back of the jaw is a large retroarticular process, which is the insertion site for the muscle that depresses the lower jaw—the depressor mandibulae.

The lower jaws of *Varanus* have a ligamentous join or symphysis at the front between the two halves. And there is a further site of flexibility between the front part of the lower jaw (the dentary and splenial) and the posterior part (all the rest of the bones).

Mobility in these areas gives monitor lizards greater scope in getting their mouths around larger prey. The pocket in the inner side of the lower jaw carries the insertions of the jaw adductor muscles, which close the mouth.

The Vertebrae of *Varanus*

Look at the vertebrae of *Varanus* and *Lacerta* with one major question in mind. What functions do the various regions of the backbone perform? The neck is primarily concerned with head mobility; the anterior part of the trunk region with lung ventilation (via the ribs) and body support; the trunk region as a whole with support and locomotion; the sacrum with support at the hind end and transmission of weight to

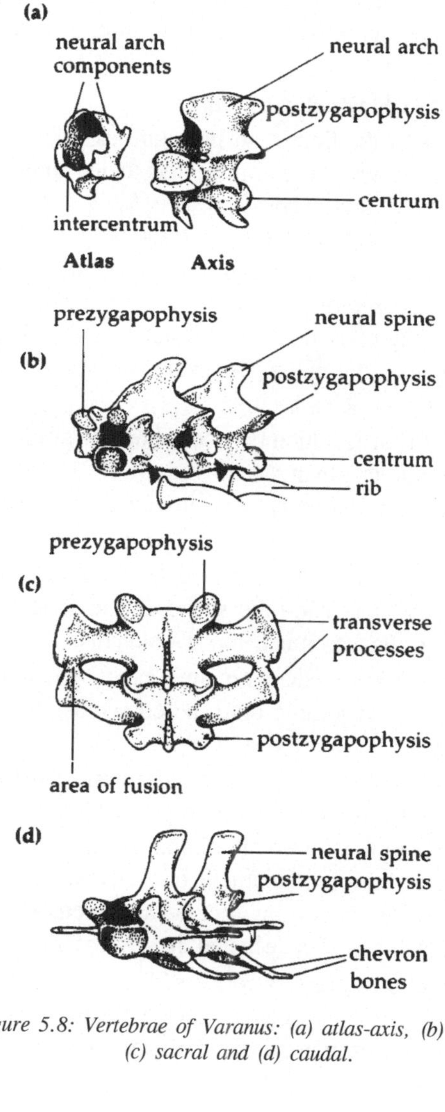

Figure 5.8: Vertebrae of Varanus: (a) atlas-axis, (b) trunk, (c) sacral and (d) caudal.

the hindlimbs; and the tail with sundry other functions. Work out how vertebrae can fulfil these roles.

Look at the shape and position of intervertebral articulations—how do they allow horizontal movement, but prevent twisting? Both centra and zygapophyses are relevant here. Where do ribs articulate? Are the two sacral vertebrae fused with each other as well as with the pelvis? Why is it important to have a strong sacrum? What is the function of the chevron bones on the tail vertebrae? The first one or two caudal vertebrae do not have these bones—can you think of a reason for their absence?

The Limbs and Limb Girdles of *Varanus*

When you look at the limbs and limb girdles, think about how the lizard moves, how its weight is transmitted to its limbs, and whether it can stand up on its toes when it walks. Look for similarities and differences between lizards and other tetrapods.

1. Starting at the anterior end, the pectoral girdle consists of scapulae, coracoids, clavicles, and interclavicles. Note the large cartilaginous dorsal extensions of the scapulae, called suprascapulae, lying up alongside the vertebral column and attached by muscles to it.
2. Where is the articulation between shoulder girdle and humerus? The scapula is always involved in it—in all tetrapods. In mammals, it is the only bone involved, because there are no coracoids.

   Lizards can retract the humerus back against the body more than salamanders can—the shape of the articulation with the pectoral girdle has much to do with this.
3. The sternum is a median structure carrying extensions of some of the ribs, and joining onto the coracoids. Was it present in amphibians?

   In reptiles, it forms a supporting ventral wall for the anterior part of the trunk. Review the way in which the pectoral girdle is attached to the vertebral column in amphibians and reptiles: note the addition, in reptiles, of an attachment via the ribs. Compare this rather indirect arrangement with the strong, direct attachment between pelvis and spine.
4. If the forelimbs are less concerned with delivering thrust than they are with steering the moving lizard, you might expect some differences in proportions between them and the hindlimbs.

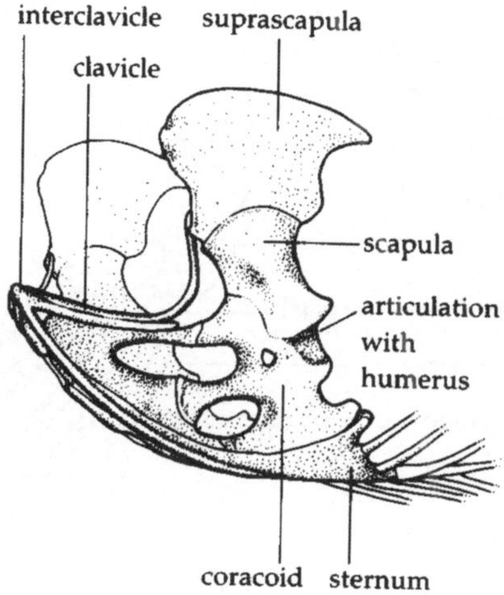

Figure 5.9: Pectoral girdle of Varanus.

Is there any difference in length? The same bones make up the forelimb as in amphibians and all other tetrapods, but their shapes and numbers (i.e. in the wrist and digits) may differ. Radius and ulna can rotate on the humerus in lizards. The ulna is broader at its ends than the radius in *Varanus;* note the olecranon, where the triceps muscle attaches.

5. In the wrist, there are fewer central elements than in salamanders. This will give a more consolidated flexibility compared with the broad base of the newt hand.

   There are three proximal carpals, one central element (the centrale), and five distal elements opposite the base of the fingers. All the fingers bear strong claws.

6. In the pelvis, ilium, ischium, and pubis are present as usual. The main difference in the hindlimb and its girdle between lizards and amphibians is the number of sacral vertebrae and some changes in the ankle.

   However, the bones of the pelvis are not the same shape as in the newt. The ilium particularly is much expanded to accommodate the additional sacral vertebrae, and more extensive limb muscles. The articulation with the femur allows movement almost entirely in a horizontal plane.

7. The femur is longer and more slender than the humerus. It can be brought in towards the body more than in urodeles during fast walking, so that a lizard is able to lift its body further off

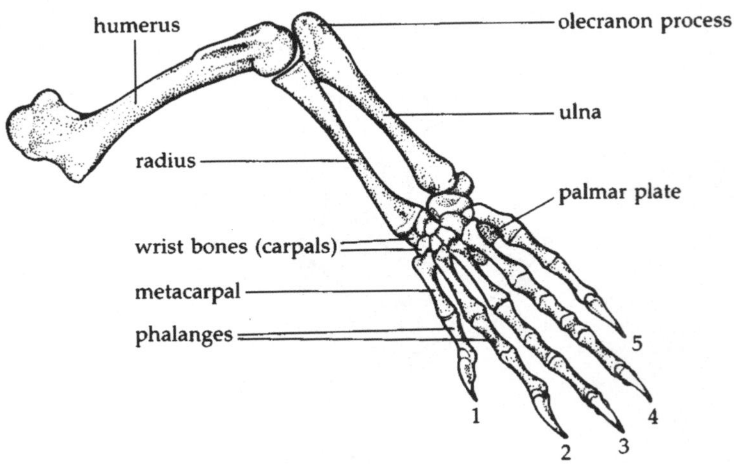

Figure 5.10: Forelimb of Varanus.

the ground and move faster.

Tibia and fibula are unmodified (cf. the frog), and articulate with one large tarsal bone. This is the major innovation in reptile feet compared with those of urodele amphibians: there has been extensive consolidation of ankle bones.

Early reptiles had two tarsal bones here—the astragalus and calcaneum; some living reptiles (e.g. alligators) also have two proximal tarsal bones. In lizards, these fuse to form one bone—the astragalocalcaneum. A suture can be seen in *Varanus*.

8. What is the functional effect of this 'new' type of ankle joint? It turns out that the joint between tibia and fibula and the astragalocalcaneum is rigid, because ligaments bind them strongly together.

   The main ankle joint is between the astragalocalcaneum and an enlarged distal tarsal bone. This is where the movement between leg and foot occurs; so it is an 'intratarsal' joint. It provides mobility in a precisely controlled direction.

   When a lizard pushes against the ground with its toes, force is efficiently transmitted through the metatarsals to the tarsal joint, and thence via the bony levers in the leg.

9. *Varanus* feet have five clawed toes. Note the asymmetry of the adigits—compare with urodeles. If you want to see some variation in lizard feet, look at those of geckos and chameleons.

   It is odd that so many lizards have gone in for reduced limbs;

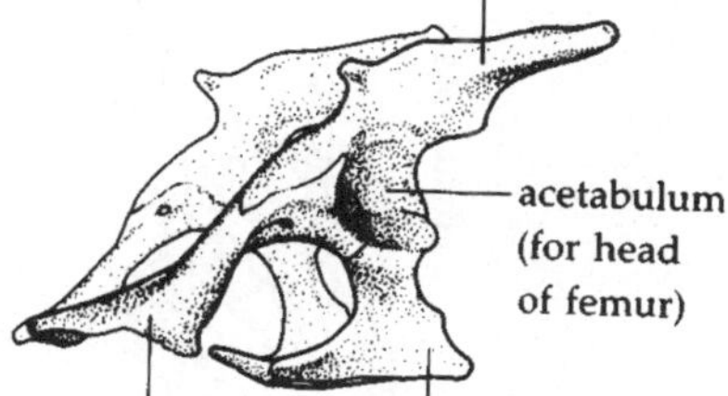

Figure 5.11: Pelvic girdle of Varanus.

many skinks have this feature and slow-worms and amphisbaenians are legless.

We now turn to the snakes, which are the most well-known offshoot of the lizards, and which have specialised in leglessness.

Snakes—an Introduction

Snakes are supposed to have evolved from burrowing lizards, and so to have been the most specialised outcome of a widespread tendency among lizards towards reduction of the legs and elongation of the body.

No lizard carries these tendencies as far as snakes do: snakes have much more elongated bodies than legless lizards, and only the most primitive ones show any sign of limbs, which are always the posterior pair. No vestige of forelimbs remains.

Why dispense with limbs and become elongated? It is likely that this was originally an adaptation for moving through dense undergrowth, as much as for burrowing.

Snakes are now adapted to several other habitats, such as trees, where their long bodies are adept at moving along, up, and around branches, and where their weight can be distributed over several supports at once.

In this section, we shall look at various aspects of the body form of snakes, and then their feeding, which is also peculiarly specialised.

Some General Features of Snakes

Ideally, you should have both, a live snake (or snake skin) and a whole skeleton in order to understand snake form. With a live snake such as the garter snake, *Thamnophis,* observe the following:

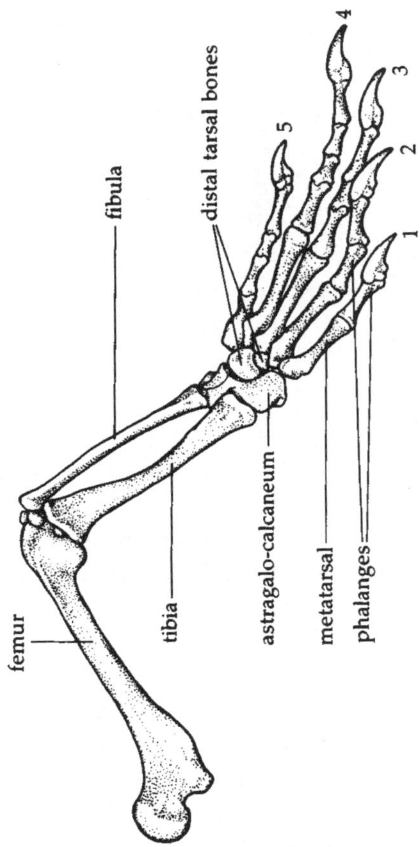

Figure 5.12: Hindlimb of Varanus.

1. Note the overall length of the animal; then gently turn it over and find the vent. Now you know how much of the snake is 'body', and how much of it is tail. What are the proportions? If you can, compare your measurments on a snake with some on a legless lizard (e.g. the slow-worm, *Anguis)*.
2. Finding out how much of the snake's body is 'neck' is more difficult without dissection, and is also rather meaningless because there is no pectoral girdle. But it is sometimes useful to know where the heart is, for example.

   This can be done by counting ventral scales, which have a constant distribution in relation to the position of the internal organs, because they are related to the primary segmentation of the body. The exact relationship between scales and internal organs will vary, though, between species.

3. Notice the pattern of scales over the body. Like lizards, snakes often have an array of larger scales on their heads. These are often paired and have names reflecting those of the paired dermal bones in the skull underneath.
4. On the ventral side of the body are the broad belly scales. Do they extend onto the tail? The scales on the sides and belly of most snakes are essential for locomotion.

   Watch a snake moving; place it on loose gravel or sand, and observe how the curves of its body push the substrate laterally as they move. When you hold a moving snake, feel the way its body presses against you.

   Without legs, snakes have devised other ways of moving themselves, using the friction of their scales against irregularities on the substrate—whether it be the wall of a burrow, a branch, or stony ground.

   They cannot progress on entirely smooth surfaces. Each lateral bend in the body applies force to the ground in an obliquely backward direction, the overall. result being to move the snake forwards.
5. Vipers and boas stalking prey have another remarkable way of moving, called rectilinear locomotion. They do not throw their body into waves during this, but appear to glide over the ground in a straight line.

   The belly scales are moved in a series of steps, so that small sections of the body are detached, moved forwards, and lowered onto the ground again, using the muscles which run between the skin and the ribs.

   Rectilinear locomotion is an extraordinarily effective way of moving with the minimum disturbance to the environment. It would, incidentally, be much more difficult to do if the skin were not so loose.

   Other snakes have other ways of using their scales and/or bends in their bodies for movement—examples of variations on the theme are desert sidewinders and swimming snakes. Look up some details of their movements.
6. Have you noticed that snakes constantly put their tongues in and out, particularly when exploring something new? What are they doing? Why is the tongue forked, and what sense organ is associated with the tongue's activities? What about

lizard tongues?

7. Can you find an eardrum on the snake's head? Think where it would be if present—reptilian eardrums usually lie just behind the jaw articulation. In fact there is no eardrum; snakes do not have them or middle-ear cavities. The stapes, or columella, passes straight out to the quadrate bone, and vibrations are probably picked up from the ground via the jaws.
8. Look also at the eye. Snakes have no separate eyelids, and cannot blink. Instead, they have a structure called the spectacle, formed from fused eyelids and protecting the *eye*; it is shed with the rest of the skin when the snake moults. One of the first signs that a snake is going to moult is the cloudy appearance of the spectacle.

The Snake Skeleton

Snake skulls will be discussed below in the context of feeding. The python skeleton illustrated in Figure elsewhere in this chapter shows how the snake body is supported.

1. Snakes have enormous numbers of vertebrae, which are all alike throughout the neck and trunk regions. All except the first one or two bear ribs.

   The tail is supported by a further series of vertebrae with ribs fused onto them (or no ribs), and chevron bones which protect the blood vessels of the tail. Note, again, how immensely long the body is in comparison to the tail region.
2. Snake trunk vertebrae are adapted to allow lateral bending of the spine, but to resist twisting—just like lizards, only more so. They have two sets of processes for this purpose. The pre- and postzygapophyses are similar to those on lizard vertebrae; but above the neural arch on the anterior side of each vertebra are two other processes.

   These fit into depressions on the posterior face of the vertebra in front, and prevent torsion of the spinal cord during sinuous movement. The likelihood of twisting is considerably greater in snakes than in quadrupedal lizards.
3. Snakes use their ribs for respiration and locomotion, as well as body support. Watch for breathing movements in a live snake. Do they occur throughout the body?

   We already mentioned that muscles run from each rib to the skin, anteriorly and posteriorly, and are used to move the

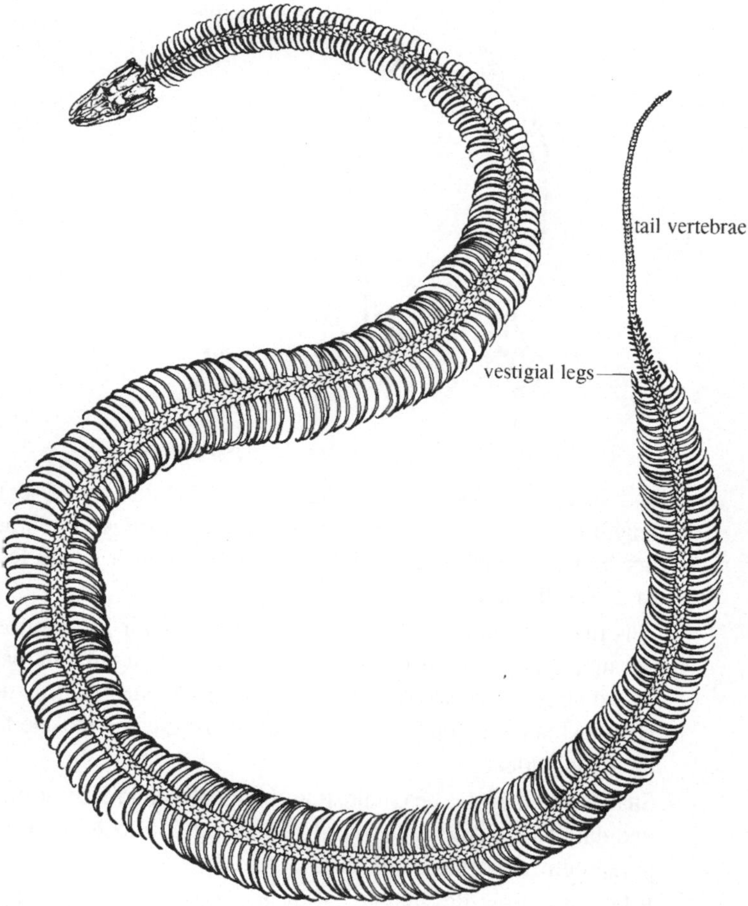

Figure 5.13: Skeleton of Python.

latter in small steps over the substrate. The edges of the ventral scales provide the resistance that gives a section of skin some purchase against the ground, while the body behind is drawn forwards.

4. Just at the junction of trunk and tail in pythons may be seen the minute vestigial hindlimbs. Pythons are one of the few types of snake to possess any sign of legs. Even so, the pelvic girdle has almost completely vanished. Claws are present on the legs, and are the only part of them to be visible externally. They may have some role in copulation.
5. Compare the snake, with its long homogeneous vertebral column

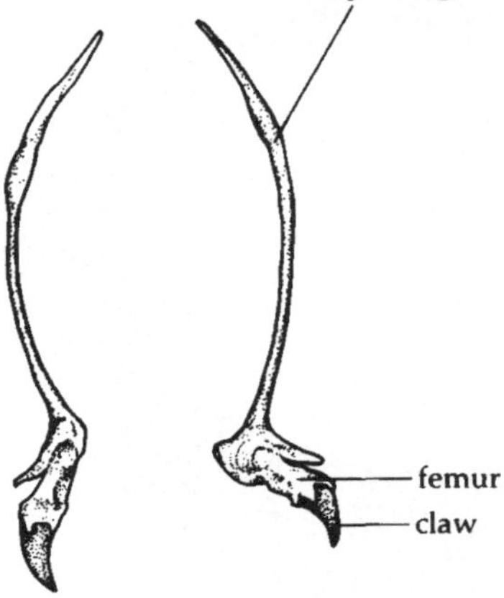

Figure 5.14: Vestigial hindlimbs of Python.

and lack of limbs, to the lizard. Note that the increase in length is achieved by increasing the number of trunk vertebrae, not by lengthening each individual vertebra (which would lead to a less flexible body).

It is the trunk muscles that provide the power for locomotion, because the tail in most snakes is a relatively insignificant part of the body. In eels, which seem to move like snakes, it is the post-anal tail which provides much of the length and muscle for the undulations.

Snakes use their bodies, adjusting the number and size of their undulations to suit each type of substrate. Flexibility is of paramount importance for this.

Ribs are present throughout, even in the neck, reflecting their important role in locomotion, and every organ system has been affected by the necessity to fit into the long, tubular shape.

How are the Organs of Snakes Arranged?

A general dissection of a snake reveals several remarkable modifications. The main ones are:

1. The lungs are modified; the left is completely missing or else vestigial, and the right is enlarged. In some snakes, it may extend down almost as far as the vent; part of the trachea may also be vascularised. If you are actually dissecting a snake, note that the anterior portion of the right lung has a thicker wall. The posterior part, which is very thin-walled, is easily pierced unless care is taken during dissection.

2. Snakes do not have a bladder. They make uric acid as their main nitrogenous excretory product, and excrete it as a semi-solid. No solutions of urea are produced.
3. The liver is long and narrow, and its right lobe is much bigger than the left.
4. The whole alimentary canal is very straight. Where it is coiled, in the intestinal region, the coils fit into a narrow diameter.
5. The kidneys are long and thin, and do not lie at the same level in the body—the right one lies more anteriorly than the left.
6. The reproductive organs also have a staggered arrangement.
7. Note, again, how long the snake's body is in comparison to its tail. So, fitting organs into a long, tubular shape has involved considerable reorganisation. Similar changes can be seen in some of the elongated, legless lizards, but none of them has gone quite as far as snakes.

Snake Skulls and Feeding Mechanisms: Pythons and Adders

Snakes have specialised in feeding on large prey, which is consumed whole and usually alive. Their major adaptations for this are twofold: mechanisms for subduing the prey, so that the snake is not injured by its attacks or struggles; and mechanisms for swallowing objects which maybe larger than the resting diameter of the snake's own mouth.

Mechanisms for subduing prey are mainly constriction and injection of venom. Modifications for swallowing are mostly to be seen in the skull, although it is worth remembering that the loss of the pectoral girdle must have vastly increased the range of food that could be eaten whole.

Since it is the skull which also delivers venom via the teeth, we shall describe below two types of snake skull. The python is a relatively unspeclalised snake for various reasons - one is that it has no venom delivery system, which means that there are no teeth modified for this function.

However, all snakes have large salivary glands to lubricate the prey and commence some digestion in the mouth. Pythons constrict their prey by throwing coils of their bodies around it, and gradually taking up the slack each time the prey breathes out, so that it is eventually suffocated.

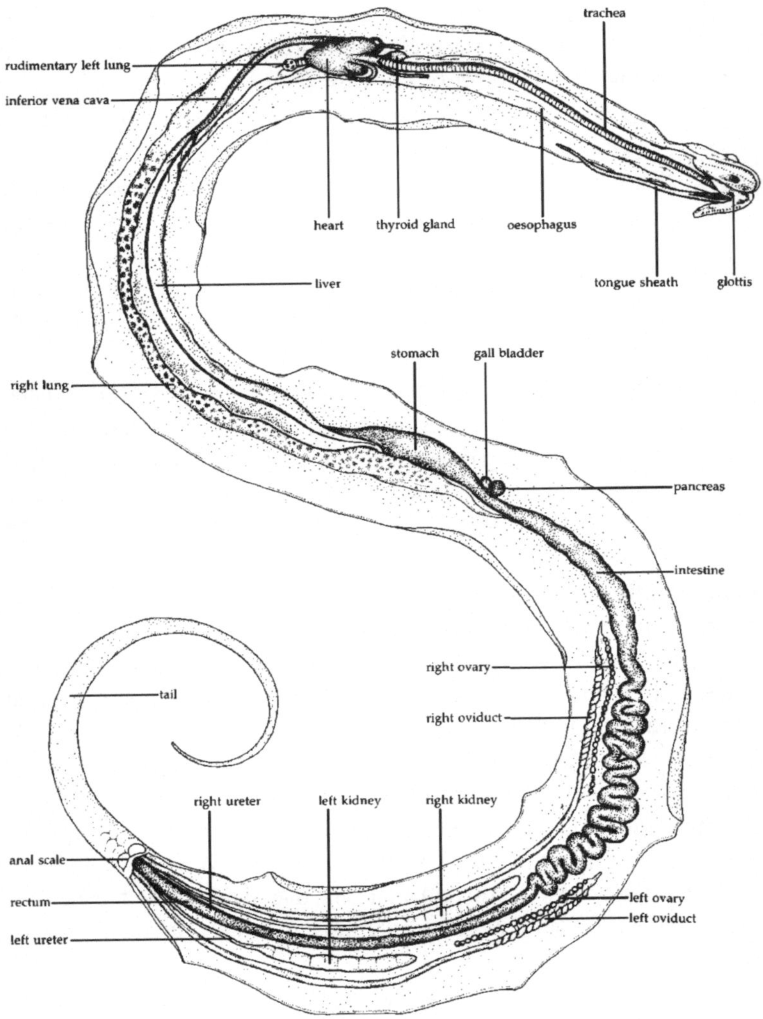

Figure 5.15: General dissection of grass snake, Natrix.

Adders are members of the family Viperidae, which inject venom into their prey with a rapid strike followed by quick withdrawal of the fangs. The prey may move away before it dies, but the snake can follow its trail by scent and will then devour it at its leisure. This avoids the dangers of being in close contact with aggressive or struggling prey. Vipers have the most specialised venom-delivery system among snakes.

The Python

Throughout what follows, keep referring back to the lizard skull for comparison.

1. Notice the flattened, broad shape of the front of the skull, and the narrow area enclosing most of the brain behind. Note also the distribution and size of the bones on the dorsal surface and compare with the lizard (*Varanus*) skull.

   Among the bones present, notice the large prefrontals, and the fact that the frontals and parietals grow down around the brain to protect its sides.

   Are there any bones on the dorsal surface that you saw in the lizard skull but which are not found in the python skull?

2. The back of the skull is very 'open'. Snake skulls are derived from a diapsid condition, but this is hard to discern because several bones are missing, particularly those that formed the temporal arcades in lizards.

   What were these bones? The result of their loss is to free the quadrate and the posterolateral parts of the palate to an even greater extent than in *Varanus*. Snake skulls are highly kinetic.

3. Find the quadrate bones. Notice that they abut onto large supratemporals dorsally, and onto long strut-like pterygoids ventrally. These connections are fibrous, not rigid. There is also, of course, a joint with the lower jaw.

   Thus, all joints between the quadrate and other bones are mobile, and it is primarily this that gives the mouth its extraordinary gape.

   The gape is also increased by the position of the jaw articulation, which is placed far back beyond the occipital condyle because the quadrates themselves can slope back. Furthermore, the mobility of the quadrates allows spreading outwards of the lower jaws.

4. Turn to the palate, and notice the distribution of teeth. One of the primitive features of pythons is that they have teeth on the premaxillae as well as on the maxillae.

   They also have numerous palatal teeth. Does *Varanus* have palatal teeth? All python teeth are sharp and recurved—effective at piercing and holding prey.

   There is little regional differentiation of the teeth, except that those at the rear of the palate are smaller. Specialisation of the teeth in pythons would not be expected, because all the

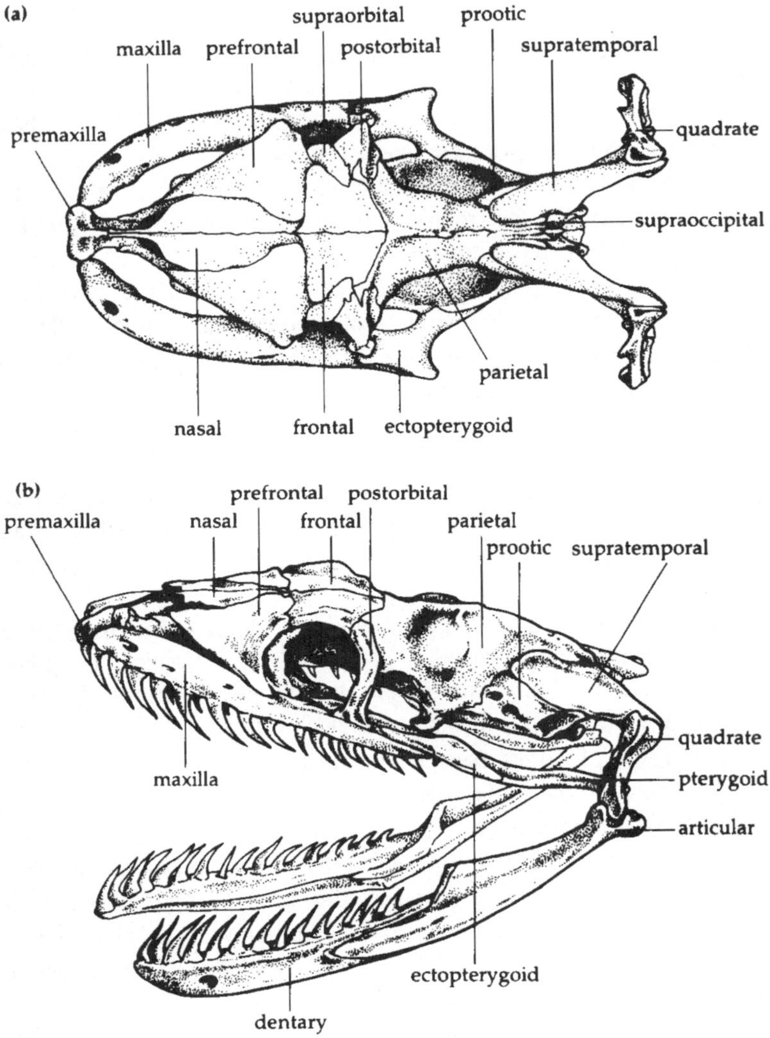

Figure 5.16: Python skull: (a) dorsal and (b) side views, with lower jaw.

teeth are employed in the same process of seizing, holding, and ingesting food—none is specialised for venom injection.

5. The maxillae in pythons are long and robust—remember this when looking at the adder skull later. They are not rigidly attached to the skull at any point.
6. A remarkable feature of snake palates is that the ptyergoids and palatines (the tooth-bearing palatal bones in pythons) can

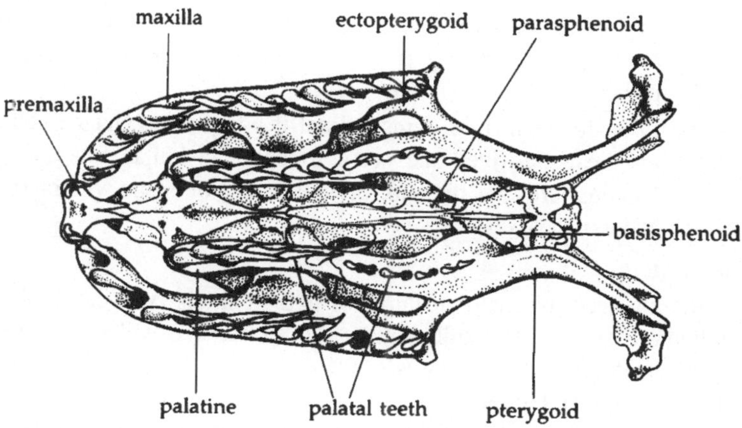

Figure 5.17: Python skull, palatal view.

slide forwards and back.

The pterygoid-palatine rod of each side is joined to the maxilla via the ectopterygoid, and the whole assemblage can move independently of the opposite side. Thus, the python can engage the teeth on one side of its mouth, while those on the other are being disengaged and moved forwards.

Try to watch film of a snake feeding: the prey is swallowed in a series of steps made by each half of the mouth alternately.

7. All this mobility means that the mouth can be distended and moved to engulf large prey. Of course, the lower jaws are also very mobile. They can be spread sideways, not just at the jaw articulation with the skull but also at the front where the two halves are joined by a highly extensible ligament.

   No snake has a fused jaw symphysis. The skin of the throat' is very flexible between the scales, and can be stretched around the prey. The whole set-up is a remarkable example of functional specialisation.

8. With a mouth full of struggling prey, snakes could be vulnerable to brain damage through the palate. Even if the prey is inert, it is still likely to be large in relation to the snake's head, and may have sharp projections—all of which makes eating hazardous. The brain is protected by extensions of frontal and parietal bones, mentioned before, and also has a robust base to the braincase composed of large parasphenoids and basisphenoids.

9. Did you notice the pits on the outer anterior edge of the

maxilla? These are openings for nerves which supply, amongst other things, sensory pits in the scales along the mouth of pythons.

Look for them in a living animal if you get the chance. They are heat-sensitive, and seem to have a similar function in locating prey to the pits on the heads of some vipers (not adders).

The Adder

Having seen the major features of python skulls, you can look at a still more specialised skull, that of the adder. We will concentrate on those features that illustrate why the adder skull is more specialised in its feeding adaptations:

1. Look first at the maxilla. It is very short and deep, and bears one large, curved fang (replacement fangs may also be visible beside it). This is the venom-injection system.

   A duct from the venom gland passes venom forwards into the hollow fang, which injects it. Muscle fibres from one of the jaw muscles are attached to the venom gland, and can increase the force of injection.

2. Less-specialised venomous snakes have open grooves in their venomdelivering teeth, which are permanently erect and situated towards the rear of the mouth (e.g. family Colubridae).

   Kraits and cobras (family Elapidae) are more advanced, with

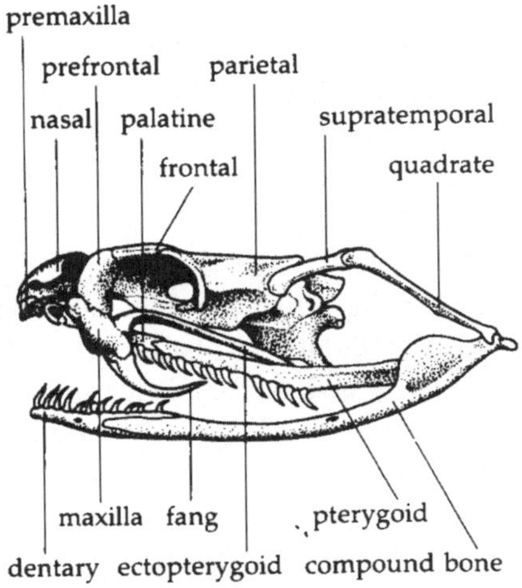

Figure 5.18: Skull and lower jaw of adder, Vipera berus.

fangs at the front of the mouth, and closed grooves (i.e. canals) for delivering venom—but the fangs cannot be folded back as in vipers.

3. The way the viper's fangs are erected as the mouth opens is as follows. There are movable quadrates just like in pythons, and as the mouth opens the quadrate, from pointing obliquely backwards, pivots forwards on the supratemporal.

   Its movement is transmitted to the pterygoid, which acts on the maxilla via the ectopterygoid. It can also move the palatine, which, as in pythons, bears some teeth. These teeth are not involved in venom injection, but are important in holding and ingesting prey.

4. The effect of the sliding motion of the pterygoids and ectopterygoids on the maxillae is to cause them to rotate through almost 90° on the prefrontals.

   This is possible because the maxillae are short, and because of the nature of the maxillary-prefrontal joint. As the maxillae rotate, the fangs are erected. Thus, a series of bones acts as a set of levers, transmitting force forwards to the fangs.

5. By the time the fangs are fully erect, the snake has its mouth

Figure 5.19: Skull and lower jaw of adder with fangs erected.

wide open, and strikes. It is not obligatory for it to erect its fangs every time it opens its mouth—but most people see things this way, and have assumed the two processes are necessarily connected.

6. Large prey is swallowed in much the same way as in pythons, in the sense that the two halves of upper and lower jaws can move independently over the prey. The throat is very distensible, and the lower jaw halves become dislocated from the skull and widely separated during swallowing.
7. One other point may have occurred to you. How do snakes breathe during swallowing when the mouth is crammed full of prey? Swallowing, after all, takes a long time—unlike in a lizard. What happens is that the glottis can be projected forwards over the floor of the mouth, so that it protrudes beneath the prey on one side.

   The trachea does not collapse under external pressure, so breathing can then continue. If you see film of a viper feeding, look for the glottis emerging from the throat. Crocodiles can also breathe with their mouths full of water and food—read the next section and find out how they do it.

Snake feeding is a fascinating subject upon which much more might be said. The main aim here has been to show how the skull is modified.

It is really extraordinary to see animals that have on the one hand specialised in long, thin bodies and on the other become adapted for eating prey that is wider than themselves. The whole arrangement seems paradoxical, but has proved extremely successful.

CROCODILIANS

All members of the order Crocodilia are adapted for living in and around water. They are the only surviving representatives of the subclass Archosauria, to which dinosaurs belonged and from which birds evolved. Thus, unlikely though it may seem, crocodiles are the closest living relatives of birds.

Zoologists find them tantalising animals for this reason, and because they are the nearest—in terms of a living breathing animal—that we shall ever get to dinosaurs. Of course, they also have their own particular adaptations.

Some of these can be discerned by looking at a crocodilian skull. You can see others by looking at film of live animals, or going to a zoo or museum.

(a)

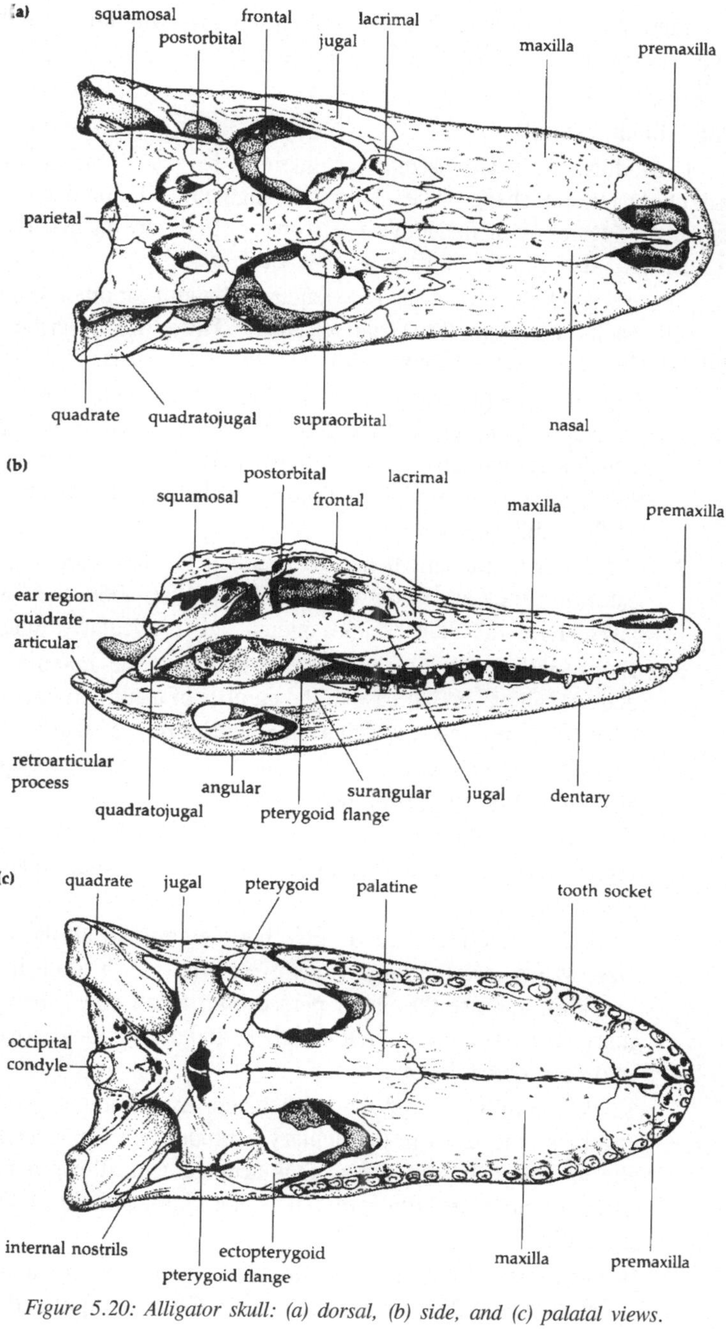

Figure 5.20: Alligator skull: (a) dorsal, (b) side, and (c) palatal views.

Find out, for example, how crocodilians swim—with tail or limbs? And how do they hold their limbs when walking? They have two different walking postures.

The Alligator Skull

Crocodilian skulls are instantly recognisable, because of their unusual and characteristic shape. The skull is elongated and dorsoventrally flattened. Species with the longest narrowest skulls are primarily, or exclusively, fish eaters (like the gavial, *Gavialis).*

Those with skulls of intermediate length and width eat other animals as well, including large terrestrial tetrapods. Here, we describe the skull of the American alligator, *Alligator mississippiensis:*

1. Note the general proportions and shape of the skull. Its surface is deeply sculptured, owing to the presence of osteoderms which adhere tightly to all the major dermal bones. It has been suggested that the sculpturing increases the mechanical strength of the skull and lower jaw.
2. What bones are lengthened to produce the flat snout? Look carefully: they are nasals and maxillae. What about the lower jaw? Here, the dentary and splenial are particularly long.
3. Elongation of the two tooth-bearing bones, the maxilla and dentary, allows an increase in the number of teeth. Crocodilians have 'fish-trap' jaws, which snap at and sieze prey that is often slippery or struggling. The long battery of teeth is very effective at holding on, and preventing escape.

   The jaws can also make broad sweeps when catching food, and abrupt sideways movements of the head are used when subduing prey too.
4. Notice that the teeth are all alike but they are not all the same size. Where are the largest teeth (e.g. the fourth tooth in the maxilla), and are they interspersed with small ones? The jaw margins are not straight but undulate, and convexities above fit into concavities below.

   Look carefully at how the teeth in upper and lower jaws fit together—big teeth in the dentary occlude with small teeth in the maxilla and vice versa. This arrangement allows a more effective hold on large prey; it is not characteristic of those crocodilians that eat only fish.

   Alligator jaws must be able to catch, hold, and crush large animals while they are killed, and then manipulated for swallowing.

5. The teeth are set in sockets in the jaws, and the dentition is said to be 'thecodont' for this reason. Compare with *Varanus* teeth. All the archosaurs, even the extinct ones, have thecodont dentition, as did the earliest birds.

   New teeth grow up underneath the old ones throughout life, and teeth are replaced in waves along the jaws from front to back so that old teeth will alternate with newer ones. When you get to the chapter on mammalian feeding, notice the contrast between the alligator (or *Varanus),* with its numerous similar teeth, and most mammals with their highly differentiated teeth. Alligators do not really process their food in the mouth, so their teeth are not adapted for complex chewing or cutting movements. There are mammals that do have teeth rather like those of crocodilians, and do use them as fish-traps too. Which are they?

6. The other major adaptation visible in the skull is a secondary palate. No other living reptile has one, nor do other vertebrates except mammals. The secondary palate in mammals allows eating and breathing simultaneously (most particularly during suckling by the young), because the air passages are separated off from the mouth.

   The crocodilian secondary palate is an admirable innovation for an aquatic animal, because an alligator can still breathe even when its mouth is full of water or food or both. Look at the palatal view of the skull.

   Find the internal nostrils. They are far towards the back of the mouth, only just in front of the level of the occipital condyle.

7. What bones form the secondary palate, so that air is made to flow right back to the rear of the mouth? Premaxillae, maxillae, palatines, and pterygoids have all expanded inwards to form a continuous secondary roofing over the palate.

   In life, two flaps separate off the entry into the lungs from the back of the mouth. Thus, an alligator can stalk terrestrial prey by swimming silently along, submerged except for its eyes, the top of its head, and nostrils.

   Shape, and the presence of a secondary palate are the main features of the alligator skull. Now notice some other details about it.

8. Is it diapsid, like the skull of lizards? Can you find the temporal openings? How many are there? Is the lower temporal arcade complete-and, if so, what bones form it? Look carefully at Figure elsewhere in this chapter.
9. The quadrates are large and immobile, unlike those of lizards and snakes. Streptostyly (moveable quadrates) is not a feature of crocodilian skulls, and nor is kinesis generally.

   The upper end of the quadrate invests the braincase in the alligator, as you can see if you look at the ear region. Jaw adductor muscles originate on part of the anterior surface of the quadrate, which lies in a backwardly inclined position.

   The effect of this is to shift the jaw articulation posteriorly. Thus, for a given amount of opening at the articulation, the tips of the jaws move farther apart, giving a prodigious gape.
10. Notice the position of the ears. Their external openings are not behind the jaw articulation (cf. lizards), but high up on the side of the head. An external ear is formed by lateral expansions of the squamosals, which overhang a pocket, at the bottom of which is the tympanic membrane.

    Crocodilians have good hearing, and the position of their ears is perhaps not surprising considering that they spend a lot of time almost entirely submerged.

    Ear flaps close off the openings to the ears when they dive. If you get the chance to see a live animal or skin, look for the flaps. The nostrils can also be closed off in a dive.
11. The eyes are placed up on top of the head—again, an advantageous position for an alligator swimming along with most of its head under water. There is an accessory bone over the top of the eye. *Varanus* had one too. What is its name, and what does it support?
12. On the underside of the skull, notice the very large pterygoid flanges. They have a variety of functions: one is to prevent lateral displacement of the long jaws.

    Another function is as the bony origin for one of the powerful jaw adductor muscles—the pterygoideus. This muscle is very large, and when it contracts, its anterior portion bulges into the spaces provided by the large palatal vacuities;
13. At the rear of the skull, the occiput is broad and solid. It is the site of origin for important jaw and neck muscles. These

must be strong to control the heavy skull with its long jaws, and to move the head when prey is caught and jerked back into the throat.

One of these muscles, the depressor mandibulae muscle, inserts on the retroarticular process at the back of the lower jaw. Notice how large this is - its upward extension probably increases the mechanical advantage of the muscle;

14. End up by looking at the bones of the lower jaw. Compare with *Varanus*. The jaw symphysis is mobile - it is one place where the sort of flexibility you heard about in lizard and snake skulls also exists, though to a lesser extent.

Many other things about crocodilians excite the curiosity of zoologists. The heart and aortic arches are like those of birds, with an almost completely subdivided ventricle.

The Nile crocodile has complex social behaviour, with advanced parental care of the young reminiscent of birds. Some people even think that birds may have evolved from animals related to early crocodiles, because of similarities in the internal structure of the skull.

Whether this is true or not, these large aquatic reptiles are certainly one example of how the great archosaurs, or 'ruling reptiles' of the Mesozoic, adapted to life in tropical waters—and they are the only archosaurs to have weathered the mass extinctions at the end of the Cretaceous period some 65 million years ago.

6

BIRDS: FLIGHT AND BIPEDALISM

Birds evolved from *archosaurian* reptiles, and were in existence by 140 million years ago, in the *Jurassic period*. No one is sure precisely which *archosaurs* they evolved from; some think certain bipedal dinosaurs were their immediate *ancestors*, whereas others prefer to look further back in a basic *archosaurian* stock of *quadrupedal* animals close to the *ancestry* of *crocodiles*.

Whatever their true source, birds are *unquestionably* closely related to reptiles for all sorts of reasons to. do with their structure and biology. This is not immediately obvious when looking at the skeletons of modern birds and reptiles, because the *adaptations* of birds to flight and bipedalism have had such a profound *influence* on bird shape and structure.

Crocodiles are the closest living relatives of birds, for they are also archosaurs, but they make somewhat specialised models for comparison because of their various modifications for an *amphibious* life—which has a totally different set of requirements to those of flight. So, in what follows, you may find it easier to use *Lacerta* and *Varanus* as a basis for general *comparison* with reptiles.

What parts of the skeleton have changed in response to the mechanical demands of *flight* and *bipedalism*? The limbs and trunk are most affected, and it is these that we focus on here. The requirements for efficient powered flight are very stringent, and have allowed little *variation* in the shape of the bird body in comparison, for example, with the shapes of different *mammals*.

Adaptive radiation among birds is best illustrated by a visit to a museum or zoo, which, together with trips into the field, will show the variation in beaks, feet, and *plumage*.

Materials Required

- Examples of different types-of feather, e.g. flight, down, and contour.
- Whole wings, some with contour feathers and skin removed to show bones *underneath*. (Wings can be obtained from such organisations as zoos, which regularly do *post-mortems* of birds.)
- Fresh-frozen or freshly killed chickens. Other *possibilities* would be pigeons, or birds *culled locally*, such as rooks or gulls.
- *Mounted* specimens or skins of a range of birds as available.

Feather Structure

Feathers are made of the protein keratin, and are supposed to have evolved from *reptilian scales*; although it is not at all clear how this happened. They consist of an axis or rachis, and the *vane*, which is composed of *lateral barbs*.

The barbs carry microscopic barbules on each side, which interlock and so hold the barbs together. This structure is light but *stiff*, resists the passage of air, and allows *minor damage* (e.g. the *separation* of barbs) to be repaired easily.

The bird restores continuity of the feather vane by *preening*, running its feathers through its beak and thus re-engaging the hooks on the *barbules*. You can do the same thing by running a feather through your fingers.

Note the various parts of a *feather*. *Compare flight*, *down*, and *contour feathers*, noting the differences in overall structure. The fine structure of feathers can be seen under a light *microscope*.

Mount them (either dry or in alcohol) between two slides, and secure the slides with *plasticine*. Figure elsewhere in this chapter shows feather barbules as seen under a total magnification of × 200. Some additional points to note are:

1. Down feathers do not have *interlocking barbs*. This makes them much more efficient at *trapping* air close to the body. Down is one of the most efficient *insulators* known.
2. The rachis of a primary flight feather is *asymmetrically* placed and so *strengthens* the leading edge of the feather, giving it an aerofoil shape in cross-section. Compare a primary with a

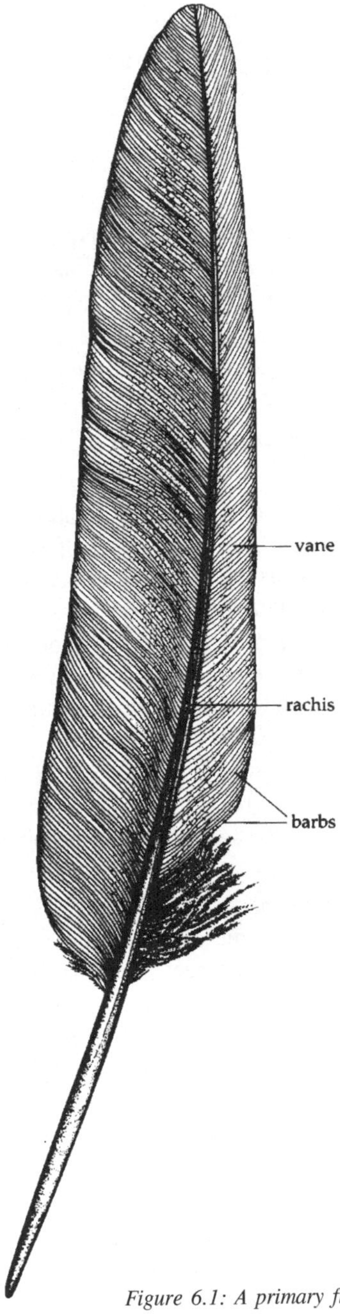

Figure 6.1: A primary flight feather.

secondary flight feather. Is the vane asymmetric in both? What about tail feather vanes?

3. Figure elsewhere in this chapter shows an interesting modification of feather structure. Owls fly silently, and the noise of air flow is reduced by extensions of the barbs on the dorsal side of the feather.

   Note the hair-like structures. If you hold an owl flight feather horizontally towards the light and look along the dorsal side, you will see that the feather appears *blurred*, or as if coated with dust.

   If an owl is available, look at the leading (first) primary feather on the wing. Can you see any other modifications?

THE ARRANGEMENT OF FEATHERS ON THE WING

Note the arrangement of feathers on the wing in Figure elsewhere in this chapter. The flight feathers provide the main flight surface and are strongly attached to the wing so as to *withstand* the forces of *flight*.

The other feathers on the wing are called *contour feathers*, because they together shape the anterior surface, both *ventrally* and *dorsally*. The wing thus has an *aerofoil shape*, which is streamlined and will produce lift when air flows over it.

Contour feathers are attached to the skin or patagium of the wing. When most of them are removed, the bones of the wing are visible. You can also see how the flight feathers are attached; they are set onto the bones of the forearm and hand, and held there with connective tissue.

When you look at the *bird skeleton* later, you will see exactly which bones are involved. Note the small group of feathers just distal to the wrist; this makes up the alula or '*bastard*' wing.

It can be raised when a bird is flying slowly and requires additional lift. The alula acts like the slots on an aircraft wing, and directs the flow of air down over the wing surface so that the wing can be tilted at *steeper* angles at slower speeds without *stalling*.

You can see large birds using their *slots* when they come in to land. Smaller birds have them too, but it is much less easy to see them in use in the wild. What is the structure of the body and tail feathers? Are they like down or flight feathers?

Is the density of feathers constant all over the body? The tail fan is often spread in flight; what do you think it is used for? (Note that the landing gannet in Figure elsewhere in this chapter has its tail fan spread.) Do the body feathers have *asymmetric* vanes like the flight feathers?

THE BIRD SKELETON

We shall concentrate mainly on the trunk and limbs, but first notice the general features of the *skull* and *neck*. Bird ancestors had diapsid skulls—all archosaurs did. Remind yourself what this means by looking at the sections on *lizards* and *crocodilians* in the previous chapter.

But modern bird skulls are highly *specialised*, and it is not easy to see any sign of their diapsid origin. Keep in mind the general features of the *reptilian skulls* you know, and make general comparisons between them and bird skulls.

The skull is lightly built; and lightness is achieved both by the

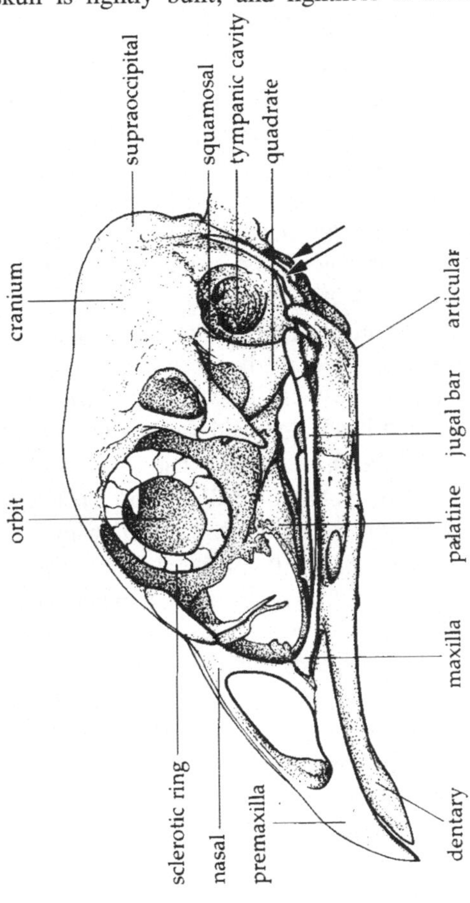

Figure 6.2: Chicken Skull.

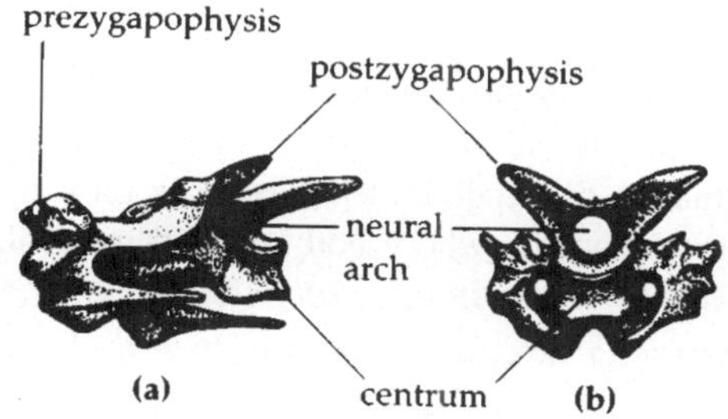

Figure 6.3: Chicken cervical vertebrae: (a) side and (b) posterior views.

internal structure (which contains air spaces) and by the shape of the bones. An example of a thin strut-shaped bone, which yet has great strength for its weight, is the bony bar that extends from the region of the jaw *articulation* to the posterior edge of the *nasal* opening.

This bar is made up of three bones—from the posterior end, the quadratojugal, jugal, and part of the *maxilla*. The first two are the same bones as those bordering the lower temporal arcade in the alligator skull.

In birds, the bar that they form with the maxilla is important as a lever in opening the upper part of the beak. Some birds have kinetic skulls, with movable *quadrates*, *jugal bars*, and *palatal* bones that together allow the beak to tilt up on the facial part of the skull (e.g. parrots).

What are the slender bones *slung* below the skull and between the two halves of the lower jaw? What structure do they support? Many skull bones have fused with each other so that it is not easy to distinguish separate bones in an adult bird.

Look particularly at the roof of the skull. Its shape is determined by the large brain underneath, which has large cerebral hemispheres and a large cerebellum, but sutures between bones are unclear. Fusion of bones could be another way of achieving greater strength in a light structure like the bird skull.

If you look at a fish or reptile skull, you will see that sutures are readily visible between bones in the *skull roof*. The neck is the most flexible part of the bird skeleton.

By comparison, the trunk is rigid because vertebrae' fuse with each other and with the *pelvic girdle* to withstand the forces imposed during life. What produces these forces? If the neck was also this rigid the bird's movement (e.g. when it is feeding) would be *severely* restricted. Thus, bird necks are very *mobile*, and the number of neck vertebrae varies from one species to another. Look at the neck vertebrae; they have complex articulations.

In what directions can movement occur? Look also at the shape of the *centrum*—compare it with the centrum of a *reptilian* neck *vertrebra*. Compare this situation of a mobile head and neck on a rigid trunk with the arrangement in a *tortoise* whose body is rigid for different reasons, but which as a result faces similar *problems*.

Another interesting functional aspect of bird neck structure is that when a bird is flying, it can keep its head' absolutely still or level in space, while the body moves in relation to it.· Thus, the bird can obtain an accurate fix on *distant* objects—for instance, the sun, or stars, used as navigational aids. If the head was rigidly fixed to the body, this would be impossible.

The pectoral Girdle and Sternum

The pectoral girdle consists of scapulae, coracoids, and fused clavicles. The long blade-like *scapulae* are placed high up on the dorsal side of the rib cage. At the shoulder joint, each *scapula* meets a *coracoid*.

The coracoids of the two sides extend *ventrally*, *converging* towards each other until they abut onto the breastbone, or sternum. Notice that the coracoids are placed and constructed so that they brace the shoulders against the *sternum*. The forces that the *coracoids* must bear are those produced by the movements of the wing in flight.

The clavicles are fused to form the *wishbone* or *furcula*: it is characteristic of birds. It carries important muscles concerned with flight, and may act like a spring to keep the shoulders correctly spaced. Movement of the wings will tend to compress the *thorax* and bring the shoulders towards the *sternum*.

Note the broad, *well-ossified* ribs with their uncinate processes, which resist compression and together with the scapulae help to brace the shoulders. Note that where the scapula, coracoid, and furcula meet, there is an opening.

It is called the foramen triosseum, and is not the articulation for the humerus; look carefully at this. The *foramen triosseum* has another function which will be explained when the role of the flight muscles is analysed. The *sternum* is large and bears a large *keel*; it is a much more striking part of the skeleton than it is in lizards.

Flightless birds do not have a *sternal keel*, which suggests that the keel carries flight muscles (see the later dissection of *flight muscles*). You already know, from eating chickens, that the bulk of the muscle is on the breast—so the large flight muscles, which are heavy, are not in

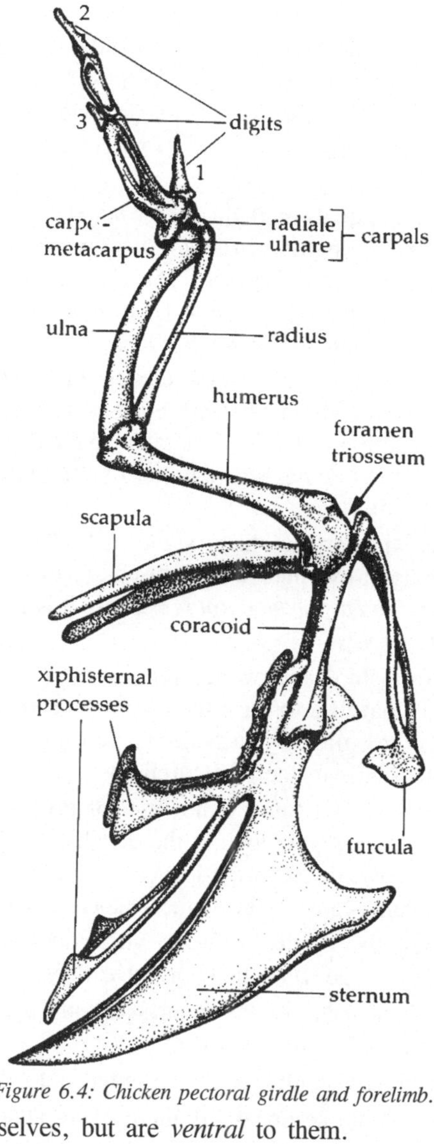

Figure 6.4: Chicken pectoral girdle and forelimb.

the wings themselves, but are *ventral* to them.

Thus, the centre of gravity of the bird is below the wings, as it must be for stability in flight; and the bulk of the main flight muscles does not add to the weight of the wings, which therefore require less energy to move.

The Wing

The bird wing articulates with the shoulder via the humerus, as does the forelimb of all land vertebrates. A dorsal ridge on the *humerus* carries flight muscle *insertions*—it is called the deltoid ridge or crest. The radius and ulna run from elbow to wrist, and the *ulna* is much larger than the *radius*.

From your observations on flight feather *attachment*, can you suggest a reason for this? From the wrist to the tip of the forelimb, the configuration of bones is *unfamiliar*. The bird wing is not obviously *pentadactyl*—it seems at first glance to have only one, or at most two, fingers. Compare it with the lizard *forelimb*.

If birds evolved originally from reptiles with *pentadactyl* limbs, what has happened to all the bones? Fusions and losses must have occurred. Look carefully at the wrist, and you will **see** two obvious wrist bones, one *articulating* with the end of the radius and one with part of the end of the *ulna*.

These bones are carpals—the *radiale* and *ulnare*. The '*hand*' is apparently made up of two main bones, fused together at each end. This structure is called the *carpometacarpus*, because it is composed of fused carpals and *metacarpals*.

We know from bird *embryology* that there are three carpals and three metacarpals that fuse to form the carpometacarpus. This suggests that the hand has three fingers attached. (There is *disagreement* over the numbering of the digits in the bird forelimb.

The system used here follows the work of Professor J. Ostrom of Yale University, USA.) Now look at the detailed drawing of the hand and digits—the second finger is the longest and most *robust*. It carries the primary feathers—look again at the feathered wings.

The first digit also carries feathers; which ones are they? What is their technical name and what function have they in flight?

From your knowledge of the wing skeleton, you should now be able to answer the following questions:

- Where are the *flight muscles* inserted onto the wing?
- Where are the secondary flight feathers attached?
- Where have bone fusions occurred in the wing? What bones have fused with each other?
- The first finger is much shorter than the other two. What function does it serve?
- Why do you think the second and third fingers are fused

together? Why not have separate fingers, and separate metacarpals and carpals like many other vertebrates?

Go and look at the wing skeletons of flightless ratite birds (e.g. *ostrich* and *kiwi*), then look at a penguin wing as an example of another, but unrelated, flightless bird. Do they have the same basic structure as the wings of *flying* birds? If so, what does this tell you about the evolution of *flightlessness* among modern birds?

HOW DOES THE WING MOVE?

Most of the effort of flying goes into the downstroke of the wing, which must keep the weight of the bird aloft and propel it through the air. Thus the *downstroke* is the power stroke, and only during take-off or hovering flight (e.g. of *humming birds*) is the upstroke also a power stroke.

This suggests that those muscles responsible for the downstroke will be larger. To find out how the flight muscles are arranged, we shall dissect a chicken. The two *muscles* we are looking for are called the *pectoralis* and *supracoracoideus* (or *pectoralis* minor). They together make up the breast 'meat' of the chicken.

Instructions for Dissection

1. Lay a plucked chicken (only the breast area and proximal part of the wings need be plucked) on its back on a board, and pin it out with awls through the feet and hand area of the wings.

   Cut through the skin *midventrally* and extend the cut anteriorly along the edge of the sternal keel up to the neck and along one of the wings.

   It is not necessary to cut into the abdominal wall. Expose the whole breast area and the muscles of one wing by carefully working the skin away and removing fat, membranes, etc.

2. With a sharp pointed scalpel (scissors are not nearly as good for this), cut down close beside the keel of the sternum and gently work the muscle away from the bone on one side.

   The muscle just under the skin is the pectoralis, and you should be able to find its *posterior* end on the posterior end of the sternal keel.

   As you work it away, you will see where the muscle is separated by a membrane from the underlying *supracoracoideus* muscle; it is difficult to miss this division. There is actually a small

Figure 6.5: Chicken flight muscle dissection: pectoralis muscle exposed.

air sac separating the two muscles. Birds have a whole system of air sacs. Find out where they are and what they do.

3. Having separated the *pectoralis* from the sternal keel, hold it by its posterior end and cut down along the edge of the wishbone and the membrane between it and the coracoid, separating muscle fibres from bone and membrane as you go.

   The pectoralis should come away as a *slab* of *tissue*. Now turn to the lateral edge of the muscle, and gently free it from the membrane over and between the ribs—this involves clearing muscle fibres from fat and underlying tissues.

   Hold the muscle away from the body as you free it. As you near the shoulder joint, you will see the large blood vessels supplying the pectoralis muscle.

   You will have to cut these eventually in order to lift the

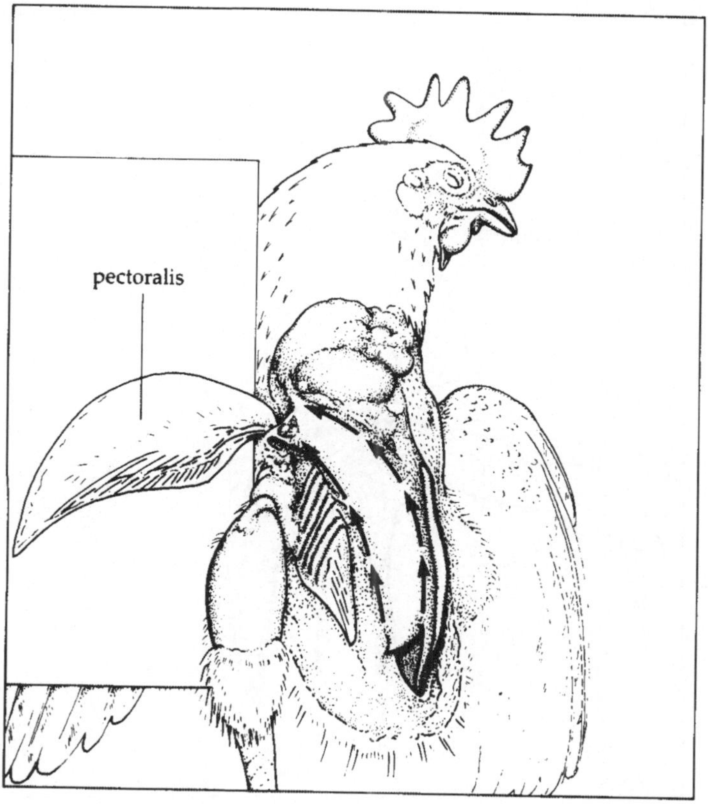

Figure 6.6: Supracoracoideus muscle exposed.

muscle away from the *supracoracoideus* underneath. If the chicken was freshly killed it is advisable to ligature the vessels before cutting them.

4. A small muscle lies over the *insertion* of the *pectoralis* on the humerus. Free this muscle at one end and turn it back. You have now completely freed the pectoralis muscle except for its insertion site. You can hold it by its sternal end and pull on it.
5. Remove the awls from the wing on the side dissected. Pull on the pectoralis muscle. *Demonstrate* that this causes the wing to move down. Check back to the chicken skeleton and remind yourself where the *insertion* site is.

Now run through all the sites of attachment of the pectoralis and list them. Is the sternal keel the only site of origin of

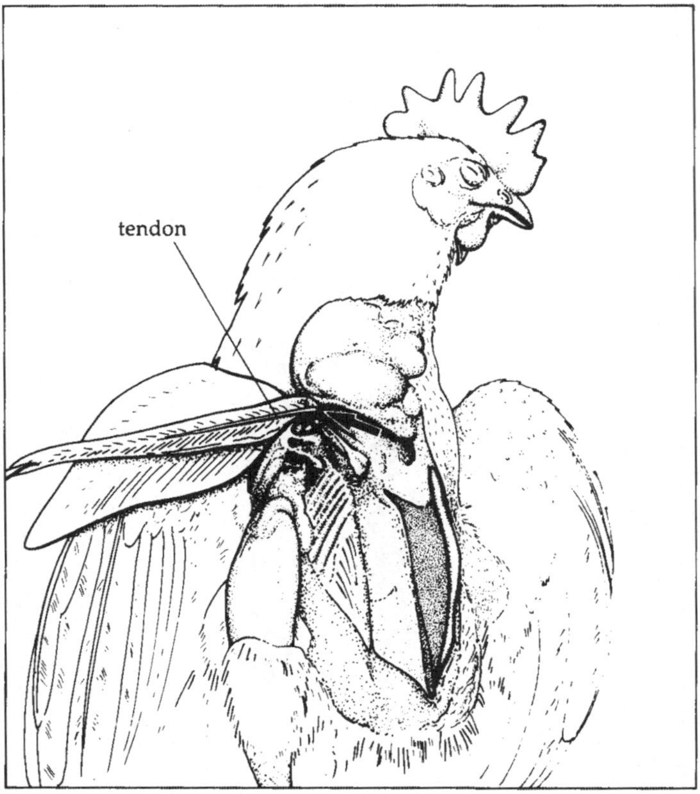

Figure 6.7: Supracoracoideus deflected to show tendon and forament triosseum (arrow).

pectoralis muscle fibres? Is it the most important site?

Is the wishbone an attachment site, or the membrane between it and the coracoid? Could you now draw in on a diagram of the chicken skeleton the exact location of the pectoralis?

6. Lay the pectoralis muscle on one side. Do not cut it off! You ought to be able to see the supracoracoideus as a leaf-shaped muscle attached mainly on the sternal keel.

   It lies entirely beneath the pectoralis and cannot be seen until the pectoralis is dissected away. Free the posterior end of the supracoracoideus and hold onto it. Cut along between the muscle and the sternum, keeping as close to the bone as possible, until you reach the anterior end of the sternum.

   Gently pull the muscle away as you free it. At the same time,

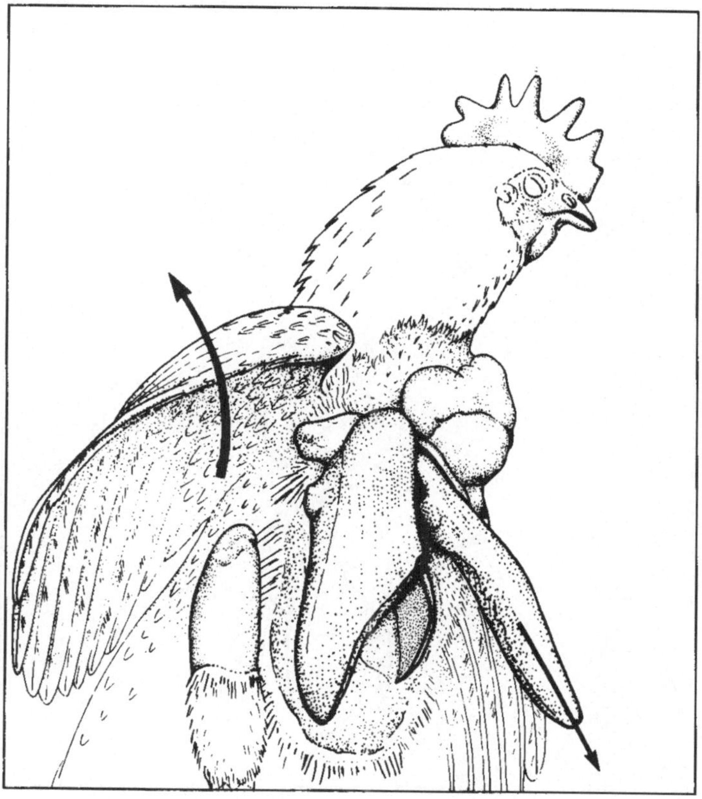

Figure 6.8: Action of Supracoracoideus muscle.

cut the fibres that originate on the membranes over the ribs. Work gradually along the rib edge of the muscle towards the shoulder joint.

7. The supracoracoideus also attaches to a membrane between the wishbone and the coracoid. This is the most difficult part of the dissection as it is not easy to see where to cut.

   Keep your scalpel blade close to the wishbone, making very small cuts and working the muscle away with your fingers.

8. Eventually, you will have freed the supracoracoideus from its origins to its insertion in the shoulder region, so that you can turn it back.

   This will reveal the tendon at its anterior (dorsal) end, and you can see it as a white strap disappearing into the shoulder joint between wishbone and coracoid.

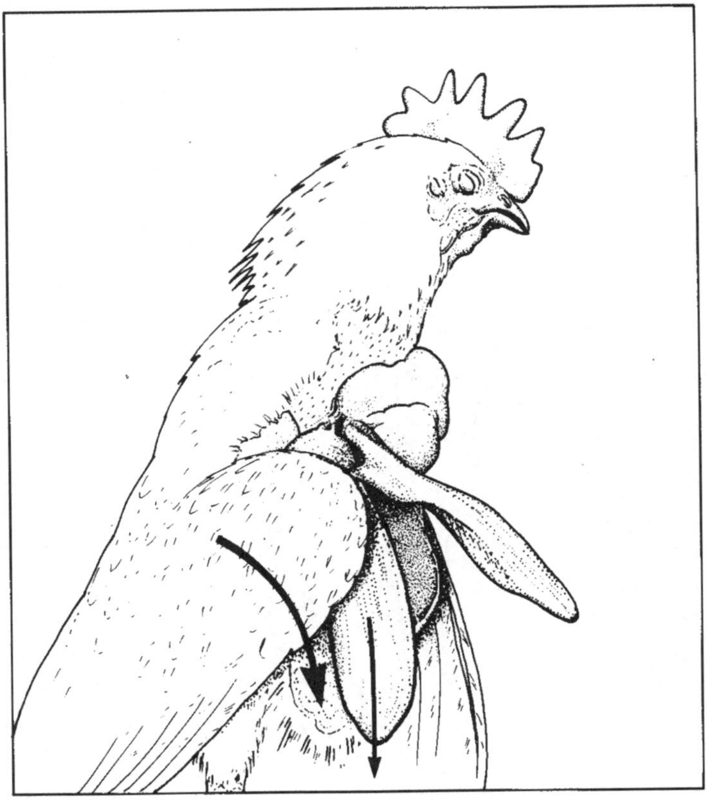

Figure 6.9: Action of pectoralis muscle.

Here it enters the foramen triosseum, indicated by an arrow on the figure.

9. Now turn to the dorsal surface of the shoulder joint. Cut away the muscles overlying the joint and inserting further down the wing. Also cut the muscle spanning the ends of the wishbone and coracoid.

   Remove any fat around the joint. You should now see a large tendon emerging from the shoulder and inserting further down on the upper surface of the humerus. It is the largest of the tendons.

   A smaller one lies partially on top of it—cut this to obtain a better view. The large tendon is the distal end of the supracoracoideus tendon. It acts as a rope from muscle to humerus, via the pulley formed by the foramen triosseum, enabling the muscle to raise the wing.

10. Now, with the chicken on its side and the wing folded along the body, hold the pectoralis in one hand and the supracoracoideus in the other. Pull first on one and then the other, and thus demonstrate the action of the two major flight muscles. Arrows on the figures indicate the direction of pull on the muscles, and the direction of movement of the wing.

You have now seen where the flight muscles are and how they work. Note that the pectoralis is indeed larger than the supracoracoideus as we predicted. Some birds have very small supracoracoideus muscles in comparison to the pectoralis; an example is the herring gull *(Larus argentatus)*.

Can you suggest why this might be so? If you can obtain a selection of birds for dissection, measure the weights of the two muscles, and express them as a ratio of weight of pectoralis/weight of supracoracoideus for each bird. Compare the ratios between species.

See if you can account for the differences by thinking about how each species takes off and flies. To what extent does each of your species use powered flight or a powered upstroke? What factors other than the requirements of flight might determine the mass of a muscle?

The total weight of both flight muscles in comparison to total body weight will also give an indication of the load on the wing (see later), and the extent to which a bird uses powered flight. In some birds, a difference in colour is visible between the fibres of the pectoralis and supracoracoideus muscles, because the nature of the muscle fibres differs.

This is also visible if you compare, say, the colour of the breast muscles in a chicken and a pigeon—they are much darker in pigeons. White muscle, as in other vertebrates, appears to be used for short bursts of intense activity, whereas red muscle is used for prolonged activity.

The biochemical basis for this functional difference is that white fibres operate on their glycogen stores, which they break down anaerobically to lactic acid. This builds up an oxygen debt, and so is most appropriate for powering short spells of activity.

Red fibres contain stores of fat and operate aerobically; they have myoglobin and many mitochondria in their cells, and are so able to function for long periods without accumulating an oxygen debt.

Next time you eat a chicken, notice that the leg muscles are redder than the breast muscles. Why do you think they contain more red fibres? Can you find any other chicken muscles that are dark like the leg muscles? Note that the supracoracoideus, *even* though it is below the wings, acts via its long tendon to raise the wings.

Considerable leverage is thereby achieved. Obviously, this would not work, even with the pulley arrangement, if the tendon inserted on the ventral surface of the humerus.

Look back at the bird skeleton. Supracoracoideus and pectoralis insert on the humerus quite close to each other. Can you now say exactly where? What other muscles act through long tendons? Where else could muscles that raise the wings be attached—at least *theoretically*? (Think of how your own arm is raised above shoulder level.)

Would these other sites provide as much mechanical advantage as the supracoracoideus pulley system? Finally, to reiterate an earlier observation, the flight muscles, which are dense and heavy, are not in the wings themselves.

If they were, the flight surface would be more massive and harder to manoeuvre. Instead, they are below the level of the wings and closer to the centre of gravity of the bird. It is thus easier for the bird to maintain stability both in flight and when balanced on two legs on the ground.

FLIGHT PATTERNS AND WING SHAPE

Birds have many different shapes of wing, which are correlated with flight pattern. We shall illustrate just a few examples of this, although the actual variation is enormous. Any visit to a museum or into a diverse habitat will confirm this.

Fast Flapping Flight

Birds that fly fast for long periods have long, narrow wings with a high aspect ratio (the ratio of length to average width). This shape is aerodynamically efficient in that it causes minimum drag for a given amount of lift.

However, it cannot easily keep the bird airborne at low speeds. The best example of such a wing is that of a swift, whose fast continuous flight is well-known. Length is provided by the primary feathers, of which the first few are much longer than any of the secondaries.

Note that the tip of the wing is pointed, without *slotted* primary feathers. High aspect ratio shapes which are efficient at high speeds can also be seen in the tails of fast-swimming fish (e.g. tuna and mackerel).

Slow Flapping Flight

Owls fly very slowly and silently. They can fly this slowly because they have a large wing area for their body size, and hence a low wing loading (wing loading = weight of bird/wing area). In Figure elsewhere in this chapter, note the long, but-broad and blunt wing shape. There is no sharp change in length of the feathers along the wing, but a gradual decrease from tip to elbow.

Soaring and Gliding

Many large birds make use of the kinetic energy of the atmosphere to assist their flight. They use upcurrents near cliffs or hills, or over warm land to gain height, and then glide downwards. *Eagles*, *storks*, and *vultures* are all birds which soar—in fact, vultures are absolutely dependent on upcurrents of air for gaining height, and will not fly in the morning until the sun has *warmed* the ground and *upcurrents* have become established.

Various seabirds also habitually soar and glide, but at speed over water—examples are fulmars, albatrosses, and gannets. The shape of their wings is very different from that of an eagle's. Figure elsewhere in this chapter shows an osprey with wings *outstretched* as they would be if it were soaring.

Watch some eagles or buzzards in the wild if you can. Note the gaps between the primary feathers, which have vanes that are shaped so as to accentuate these, gaps. Because of them, air flows more smoothly around the wing tip where considerable turbulence can arise.

Reducing turbulence allows slower flight—and a soaring eagle is moving slowly. The primary feathers at the wing tips are also tilted by the air flow and can act as individual aerofoils, giving additional lift. The wing is relatively long and broad, and the tip as a whole has a rounded profile.

Long, broad wings with slotted primaries are characteristic of large, soaring birds. The weight of the bird is considerable, and some of these birds also carry heavy prey in flight. Thus, the wing must be such as to support all this weight, whilst at the same time allowing slow *soaring flight*, and providing the *manoeuvrability* to turn within an upcurrent of air.

All of these factors have shaped the wings of these birds. In contrast gannets, fulmars, and albatrosses all have high aspect ratio wings with pointed tips. Such *turbulence* as there is around the tip of the wing is far removed from the body, because the wings are very long and narrow. Find out what wing bones provide all the length.

Such birds are not concerned with *manoeuvrability*, because they do not turn within small columns of air or confined spaces. They have settled for speed at the expense of manoeuvrability. Compare all this with the osprey's shape and flight requirements.

How do you think the wing loadings compare in a gannet and an osprey? Can you see differences between the high aspect ratio wings of swifts and fulmars? Soaring and gliding birds flap their wings rarely, whereas swifts and owls flap constantly—the former fast and the latter slowly.

Short Take-off, Heavy Payload

The last example is a game bird—the grouse. Many game birds have high wing loadings; their bodies are heavy, their wings short and broad with a convex profile.

Enough power must be provided to allow them to take off, but once airborne these birds do not fly far, for although their wings flap fast, their speed cannot be maintained for long. What other groups of birds have similar flight characteristics? These examples of wing shapes have provided some insight into adaptive radiation amongst birds.

How could you express what you see more quantitatively? A possible exercise, if you have appropriate material, would be to measure wing loadings. You will find correlations with overall size and also with the kind of flight (powered or soaring) used by the bird.

Other structures which reflect the adaptive radiation of birds are beaks and feet, which vary according to feeding habits and the requirements of locomotion on the ground.

ADAPTATIONS TO BIPEDALISM

Birds are unique among vertebrates in being efficient movers in all media—on land, in water, and in the air. They can do this because their fore- and hindlimbs have different functions.

Birds are completely bipedal animals when on the ground; that is, they stand on their hindlimbs, and their forelimbs are not involved in ground locomotion or in supporting the bird on land.

We may therefore expect the hindlimbs and pelvic girdle to be adapted very differently from the forelimbs and pectoral girdle.

The Pelvic Girdle

The pelvic girdle must support the bird's weight on the ground, and must withstand the impact when the bird lands; yet as with other parts of the bird's skeleton, it is a light structure for its size. It consists of ilium, ischium, and pubis on each side, but the sutures between the bones are impossible to see.

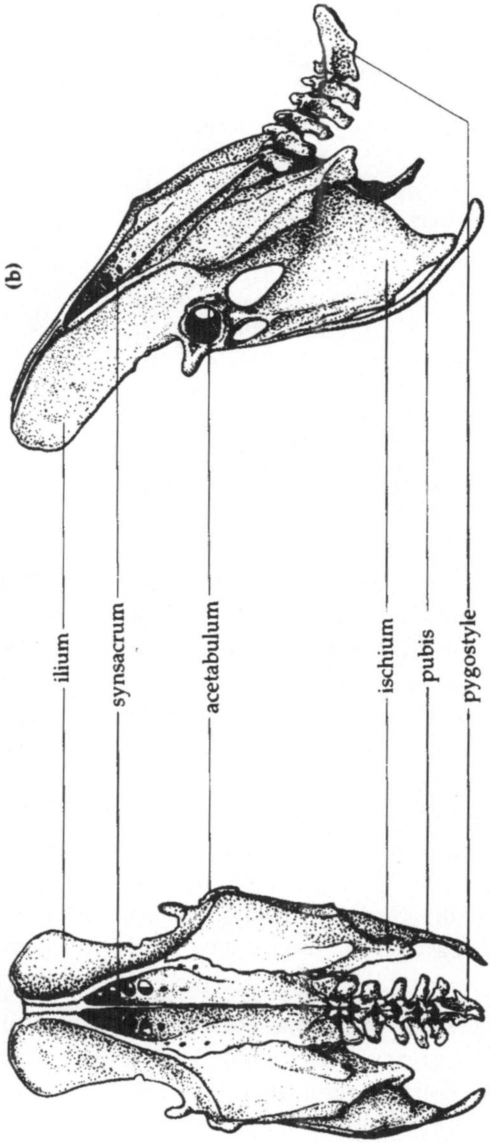

Figure 6.10: Chicken pelvis and synsacrum: (a) rear and (b) side views.

As in other parts of the skeleton, bone fusions have occurred. Note the large ilium flaring forwards both in front of and behind the articulation with the femur (acetabulum). The pubis is slender and projects backwards alongside the ischium.

Now look at the vertebral column. Lumbar, sacral, and caudal

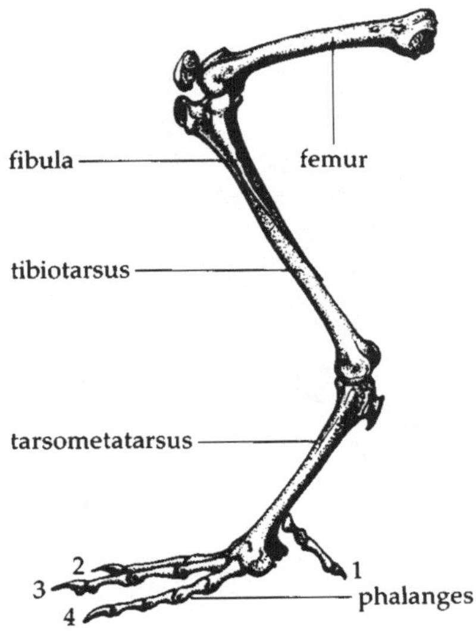

Figure 6.11: Chicken hindlimb.

vertebrae all tend to fuse together with each other and with the pelvic girdle. Note that between the two halves of the pelvic girdle is a bony area in which individual vertebrae cannot be distinguished.

This is composed of fused sacral and caudal vertebrae, and is often called the synsacrum. The tail contains some fused and some free vertebrae. The last tail bone is the pygostyle, consisting of at least four fused vertebrae.

Note that even in birds with long tails, the vertebrae do not form a long bony tail axis. It is the length of the tail feathers that determines tail length. So the pelvic girdle, through fusion of its own bones, and between them and the vertebral column, achieves great strength for its weight. It also has a large surface area for muscle attachment.

The Hindlimbs

Note first the stance of the bird. Where is its centre of gravity? The femur lies almost horizontally from acetabulum to knee. Why? Imagine the femur pointing vertically downwards. Would the bird be balanced?

Remember, most of the weight of the bird is anterior to the point at which the legs join the body, and there is no heavy tail behind to counterbalance it. If you have the chance, go and look at a bipedal dinosaur skeleton which does have a counterbalancing tail. Note the different angle of the femur.

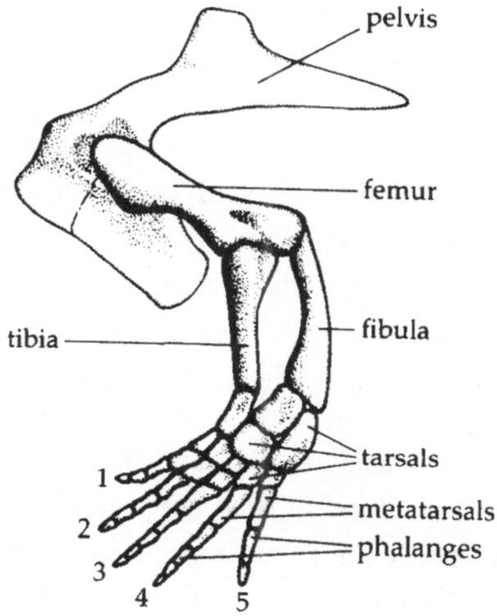

Figure 6.12: Diagram of bones in the hindlimb of a generalised fossil amphibian.

The knee of the bird is held flexed, and the tibia passes obliquely back from it so that the knee forms almost a right angle between femur and tibia. The small splint of bone along the tibia is the fibula.

Note again, that without this arrangement of femur and tibia the bird's weight would not be balanced over its feet. Now try to work out the ankle and foot. The bird is standing on its toes; there are three pointing forwards, and one pointing back or opposable.

The fifth toe of the tetrapod pentadactyl limb is missing. Some dinosaurs had feet like this. The foot bones (metatarsals) are very elongated and fused to each other, and together with some of the ankle bones (tarsals) make what is effectively an extra leg joint.

It is called the tarsometatarsus. This lengthens the whole leg and makes the bird's stride longer. It also means a bird can apply force to the ground for longer as it pushes off when running, hopping, or taking off.

Can you think of other vertebrates with similar forms of locomotion that have lengthened their hindlimbs in this particular way—by lengthening the metatarsals and/or tarsals. Some tarsal bones are also fused to the end of the tibia, which is consequently referred to as a tibiotarsus.

This provides greater strength at the ankle. Length alone is not enough—a limb that must withstand the forces of landing and running must also be strong; separate ankle bones in a bird's leg could weaken the leg. Frog hindlimbs do have separate *ankle* bones, yet they hop and jump. Can you suggest a reason why the bird leg requires greater strength?

To sum up, compare the whole bird leg with a diagram of the pentadactyl limb of a generalised land vertebrate. Note:

- Angles of the bones.
- Relative size of tibia and fibula.
- Fusions of bones at the ankle, and loss of some bones.
- Position of the ankle joint in the middle of the *tarsal* region (i.e. it is a mesotarsal joint). Proximal tarsals have fused to the tibia, and distal tarsals have fused onto the metatarsals.
- Metatarsals are fused to each other and to some of the tarsals.
- The bird stands up on its toes. Supporting toes are mainly digits II, III, and IV; toe III being the longest and toe I opposable.

Now look back at a whole chicken. Make comparisons with your own leg. Which are the 'leg' bones; where is the knee, the 'ankle', and also the 'foot'?

Can you see the knee externally on a whole chicken? Do the same sort of exercise with the wing—where is the equivalent of your elbow and wrist? The position of the wrist in a bird's wing is often mistaken for that of the elbow which is actually held very close to the body.

You should now understand the bird skeleton in terms of its functional adaptations to flight and bipedalism. It is these adaptations that really form the essence of bird structure.

7

Mammals: Form and Feeding

Mammals evolved long ago from reptiles, and by the time the dinosaurs and other major groups of reptiles were dying out, they were well established. Since the end of the Cretaceous period, about 65 million years ago, they have been the dominant land vertebrates.

Mammals are such a diverse group of vertebrates that it is difficult to decide which set of adaptations to discuss. The chapter will restrict itself to the parts of the mammal body most concerned with feeding—that is, the jaws and teeth, and the digestive system.

One reason for discussing feeding adaptations is practical—skulls are familiar objects, and are relatively easy to come by. It is less easy to assemble material for a large class on other sorts of mammalian adaptations (e.g. locomotion).

Nutrition is, in any case, a central activity of mammals, and the methods which they have evolved for catching and processing food provide a fascinating example of adaptive radiation.

This is particularly true because mammals begin the processing of their food in the mouth, and the variety of foods which they eat is reflected in the structure of their teeth to an extent unrivalled in any other group of vertebrates.

We begin with a general account of the mammalian skeleton, as a way of introducing terminology that will be useful in this and the other two chapters on mammals.

Remember that mammals evolved from reptiles, and so useful

comparisons can be made with the lizard skeletons you saw in other chapter of this book.

Materials Required

- Articulated skeleton of rabbit, *Oryctolagus cuniculus,* or equivalent.
- Disarticulated rabbit skeleton for investigation of vertebral structure, etc.
- Laboratory rats, *Rattus norvegicus,* for dissection of jaw milscles.
- A selection of other mammals with different diets for comparison of jaw muscle arrangements. Examples used here are: domestic dog, *Canis familiaris;* and roe deer, *Capreolus capreolus.*
- A selection of mammalian skulls to illustrate as wide a range of dentitions as possible. Examples used here are: insectivore - hedgehog and giant anteater, *Erinaceus europaeus* and *Myrmecophaga;* frugivore - fruit bat, *Pteropus;* omnivore - domestic pig, *Sus scrofa;* carnivores - domestic dog and cat, *Felis domesticus;* piscivore - dolphin, *Delphinus delphis;* rodent - rat; herbivores - horse, *Equus caballus,* and roe deer.
- Examples of different mammalian digestive systems, to allow comparison between herbivores and carnivores. Examples used here are: hedgehog; fox, *Valpes vulpes;* roe deer; and rabbit.

THE MORPHOLOGY OF THE RABBIT

The rabbit (order Lagomorpha: *Oryctolagus cuniculus),* though not a particularly generalised mammal, has the advantage of being common, familiar to most people, and easily obtainable for class use. All the major features of mammalian skeletal morphology are clear, with no extreme specialisations except in the dentition.

The Skull

It is worth knowing the main bones in the skull in order to avoid a lot of circumlocution when talking about such things as jaw mechanisms. You will recognise many of the names from earlier chapters, and you can relate back to the basic tetrapod skull and to lizard skulls for comparison.

In mammals, the shape of the skull closely reflects that of the brain it encloses, because the dermal bones of the skull roof and sides fit directly around it, rather than forming a loose outer box around the braincase with the jaw muscles filling the space in between. Diet also has much to do with shaping the jaws and the teeth which they bear.

What are the major features of mammalian skulls, and what can be learnt from rabbit skulls of the changes that took place during the evolution of the mammalian skull from that of the mammal-like reptiles?

1. Of the dermal bones in the roof and sides of the skull of early tetrapods, several are not present in mammals. There are no prefrontals, postfrontals, supratemporals, or postparietals - though the latter two may have fused with the occipital bones.
2. The brain has expanded tremendously, and as a result has outgrown its original braincase. Endochondral bones which almost completely enclose the brain in reptiles, form only the floor and back of the braincase in mammals.

   The bones that now enclose most of the brain are dermal ones from the skull roof and sides - that is, the frontals, parietals, and squamosals. These have expanded ventrally and laterally beneath the jaw muscles to cover the brain as it grew.

   Another bone involved in covering the mammalian brain is the alisphenoid, which is derived from the reptilian epipterygoid. Underneath the brain, basisphenoid and basioccipital elements are present as in reptiles.
3. Running laterally along the lower border of the eye socket is a bridge of bone called the zygomatic arch. It is composed of two bones, the jugal and a process from the squamosal; in some mammals the maxilla also participates.

   The zygomatic arch is characteristic of mammals, and is a site of attachment for one of the jaw muscles. It is derived from the bones bordering the lower edge of the temporal opening of synapsid reptiles from which mammals evolved.

   Note that between the zygomatic arch and the skull wall is a space, small in rabbits, but very large in some mammals. This contains not only the eyes but also the temporal muscles which close the jaws. The zygomatic arch is the only remnant of the original outer dermal shell of the temporal region.

   Note that whereas in early tetrapods the jaw adductor muscles were entirely enclosed between this shell and the braincase, in mammals they are not restricted in this way; and have expanded and differentiated to produce the complex jaw movements characteristic of mammals (see later).

4. At the back of the skull, the spinal cord leaves the brain via an opening called the foramen magnum. The precise position and angle of the foramen magnum in a skeleton give a clue to the whole posture of the animal, for they show the position of the head in relation to the trunk.

   Two bony facets, the occipital condyles, articulate with the first neck vertebra (the atlas) in mammals. Oddly enough, amphibians also have two occipital condyles, but reptiles and birds have only one.

5. On the underside of the back of the skull is the ear region, and most eutherian mammals have prominent tympanic bullae. Rabbits have large ears, and the opening (external auditory meatus) into the middle ear is very prominent.

   Tympanic bullae are a new addition to the skull (cf. amphibians and reptiles); they surround the middle ear on each side and protect the ear ossicles (malleus, incus, and stapes) from damage.

   Some mammals have incomplete tympanic bullae, and the tympanic bone forms a ring here—look at a hedgehog skull, for example. This 'new' tympanic bone of mammals is actually derived from the angular bone of the reptilian lower jaw.

6. You may have noticed that mammal skulls apparently have no quadrates. Each has been incorporated into the middle ear as the sound-conducting incus; so has the articular bone of the reptilian lower jaw, which is the malleus in mammals.

   Thus, the bones which formed the jaw articulation of reptiles have totally changed their function, while nevertheless maintaining their original contact—a contact which originated in the earliest fishes.

7. The skull narrows drastically between the eyes, whose sockets are large in rabbits. This narrowing allows space for the eyes, and also emphasises that the bulk of the brain (i.e. the cerebral hemispheres) is just posterior to the eyes.

   Note the opening for the optic nerve in each eye socket. The anterior part of the skull is long and narrow, covered above by the long nasals, and laterally by maxillae and premaxillae.

   It houses the olfactory epithelia and nasal passages, as well as bearing the teeth. It is usually possible to make some assessment of the importance of the sense of smell to a particular mammal by looking at the relative size of the nasal region. Rabbits have a well-developed sense of smell.

In all mammals the air is also warmed and cleaned as it is breathed in. This is achieved by passing the air through passages which are lined with ciliated epithelial tissue that secretes mucus and is well supplied with blood vessels.

This tissue is housed on the turbinal bones, visible underneath the nasal bones. Note the fenestrations in the maxillae on the sides of the rabbit skull.

8. Look at the palatal side of the skull. Note the flanges of the pterygoid bones. Where do the internal nostrils open? All mammals have a secondary palate, and would not be able to breathe and suckle at the same time if they did not.

   Which bones on the side of the nasal region are involved? Is the secondary palate complete? What do we mean by the soft palate? Remember that what appear to be openings in skulls may in life be covered over by tissue.

   Check back to the alligator skull to remind yourselves that-crocodilians also have a secondary palate. Is it formed from the same bones as in mammals?

9. Now look at the lower jaw; it is composed of only one bone. Unlike all other tetrapods, mammals have only a single lower jaw bone—the dentary or mandible. This has increased in size and formed a new joint with the skull (via the squamosal) during mammalian evolution.

   The rabbit dentary has an ascending ramus which bears the articular surface, and this can assume various shapes in different mammals. In rabbits, it fits into a groove (the glenoid) in the squamosal which allows some fore and aft movement of the lower jaw, but only slight lateral movement.

   In carnivores, the articular condyle is not on an ascending ramus but is level with the tooth row, and there is a separate ascending process called the coronoid process. Rabbits have a very reduced coronoid process.

   The dentary also has an angular process at the back, and then passes forwards as the tooth-bearing mandible. Note that rabbits carry their teeth in two groups; one at the front—the incisors (rabbits have no canines)—and another further back. These are the cheek teeth, which include premolars and molars. Note that all the cheek teeth look alike.

The gap between incisors and cheek teeth is called a diastema, and is characteristic of herbivorous mammals. Teeth and jaws are discussed in later sections of this chapter.

10. Just beneath the back of the skull is a small structure, partly bony and partly cartilaginous, called the hyoid apparatus, which is sometimes missing from mounted skeletons.

    It is a remnant of the hyoid arch of fish, but its functions are not at all negligible in mammals, where it is involved in moving the tongue, swallowing and opening the mouth. Other components of the hyoid arch help to form the larynx, and support laryngeal muscles.

The Vertebral Column and Ribs

Mammals are characterised by an S-shaved vertebral column. with twn flexures in the shoulder and lumbar region. Ribs are only found in the fore part of the trunk, and the posterior boundary of the ribcage is occupied in life by the diaphragm.

This arrangement of backbone and ribs appears during the earliest evolution of mammals from mammal-like reptiles, and signals the development of dorsoventral flexibility in the spine, and a diaphragm—neither of which is characteristic of reptiles.

The vertebral column is like a bipartite girder cantilevered out from two supports, the fore- and hindlimbs. The component vertebrae vary along the girder, and are shaped by the forces they bear.

The ties (muscles and their tendons) that hold the whole structure together are attached particularly to the transverse processes and neural spines, which act as struts. In the thoracic region is an 'anticlinal' vertebra, which marks the meeting point between the anterior girder, in which the vertebrae have backwardly pointing neural spines, and the posterior girder with forwardly pointing neural spines.

The ribs also act as struts, besides their other functions. As you look at different mammals, notice how the vertebrae and their processes are modified in correlation with the overall shape and size of the animal and with the distribution of its weight.

Between the head and thorax of almost all mammals are seven cervical vertebrae, including the atlas and axis. The neck allows mobility of the head on the shoulders. Compare with birds, which have very mobile necks but variable numbers of neck vertebrae. What about the

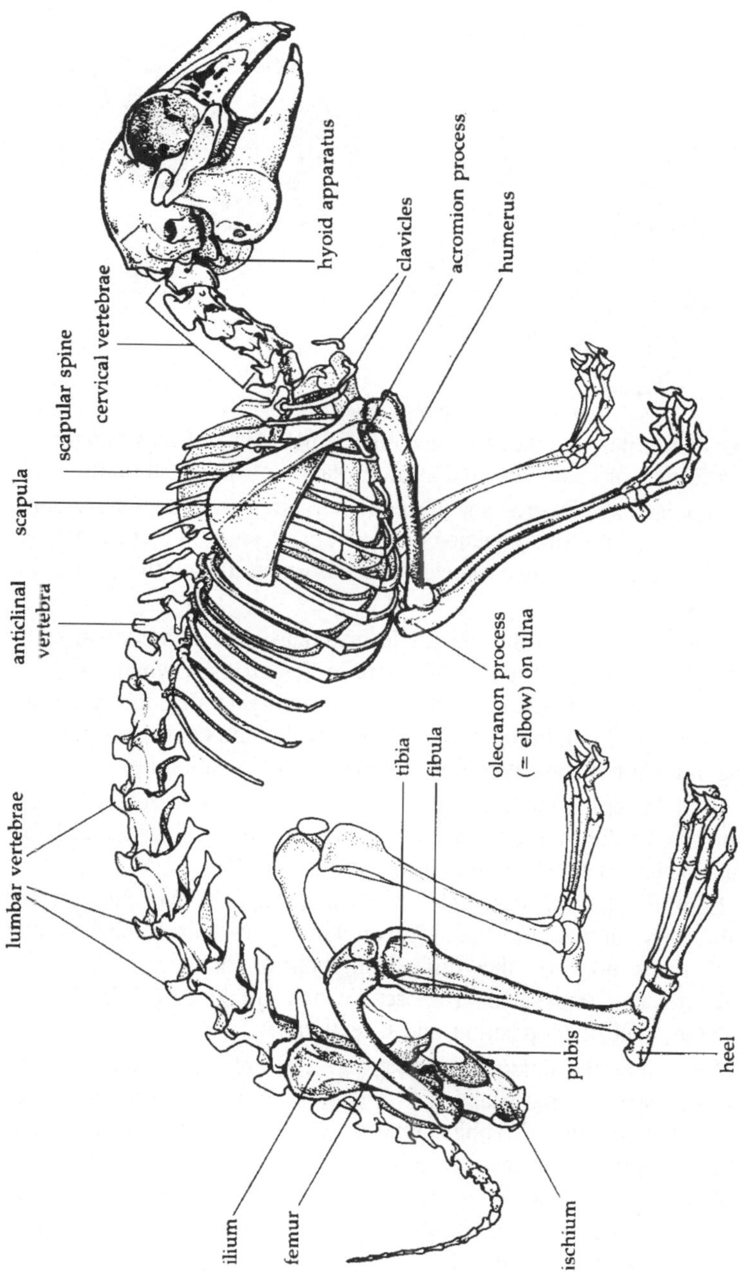

Figure 7.1: Skeleton of rabbit.

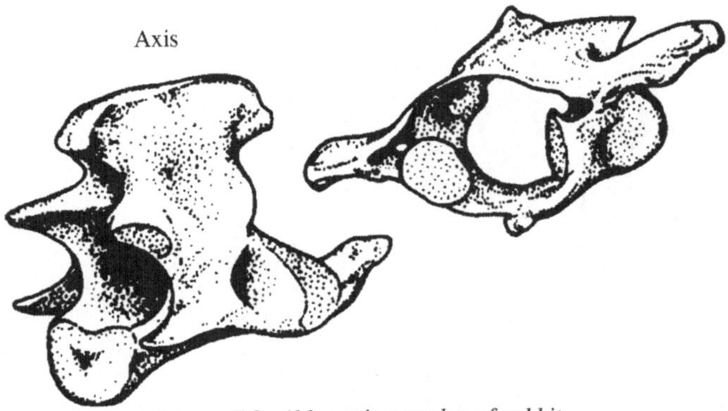

Figure 7.2: Altlas-axis complex of rabbit.

necks of reptiles, amphibians, and fish? The atlas and axis complex is also a feature of mammals, and allows rotation of. the head on the neck.

Rabbits have twelve or thirteen thoracic vertebrae which carry ribs. How are the ribs attached at their dorsal ends? The ventral ends are either free or attached via cartilaginous extensions to the breastbone or sternum.

Note the extent of the ribcage in mammals, and then compare with the lizard skeleton in Figure elsewhere in this chapter, where there are ribs all along the body. The mammalian ability to flex the spine and bring fore- and hindlimbs close together under the centre of the trunk is essential for certain types of locomotion (e.g. galloping).

Could a reptile move like this? Long neural spines project dorsally from most of the thoracic vertebrae. Why are they longer towards the head? Where is the anticlinal vertebra?

Look carefully at the angle of the neural spines. Are they present on the cervical vertebrae? All seven lumbar vertebrae have similar neural spines; note how they differ from those on the thoracic vertebrae. There are also transverse processes, which are large on the lumbar vertebrae; note their position and direction.

Next, note the flexions of the spine. The human vertebral column is not this shape; what shape is it, and why? Four vertebrae are fused to form the sacrum of rabbits. One of the four attaches to the pelvic girdle, forming the sacro-iliac joint.

Caudal vertebrae support the tail, and their number varies considerably in different mammals. Why might it be functionally adaptive for several vertebrae to fuse in the sacral region, even though only one is actually involved in the articulation with the pelvic girdle?

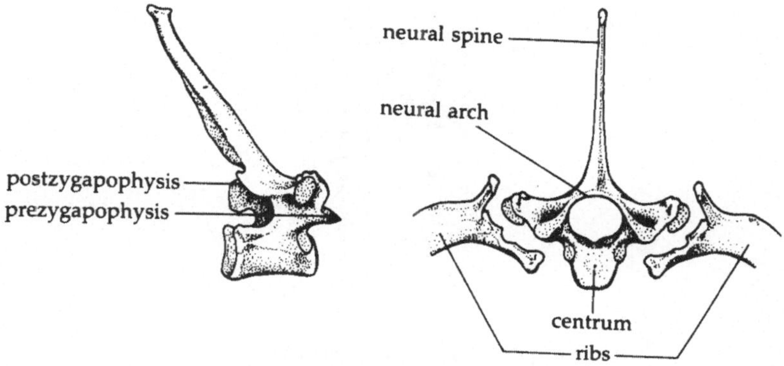

Figure 7.3: Thoracic vertebra and rib of rabbit.

The Limb Girdles

The limbs of land vertebrates carry the weight of the body slung between them, and must support it above the ground. They also produce the propulsive forces necessary for locomotion. The limb girdles transmit these forces to the vertebral column.

As noted previously in other chapter of this book, the pelvic girdle of all land vertebrates is attached directly to the sacrum, whereas the pectoral girdle has no direct connection with the spine. Instead, it is attached to the ribs by muscles, and in many mammals the clavicles connect with the sternum as well.

Flexibility in the connection between pectoral girdle and vertebral column seems to have been a more compelling requirement than rigidity. The mammalian pectoral girdle consists of two bones on each side, the scapula and clavicle. Note the flared shape of the scapula, its spine, and acromion process.

The scapula carries the muscles which attach it (and hence the whole forelimb) to the ribcage, and obviously provides a large surface area for them. It can also be moved forwards and backwards alongside the ribcage, and in some mammals this movement is an important source of extra leverage during fast running.

The scapula effectively becomes another limb bone. The clavicles can act as braces between the shoulders and sternum, but are often reduced or completely absent in mammals.

Their bracing function is not critical if the forelimbs are only moved backwards and forwards, and would actually be a hindrance to anteroposterior rotation of the scapula and glenoid in fast cursorial mammals. Rabbits have reduced clavicles, but the human clavicle is well developed.

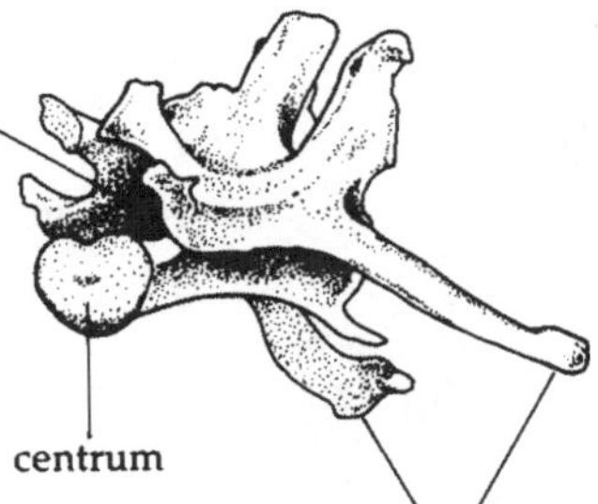

Figure 7.4: Lumbar vertebra of rabbit.

What arm movements can you make which a rabbit would find impossible? Finally, look at the glenoid cavity, which is the point of articulation with the humerus. It is not a deep ball and socket articulation like the hip joint, but is more saucer-shaped.

This also has important implications as regards mobility at the shoulder joint. The pelvic girdle is long and slender, with the hip joint almost in the centre of its long axis. It is often difficult to distinguish ilium, ischium, and pubis in adult animals.

All three bones carry muscles that move the legs, but particularly the ilium and ischium, which are elongated to accommodate them. The pubic symphysis braces the two hips, and prevents them from tending to spread apart.

The bones of the pelvic girdle never become as reduced as those of the pectoral girdle, although their shapes certainly change. Indeed, the three components have remained essentially the same throughout vertebrate evolution since the amphibian pattern developed.

This suggests that the prime function of the tetrapod pelvic girdle is to provide a strong joint between the body and the propulsive hindlimbs, and that the design first evolved was well adapted for this.

The Limbs

Mammalian limbs are held in close to the body and generally support it well above the ground because of their vertical orientation. The forefeet are generally placed beneath the shoulders, and the limbs move in a vertical or parasagittal plane.

All this is largely true of cursorial mammals (e.g. horses) and large graviportal ones (e.g. elephants). Other mammals may hold their limbs more horizontally, particularly if they dig or swim—and many noncursorial mammals swing their limbs forwards and back at various angles from the parasagittal lane. So mammals show a variety of limb positions and movements, defending on their modes of life. It is interesting that reptiles, which generally hold their limbs and feet well out to the side, never evolved fast cursorial quadrupedal forms.

However, fast bipedal movement did evolve (in the dinosaurs) and, in the process, the hindlimbs became positioned vertically beneath the pelvis. This also happened with both pairs of limbs in large graviportal dinosaurs.

Laterally held limbs are inefficient not only for fast movement but also for supporting very heavy weights. Note the position of the humerus in the rabbit. It points posteriorly at an acute angle to the scapula, and so brings the forelimb in beside the body. The radius and ulna are semi-vertical, and the elbow points backwards.

Note the olecranon process for insertion of the muscles that extend the forelimb - mainly the triceps muscle. Look at the position of the radius and ulna, and their relative sizes. These two bones are responsible for any rotatory movements in the forearm.

Which bone carries the olecranon process? Rabbits can only flex and extend their lower forelimbs, but some other mammals (e.g. primates) can rotate them as well. Others still have simplified their forelimbs and retain only the radius, with a greatly reduced ulna fused to it (e.g. horses).

Do both radius and ulna articulate with the humerus in the rabbit? Is the situation the same in the human elbow? Look at the plan of the bones in the rabbit forelimb and digits. Numerous modifications to this plan occur in different mammals.

One major influence on the pattern of bones is the position of the digits during standing and locomotion, and this of course applies to the digits of the hindlimb as well.

Mammals which move with the whole sole of each foot on the ground are said to be plantigrade; those which touch the ground only with their digits are digitigrade, and those which walk up on the tips of their digits are unguligrade.

Heavy mammals such as elephants and bears are plantigrade or semi-plantigrade, dogs are digitigrade, and horses, pigs, and deer are unguligrade. Rabbits vary the area of sole that touches the ground depending on their gait, and whether they are moving on snow, for example.

The most complete arrangement of foot bones is found in plantigrade mammals, which have the more primitive method of locomotion. A plan of the bones in the forelimb of a horse provides an indication of the scope for reduction of the bones in the wrist and hand.

All the manifold adaptations of mammalian forelimbs involve chiefly the bones distal to the elbow. Hindlimbs in mammals usually retain their role as weight bearers and propulsive organs, and, unlike the forelimbs, do not adopt other major roles or become modified for unusual methods of locomotion (e.g. flight).

When they are not used for weight bearing or propulsion, they tend to become reduced, as in whales. Thus, there is a conservatism about the function of the hindlimb, which is not characteristic of the forelimb.

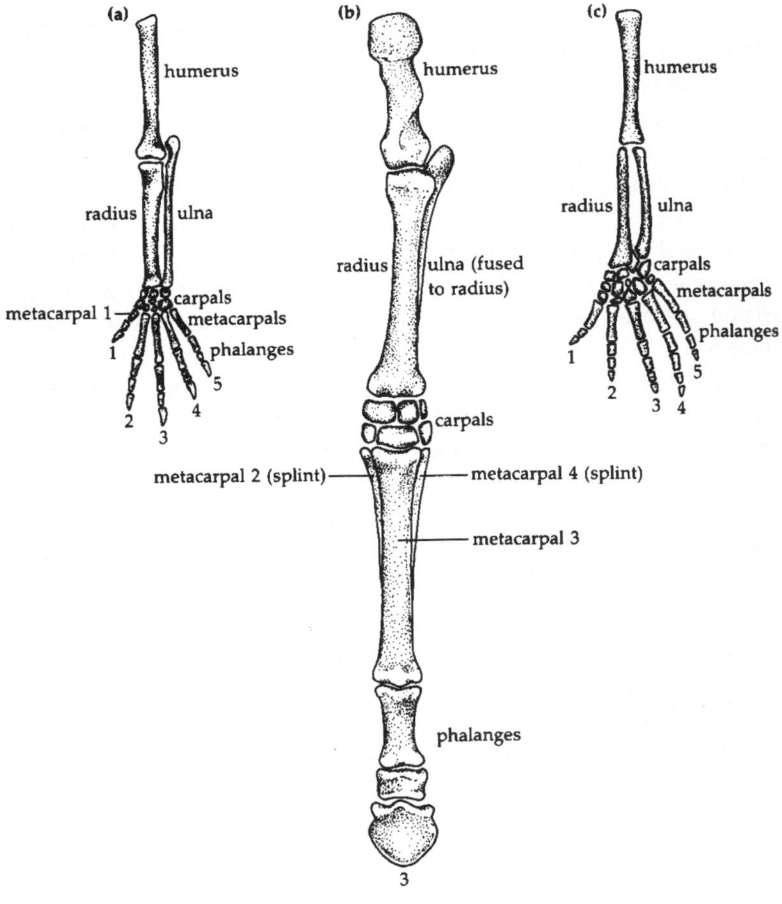

Figure 7.5: Plans of forelimb in (a) rabbit, (b) horse and (c) primitive tetrapod.

From the acetabulum the femur points anteriorly, and the knee joint is directed forwards.

The limb is thus brought in close beside the body. Compare with the humerus and elbow. Tibia and fibula pass semi-vertically to the fully plantigrade foot. Note the relative sizes of tibia and fibula, and their fusion into a single bone distally.

As in the forelimb, many mammals have only one bone in the lower leg. Can you think of some examples? Note the heel - it is a mammalian feature, and is prominent in rabbits. What muscles does it carry? Is it in the same relative position as the olecranon process in the elbow?

What bone is modified to form the heel? Check back to lizard feet for comparison. There are only four digits in the rabbit foot. It is the fifth digit that is lost (i.e. of the five originally present in primitive mammals).

A reduction of the number of digits in the hindfoot is common in mammals, and is most extreme in unguligrade species. Note the proportions of the various bones and compare with those of the forefoot, which is shorter.

Then compare the whole hindlimb with the forelimb—it is much loneer in rabbits. Long limbs indicate that they are used for providing powerful leverage during locomotion; so why are rabbit hindlimbs longer? The relative lengths of the limbs are very instructive when working out how animals move.

If a mammal had very long arms, what sort of locomotion would you predict for it? By looking at the rabbit limbs you can work out the main points of movement between the component bones. They are moved by muscles intrinsic to the limbs, whereas movement of the whole limb in relation to the body is produced by extrinsic muscles.

The positions of all these muscles are readily revealed by dissection. Before leaving the rabbit skeleton, can you sketch its proportions, the stance of the limbs, the 'shape of the backbone, the ribcage, and the angle of neck and head?

The essence of mammalian form lies in the overall shape of the skeleton, and detailed drawings of parts of it can prevent you from seeing it as a whole. From such a general construction as that of the rabbit, all the manifold mammalian forms may be derived.

THE JAW MUSCLES OF MAMMALS

The next two sections of this chapter are concerned with jaw muscles, teeth, and jaws. These are the structures which most directly reflect the dietary specialities of mammals.

Their digestive systems also show adaptations—these will be covered briefly in the last section. It may seem odd to look at jaw muscles before teeth and jaws; but the fact is that skull and jaw shape is profoundly affected by the size and distribution of jaw muscles.

So it helps to know their nature and location before trying to analyse different jaws and dentitions. Also, tooth shape cannot only be considered in a static context—it is absolutely essential to know how the teeth relate to each other when the jaws move.

There are three main masticatory muscles; the temporalis, masseter, and pterygoideus. Each may consist of more than one part, and parts of temporalis and masseter may merge. The temporalis muscle originates on the temporal region of the skull (parts of the parietal, frontal, and squamosal bones) and inserts on both sides of the coronoid process of the lower jaw.

The masseter originates only on the zygomatic arch or on the maxilla as well, from whence its fibres run down and backwards to insert on the outer side of the dentary and around the angle of the jaw. The masseter may have at least two parts—deep and superficial—which are clear in the rat, described later.

The pterygoideus muscle also consists of two parts in the rat. Both originate on the pterygoid bones and run laterally to insert on the dentary, at the articulation with the skull and lower down. All of these muscles act to close the mouth by raising the mandible.

However, they pull in different directions and so can cause more subtle movements than simple closure—they can pull the jaw to one side by differential contraction, for example. A further muscle is also important—the digastricus.

It runs from the paroccipital process to near the jaw symphysis in the rat, and opens the mouth by lowering the mandible; it can also act to pull the jaw back.

Other muscles are involved in mastication and swallowing, particularly those attached to the hyoid apparatus and those operating the tongue and cheeks, but we shall here confine ourselves to the main (and hence most visible) muscles already mentioned.

They are also the ones that show the most obvious differences in mammals with different diets.

Dissection of the Jaw Muscles of the Rat

Laboratory rats provide a good source of material for investigating jaw muscles. The dentition of rats is specialised (see next section), but all the relevant muscles are nevertheless easily visible by dissection; in fact their component parts are more distinct in rats than in some larger mammals such as dogs and rabbits.

Some simple instructions follow. It is helpful to have a rat skull available as well.

1. Remove the skin carefully from one side of head, neck and shoulder, and clear away glandular tissue from throat and ear region.
2. Expose the masseter muscle; it is a dark-red mass bulging around the outside of the back of the lower jaw. Locate a tendon which attaches the superficial part of the muscle to the side of the face (maxilla). Uncover the tendon and follow it to

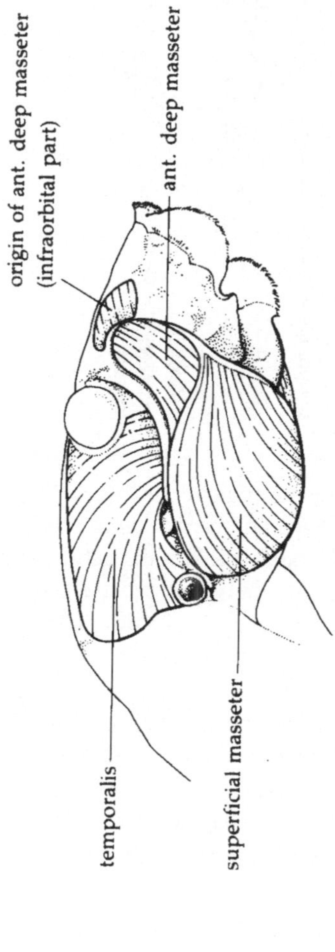

Figure 7.6: Dissection of jaw muscles of rat, Rattus norvegicus; undisturbed.

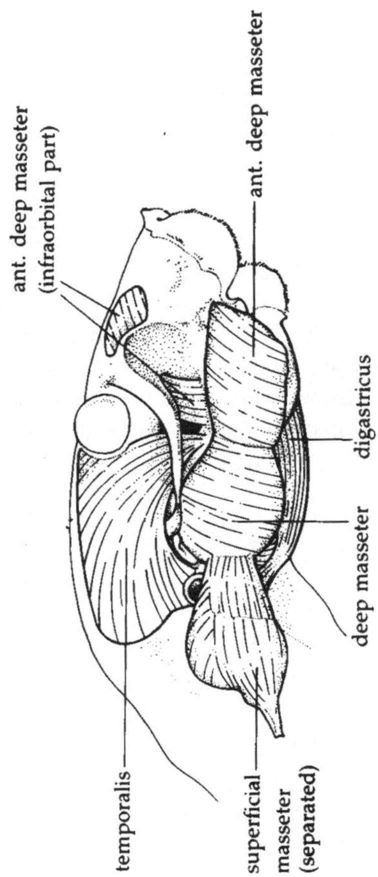

Figure 7.7: Rat jaw muscles: parts of masseter, separated and detached from skull.

the maxilla.

3. You will have to remove the masseter in order to see the insertion of the temporalis, but do not cut it out indiscriminately, for the whole point of this dissection is to find out exactly where the various muscles are attached, and so to work out what movements each performs. The masseter is the most complex of the jaw muscles, since it consists of several parts.
4. Cut the tendon attaching the superficial masseter to the maxilla, cutting close to the bone. Then hold the tendon with forceps, and free the muscle from in front back along the jaw and around the jaw angle.

   There is a flange at the back of the jaw to accommodate it. As you do this, you will see the fibres of the deep masseter

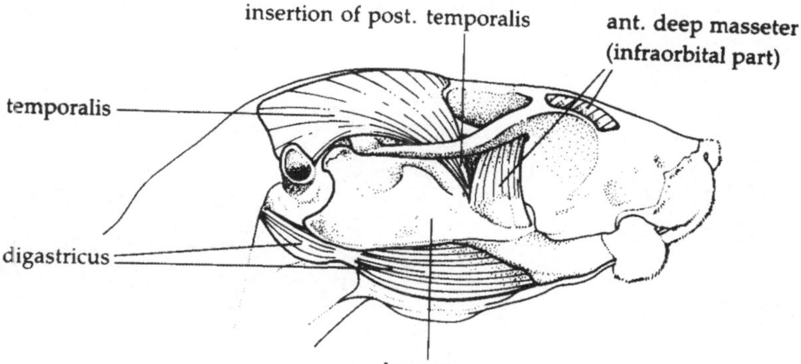

Figure 7.8: Rat jaw muscles: temporalis and digastricus muscles.

lying under the superficial masseter. They run vertically from zygomatic arch, to dentary.

5. Having freed the superficial masseter from the back of the jaw, deflect it ventrally and shave carefully along the ventral edge of the zygomatic arch from behind forwards. Be careful not to cut the temporalis muscle underneath.

   At about mid-eye level, you will see that part of the deep masseter goes into the orbit underneath the anterior end of the zygomatic arch. This is the infraorbital part of the anterior deep masseter; leave it in place.

6. Now free the rest of the deep masseter, which originates on the maxilla, just ventral to the anterior end of the zygomatic arch, and runs down to insert on the lower jaw. Note that the nearly vertical orientation of this section of the masseter is in contrast to the almost horizontal arrangement of the superficial masseter fibres.

   Shave away the fibres attached to the jaw, so that the whole masseter is now connected to the skull only by its deep infraorbital component.

7. Remove the eye, so that you can see into the orbit. Note the position of the masseter. Take hold of the bulk of the masseter and pull on it. Watch the side of the face just in front of the orbit—you will see movement there.

   It marks the point where anterior deep masseter fibres emerge onto the maxilla from the infraorbital foramen. Clear away obscuring tissue, and convince yourself that the bony bar around

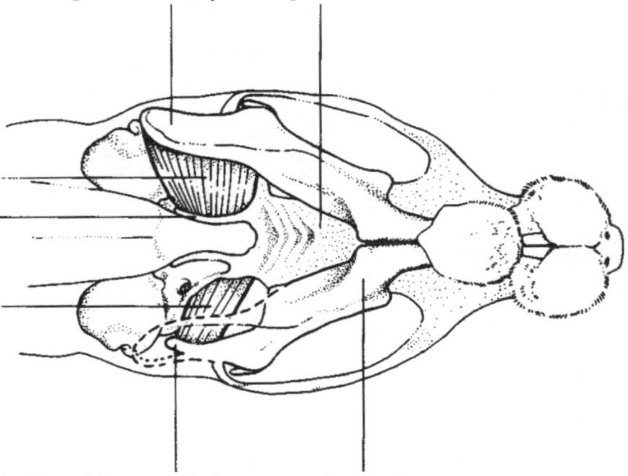

Figure 7.9: Rat jaw muscles: pterygoideus muscles, from below (longue and hyoid removed).

the outside of the infraorbital foramen is functioning as a pulley, over which the deep masseter can act.

This arrangement is a feature of myomorph rodents (rats, mice, hamsters, etc.). To complete the dissection, deflect the masseter over the snout, or cut it off where it passes into the orbit.

8. The outside of the dentary is now exposed. Look for the digastricus muscle looping around ventrally from the occiput, inside the jaw angle, to the front of the jaw.

   Find out where it originates. The digastricus is so-called because it has two bellies, connected in tandem by a tendon. Can you see this?

9. Carefully detach the temporalis muscle, starting at the back of the skull and shaving along the skull table. Hold the occipital edge of the muscle, and note that it extends down to the ear region and bulges over the posterior end of the zygomatic arch.

   It also has an anterior portion originating at the back of the orbit. Does the temporalis attach at any point to the zygomatic arch? When you have entirely freed the temporalis from the skull, look for its insertion sites on the lower jaw.

10. Pull the temporalis dorsally—it attaches on both sides of the coronoid process, and also further down towards the cheek teeth. Carefully remove the muscle from the outside of the

lower jaw. Turn the animal on its back and cut the digastricus muscle at its occipital end.

Deflect it out of the way. Cut out the larynx and hyoid apparatus from the floor of the mouth. Also remove the tongue, and expose the roof of the mouth.

11. Pull the exposed lower jaw laterally and look in behind the jaw angle, or from underneath. The pterygoideus muscles will be extended, and you can see the internal pterygoideus passing medially from the inside of the jaw angle.

    The external pterygoideus is a smaller muscle, less easy to see. Cut the internal pterygoideus at its insertion on the jaw. Look between the condyle and the skull for the external pterygoideus.

    Distinguish its insertion site from that part of the temporalis which inserts on the inside of the coronoid process. Now work out where the pterygoideus muscles attach to the skull (a cleaned skull will help you).

Comments on Muscle Function

Although some idea of muscle movements can be gained from looking at the. size and orientation of muscles, this mostly reveals what is likely to happen during free movement of each muscle.

Interactions between the various muscles and against loads imposed by the food are much more difficult to analyse, and require such, techniques as electromyography, cineradiography, and extensive measurements of the muscles concerned.

References to this work are given at the end of the chapter. From such analyses, the major roles of the rat jaw muscles have been worked out, and are summarised below:

- The main feeding movements of rat jaws are vertical and horizontal. The incisors procure and ingest food. If you look at a rat skull with its lower jaw in the rest position, you can see that the lower incisors rest inside the upper ones. So, the mandible must be moved down and forwards to engage the incisor tips.
- To masticate food, rats engage their cheek teeth against the food, which is positioned between them by the action of tongue and cheeks. Occlusion of the cheek teeth cannot occur at the same time as occlusion of the incisors (check this on a skull), so the jaw must move back to begin mastication and will simultaneously disengage the incisors. Mastication in rats

involves forwards and backwards movement. The glenoid and condyle are shaped to allow this movement.

- The temporalis muscle is the main elevator and retractor of the mandible. It probably also keeps the lower jaw stable when at rest.
- The superficial masseter is the main protractor of the jaw.
- The deep part of the masseter which attaches to the zygomatic arch is the most powerful of all the rat jaw muscles. It raises the mandible against the resistance of the food. It also acts as the external part of a sling stabilising the jaw at rest. The internal part comes from the temporalis fibres that pass to the inner side of the coronoid process.
- Think about where the deeper fibres of the masseter insert.

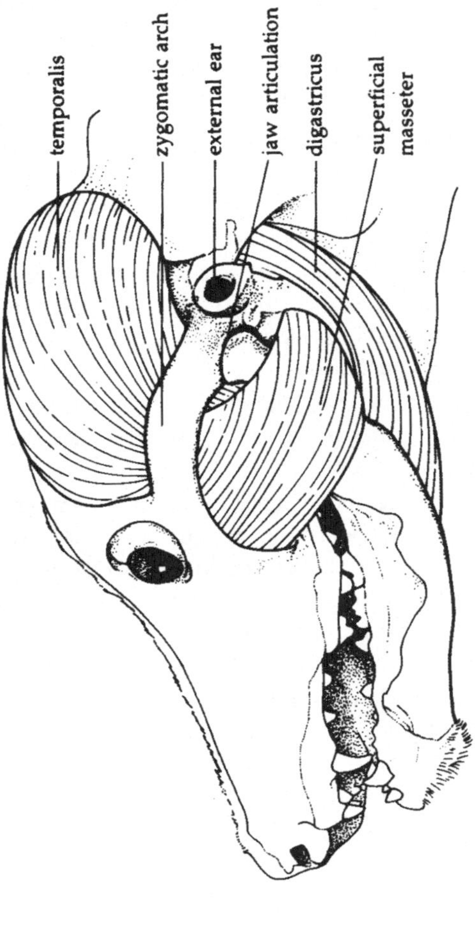

Figure 7.10: Jaw muscles of dog, Canis familiaris.

Their contraction will tend to pull the lower edge of the mandible outwards. This tendency is resisted by the internal pterygoideus—the main deep masseter antagonist. For future reference, note that if the internal pterygoideus contracted unilaterally, it would shift the jaw sideways.

- The deep parts of the masseter that run from just behind the lower incisors onto the maxilla and through the infraorbital foramen probably assist in bringing the incisors into occlusion. They have to overcome the resistance of the food between the incisors and have large moment arms about the jaw joint to produce the required force.
- The external pterygoideus is probably most important in stabilising and controlling the movement of the condyle in the glenoid fossa.

This brief summary omits all details of force magnitudes, loads, and moment arms, and gives an erroneous impression of simplicity and discreteness as regards the movements of each muscle. In fact, their interactions are very complex.

But even a rudimentary understanding of what the various muscles do allows you to attempt a functional interpretation when confronted with morphological changes in the jaws of different mammals.

Draw diagrams of the rat skull with the muscles sketched in as lines from origin to-insertion. Deduce the movements each could produce, and check your conclusions with the summary above.

Other Examples of Jaw Muscle Arrangement

If you can get the material, compare the jaw muscles of mammals with different diets. Do it qualitatively by dissection, and quantitatively by weighing the various jaw muscles and expressing their weights as a percentage of the total weight of jaw muscle (i.e. of temporalis + masseter + pterygoideus; do not attempt separation of the parts of the masseter, because your separations will not be reproducible.).

The Dog

A diagram of a carnivore head with its jaw muscles is provided for comparison with the rat. Note the large temporalis muscle - it bulges over the occiput, and the muscles from each side nearly meet in the dorsal midline.

It also completely fills the large space between the side of the skull and the zygomatic arch. By comparison, the masseter is a: much smaller muscle. The predominance of the temporalis muscle is probably due to two major factors:

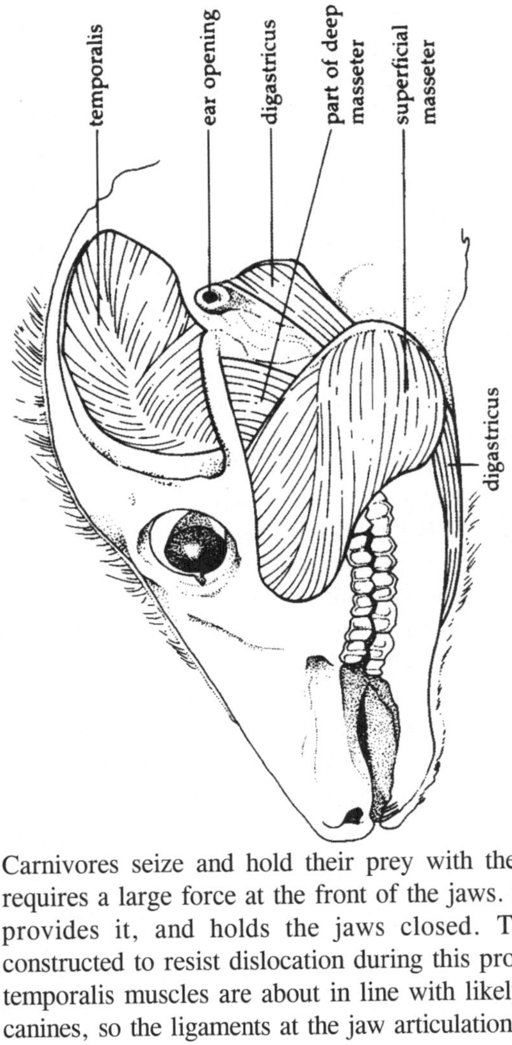

Figure 7.11: Jaw muscle of roe deer, Capreolus capreolus.

- Carnivores seize and hold their prey with the canines. This requires a large force at the front of the jaws. The temporalis provides it, and holds the jaws closed. The condyle is constructed to resist dislocation during this process. Also, the temporalis muscles are about in line with likely forces on the canines, so the ligaments at the jaw articulation are not subject to large forces.
- Carnivores process their food mostly by moving the jaws vertically, so that the cheek teeth slice past each other and cut up flesh or remove it from a carcass. The temporalis muscle is the main elevator of the jaw in the power stroke against the force exerted by the food.

The Roe Deer

It is also instructive to look at the jaw muscles of a herbivore that uses lateral movements of the jaws for mastication. Ruminant herbivores do this. If lateral movements predominate, which muscles would you expect to be enlarged? Now look at the roe deer head to see the relative sizes of the muscles. Also look at the skull (next section). What muscles does the deep jaw angle carry?

MAMMALIAN JAWS AND TEETH

It would be useful to have a lizard or alligator skull by you for comparison as you go through this section—or refer back to Figures elsewhere in this chapter. All mammals are distinguished from most other vertebrates by their heterodont dentition: their teeth are not all alike, but are functionally differentiated.

Nor are they only concerned with catching and holding food; the processing of food also begins in the mouth, so assisting in the maintenance of the high metabolic rate of endothermic mammals. This means that the teeth must be able to process whatever food is eaten into pieces small enough for effective enzyme action to start.

The requirements for one type of food will not be the same for another, and consequently tooth form and arrangement vary widely in different mammals according to their diet. It is this variation that strikes anyone looking at mammalian skulls.

The teeth must also move in appropriate ways, so changes in jaw muscle function can often explain changes in the shape of the jaw and back of the skull in different mammals. There are also other, non-feeding functions of jaws and teeth that will affect their shape (e.g. defence).

It is possible to classify mammals functionally on the basis of their feeding adaptations, and we reproduce here a pictorial guide to such a classification. This also gives a good overview of mammalian adaptive radiation, and is not unrelated to the existing phylogenetic classification.

Whereas phylogenetic relationships between the orders are often vague, the main lines of dietary specialisation are clear. We know that the basic mammalian feeding type was insectivorous—this is clear from looking at the skulls of Triassic mammals.

From this type of dentition, exemplified today by the hedgehog and other members of the order Insectivora, all other types must have evolved. In this section, we shall look at some examples of the main feeding adaptations of skull and jaws. Refer back to the previous section as you go, for it is impossible to understand teeth without knowing something about how the jaws move. The primitive mammalian tooth arrangement consists of incisors, followed by canines, premolars, and molars passing successively back along the jaw.

All are borne on the dentary below, and on the premaxilla and maxilla above. Incisors and canines are concerned with procuring and manipulating food, whereas premolars and molars (collectively referred to as cheek teeth) do most of the processing of the food.

As a general rule, incisors and canines cut and pierce, whereas cheek teeth grind and shear. This functional distinction is reflected in the different shapes of the teeth, and exceptions to the rule are likewise usually obvious from tooth shape.

The functions of procuring and processing food may be widely separated by a gap or diastema, as they are in the long jaws of ungulates. But some mammals have short jaws, with no diastema and very reduced cheek teeth, and in these cases the requirements of processing must be met by the remaining cheek teeth which suggests that the food needs less processing.

Mammalian dentitions are described by tooth formulae, which express the number of each type of tooth in one half of the upper and lower jaw. The primitive formula for mammals is: 13/3; C 1/1; PM 4/4; M 3/3. Members of the order Insectivora, some omnivores, and the more unspecialised carnivores are generally closest to this arrangement.

Insectivores

1. Hedgehog dentition is characterised by peg-like anterior teeth, and by posterior premolars and molars with several pointed cusps.

   The dental formula is: 13/3; C 1/1; PM 3/2; M 3/3. Look carefully at the shapes of the teeth. The lower incisors slope forward, so as to slip under food objects more easily - many mammals show this feature.

   Cusps on the lower molars and last premolars fit into depressions on or between the upper molars and premolars. This occlusal fit allows the molars to pierce chitin, and to crush the food; the cusps also shear past each other as the molars meet and separate.

   Little movement can occur laterally or backwards and forwards while the teeth are occluded; but grinding is unnecessary for extracting the contents of insect bodies, and chitin itself is not processed.

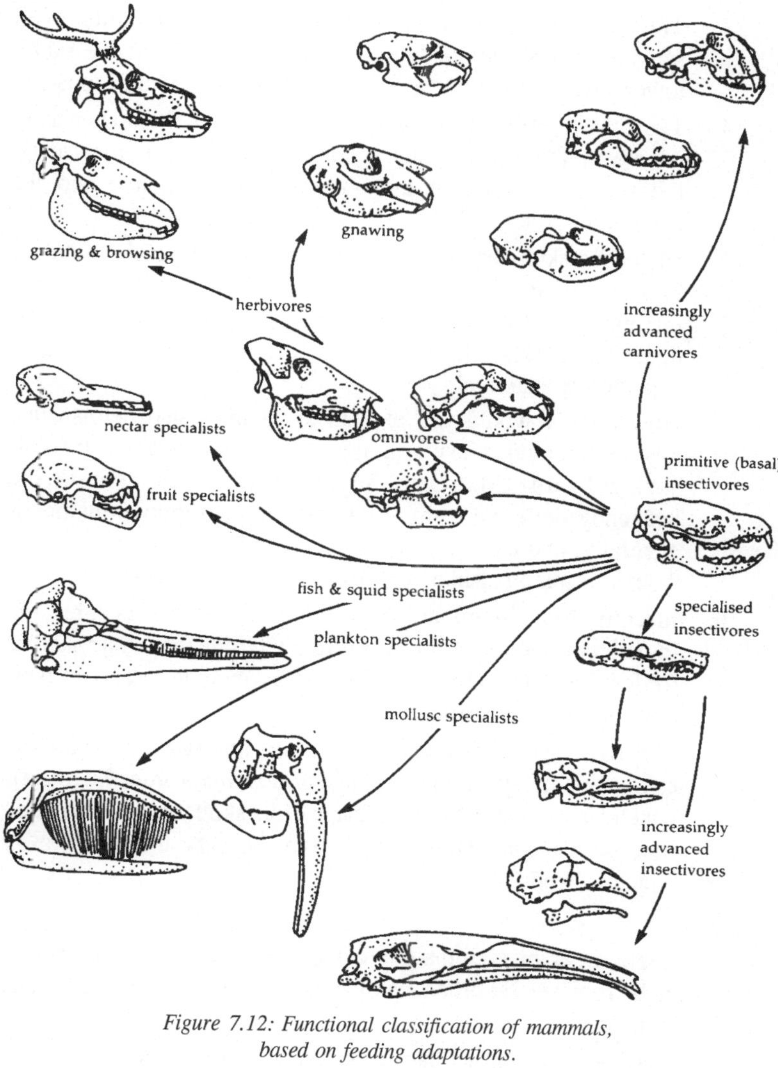

Figure 7.12: Functional classification of mammals, based on feeding adaptations.

2. The precise fit between the cheek teeth of upper and lower jaws in mammals is crucial for efficient food processing. It has influenced the method of tooth replacement, which is quite different from that of reptiles. What is the difference?

   Why would the reptilian method disrupt the occlusal fit of the teeth? How many times during the life of a mammal are the teeth replaced?

3. The coronoid process is well developed, and quite well separated from the condyle. This is different from the rabbit lower jaw. It suggests a relatively large temporalis muscle.
4. There is a pronounced angular process on the lower jaw. Above it, the condyle sits against a flat glenoid, formed by the squamosal bone at the point where it extends into the zygomatic arch.
5. Hedgehog skulls have incomplete tympanic bullae and vacuities in the palate. These are both associated with primitive mammals, and quite apart from the generalised insectivorous dentition, should tell you that you are looking at the skull of a primitive mammal.

   How exactly would you explain to an interested layman that this is a mammal skull in the first place, and not that of, say, a lizard? Many of the features you can see in the hedgehog skull and teeth are diagnostic of primitive mammals generally, and have been used to sort out the earliest mammals from the mammal-like reptiles in the fossil record.
6. Insectivorous mammals exist in other orders besides the Insectivora. Examples are bats (order Chiroptera) and armadillos (order Edentata). Other mammals may include insects in their diet, as do many primates.

   The most specialised insectivores are anteaters. An extreme example is the giant anteater, *Myrmecophaga* (order Edentata), which has no teeth. Note the shape of its skull, and the extended secondary palate. How does it trap the ants and termites on which it feeds?

Frugivores

No single order of mammals is composed entirely of fruit-eaters, but mammals from several orders eat mainly fruit. There are frugivorous bats and primates.

Fruit varies greatly in its hardness, but in some ways it resembles insects as far as initial processing is concerned. A tough outer covering conceals the nutritious contents, and so must be penetrated—but it is often then spat out.

Piercing and crushing are thus the chief functions of the teeth, aside from the bite which procures the fruit or which tests it for ripeness. Where softer fruits make up most of the diet, the cheek teeth may be reduced; and if most of the piercing is done by anterior teeth, the molar cusps are likely to be low and less pointed than in insectivores. Some fruit bats simply squeeze out the juice from fruit and discard the rest; *Pteropus* is one of these.

1. This fruit bat has a dental formula of 12/2; C 1/1; PM 3/3; M 1-2/2-3. Notice first that there are fewer teeth than in the hedgehog, and some teeth are reduced (which?).
2. It is obvious that the canines are the main piercing teeth from their shape. Look at the other teeth; could any of them be used for piercing? (Note that many mammals have large canines for defensive reasons too.)
3. The lower molars are flattened, with a longitudinal groove. What are they used for? Compare with the hedgehog molars and notice how strikingly different they are. They are obviously reflecting a major difference in function.
4. Note the other major features of the lower jaw—it is shallow, has a broad coronoid process, but no marked angular process. The condyle and glenoid are flat.

Omnivores

Omnivores need a versatile dentition to cope with a variety of food. Pigs are omnivorous, for although they eat roots and other plant matter, they also eat such things as earthworms and carrion. Their versatility is one reason for their success as domesticated animals.

1. Omnivores retain most or all of their teeth. This pig has the full mammalian tooth formula of 13/3; C 1/1; PM 4/4; M 3/3. The incisors are widely spaced, and the lower ones slope forward. The canines form tusks, which are not just of importance in feeding.
2. The mobile, sensitive snout of the pig, together with its incisors and canines, is used to seek out and dig up roots, and the long facial region is also used as a whole for digging.
3. The cheek teeth have low rounded cusps, and are described as bunodont. Compare them with the cheek teeth of specialised herbivores and carnivores.
4. There are several other features to notice about pig skulls, such as the massive zygomatic arch and the high forehead and occiput, with large paroccipital processes. Do you think that these features can be accounted for simply on the basis of the strength required for digging?

Carnivores

The order Carnivora contains all the predators associated with carnivory in most people's minds (e.g. lions, tigers, and wolves), but it also includes many other animals that are not specialised flesh-eaters. Examples are bears and badgers.

Even members of the dog family Canidae, which includes wolves, are opportunistic in their feeding habits, and will eat such things as insects and berries. Thus, there are pronounced tendencies towards omnivory amongst the carnivores.

We shall look at the dog skull, which is an example of a relatively generalised carnivore, and the cat skull, which is more specialised for flesh eating.

The Dog

Look at the dog skull and note the following:

1. The snout and jaws are long relative to the braincase.
2. There is a crest of bone between the parietals in the dorsal midline of the cranium; it is called a sagittal crest. Sagittal and occipital crests provide additional surface area for muscle attachment, and males of a species may have larger crests than females. In dogs, the top of the sagittal crest is all that separates the temporalis muscles of the two sides.
3. On the lower jaw there is a high coronoid process. What does this imply about the temporalis muscle?
4. The condyle is a horizontal bar of bone at the back of the jaw. It is about at the same level as the tooth row, and fits in front of a curved flange on the squamosal. Compare the shape of the condyle and glenoid on the dog skull with those on the rabbit or insectivore skull.
5. There is a pronounced angular process on the lower jaw, but the back of the jaw is shallow as a whole.
6. The dental formula is I3/3; C 1/1; PM 4/4; M 2/3.
7. The third upper incisors and the canines are obviously stabbing and tearing teeth from their shape. They are used for biting and holding onto the prey.
8. The major cutting apparatus is formed by the carnassial teeth. They are the largest cheek teeth—the fourth upper premolar and the first lower molar on each side. (Note: count from in front backwards —do not assume that there are always three molars.) The carnassials do not interlock (cf. insectivore molars),

but shear past each other like a pair of scissors. They cut meat off bones and slice it up.

9. Look carefully at the shapes of the other premolars and molars. Are the cusps pointed or rounded? How many are there on each tooth?

The Cat

The cat skull shows several differences from the dog:

1. The face is much shorter and the braincase larger in relation to it.
2. There is no sagittal crest, but occipital crests are present. Why might dogs require a sagittal crest, whereas cats have none? What muscles might attach to the occipital crests?
3. The coronoid process is again high and well developed.
4. The condyle is a horizontal bar of bone. Look at the glenoid; is it like the glenoid on the dog skull?
5. The angular process of the lower jaw is not as pronounced, and the back of the jaw is very shallow.
6. Now look at the tooth row. You will see one reason for the short face—the tooth row is short. What teeth are lost? Start at the front. The three incisors are all there on each side of upper and lower jaws. So are the canines, which are very well developed.

   Now find the carnassials; they are always the fourth upper premolar and the first lower molar on each side. The cat has therefore lost one upper premolar and two lower premolars. Posterior to the carnassials it has one minute upper molar and no other lower molars. Its dental formula is therefore 13/3; C 1/1; PM 3/2; M 1/1.

We can now summarise the main features of carnivore skulls. They have well-developed canine teeth for stabbing and slashing at prey and holding on to it. Members of the cat family, for instance, kill their prey by a wellaimed bite either to the back of the neck or throat.

A specialised cutting and shearing apparatus is formed by the carnassial teeth, which allows meat to be removed from a carcass and cut up. But whereas dogs will crush bones, cats do not do so. Dogs have crushing molars besides carnassials; cats do not.

Look at the cusps on the molars and note shape, sharpness, and pattern. At the back of the lower jaw, a high coronoid process suggests a welldeveloped temporalis muscle (see previous section), with a large mechanical advantage about the jaw joint. The condyle is always more or less level with the tooth row and is bar-shaped.

Its posterior movement is restricted by a shelf of bone, and in some carnivores (e.g. mustelids) it is locked in place by an anterior shelf as well. It is essential that the jaw is not dislocated when tugging at prey. The more pronounced angular process in the dog suggests a relatively larger superficial masseter muscle than in cats.

The shallowness of the jaw implies that the insertion sites for both the superficial masseter and the internal pterygoideus muscles are narrow. The deep masseter fibres in carnivores insert into the masseteric notch. If possible, investigate these suggestions by doing some dissection yourself.

Piscivores and Plankton-Eaters (Order Cetacea, the dolphin, Delphinus delphis; baleen whales)

Not all mammals have heterodont dentition, and those that eat marine fish and squid have numerous teeth which are all alike (homodont). A good example of this situation is the dolphin.

The adaptive value is obvious - the food is slippery and so difficult to hold once caught, but it is not very difficult to process. As in many fishes and fish-eating reptiles, the mouth forms a fish trap, and the food is swallowed more or less whole.

Look at the dolphin skull. Note the following:

1. The braincase is large but is, as it were, pushed to the very back of the skull.
2. The nostrils open not at the tip of the rostrum, but just in front of the braincase, on top of the head. Note the position of nasals, maxillae, and premaxillae.
3. The zygomatic arch is reduced (it is missing in the skull illustrated).
4. The coronoid process of the lower jaw is short and blunt, and the condyle points posteriorly and is flat. The angular process is not well developed.
5. The long rostrum is produced as a result of an enormous anterior development of the premaxillae and maxillae. The premaxillae, however, bear no teeth—all the teeth are borne on the maxillae. There are about forty teeth in each half of each jaw, all pointed and similar in shape.

Many of the characteristics of the dolphin skull, strange at first sight, are explained by the development of the fish trap and by the fact that the food is not chewed. Food catching is emphasised and masticatory muscles are reduced. The muscles used for swallowing might be expected to be well developed.

If you have the opportunity, look at a piece of baleen from a baleen whale (order Cetacea, suborder Mysticeti). These whales have no teeth. How is the baleen used to trap plankton, such as krill (a euphausiid crustacean)? What is baleen made of, and which part of the mouth secretes it?

Herbivores I

(Order Rodentia, the rat, Rattus norvegicus)

Rodents are a specialised kind of herbivore, adapted for gnawing. The features to notice on the rat skull are:

1. The skull is long and flat, with the snout curving down only slightly.
2. A single pair of large incisors on uvver and lower jaws form the gnawing teeth. These teeth are worn down rapidly, and grow continuously throughout life from long, open roots.

   They have a self-sharpening mechanism, because there is a layer of enamel only on the outer surface, and this wears less fast than the rest of the tooth—so maintaining a sharp edge.

   The enamel can be seen, because it is stained brown. Notice that the incisors are shaped like chisels. How do the lower incisors stay sharp?
3. Behind the incisors is a large diastema with no teeth. Which teeth are missing here? Myomorph rodents do have three molars on each side of both upper and lower jaws, so work out the dental formula of the rat.
4. Look carefully at the cheek teeth. There are three of them in each half of each jaw. Do they have cusps or ridges? Compare with hedgehog molars. Notice also the relative widths of upper and lower jaws, and that the cheek teeth on both sides can be in occlusion at the same time.
5. Now look at the back of the lower jaw. The coronoid process is quite small, but the condyle is raised up above the level of the tooth row on the mandible. It is rounded and fits into a longitudinal glenoid.
6. The angular process is pronounced, and if you look at the

lower jaw from behind, you can see that it slants in towards the midline. Check back to the dissection of rat jaw muscles to remind yourself which of them are attached to the angular process.

Rodent skulls are chiefly remarkable for their large gnawing incisors, but they also show features common to other herbivores. The diastema is one of these. The anterior teeth and their activities during feeding are separate from the cheek teeth, which process the food.

In rodents, the lips can be folded in behind the incisors, and will prevent chips of bark or whatever from reaching the throat during gnawing. Food can also be held in the diastema before it is passed back to the cheek teeth for processing.

This is most obvious in herbivores that eat grass. The longitudinal glenoid allows fore and aft movement of the lower jaw, which gets the incisors in position for gnawing, and then the jaw can shift back to engage the cheek teeth.

There are striking convergences between the skulls of lagomorphs and rodents, because both are adapted for gnawing and a herbivorous diet. The arrangement of the teeth is very similar, but look at the lower jaws.

Rabbits move their jaws laterally to masticate, not backwards and forwards. How could you tell this from the skull? These two orders of mammals were at one time classified together because they looked so alike, but they are actually different in all sorts of ways.

Could you distinguish a rabbit from a rodent skull of similar size? Look carefully at the incisors and the maxillae.

Herbivores II

(Order Perissodactyla, the horse, Equus caballus)

Horses have very long faces, and the braincase is small in comparison. Compare the general proportions of the horse skull with those of the other skulls described here, particularly with the carnivore skulls.

1. Look at the braincase and back of the skull. What measurements would you make to express quantitatively the difference in proportions of the horse and cat skull? Note the occipital crests; is there a sagittal crest? Note the paroccipital processes—what muscles attach to them?
2. Find the zygomatic arch. It is broad posteriorly, and flares laterally over the glenoid, which is a transverse groove.

3. Horses have a postorbital bar behind the eye. So do primates.
4. Now look at the skull from in front. The area housing the cheek teeth is broad—note broad nasal bones, free at their anterior end, and the large maxillae, which bear the teeth.
5. The anterior end of the skull is narrow. It narrows at the diastema, and then broadens slightly at the tip where the incisors are.
6. The teeth consist of a full complement of incisors, variable canines (depending on the species), three premolars, and three molars. Note that the premolars look exactly like the molars. The cheek teeth are high crowned, or hypsodont, with open roots, and have a characteristic pattern of ridges and grooves on them.

   These are produced by differential wear of enamel, dentine, and cement, cement being laid down between the tall cusps as they grow. In a young tooth, only the cusps protrude, but as they wear, more of the tooth erupts—several centimetres of unerupted tooth is concealed.

   Wear itself produces the ridges because enamel, dentine, and cement have different hardnesses, and therefore always maintain a rough surface. This is an exceedingly important adaptation, for the silica in grass quickly wears down the teeth during chewing.
7. The lower jaw is remarkably deep. Look at the skull from behind to obtain a good impression of this. The distance from condyle to jaw angle is about 24 times the depth of the braincase. In comparison, the coronoid process is small.

   This is an unmistakable indication that the masseter and pterygoideus muscles are very large, whereas the temporalis is small.
8. The articular condyle is a horizontal hinge-like joint. How closely does it fit into the glenoid? Compare with a carnivore skull. Note that the condyle is situated well above the tooth row. This gives the masseter and pterygoideus muscles a large mechanical advantage about the jaw joint.

   If you have a skull in front of you, try lowering and then raising the lower jaw. You should see that when it is raised, the cheek teeth are brought into apposition all at once as a level row. Try the same movements with a cat skull—the cheek teeth shear past each other in succession from behind forwards. This is exactly the sort of pattern of apposition that would be predicted for grasseating herbivores and flesh-eating carnivores.

9. Finally, look at the relative widths of upper and lower jaws. The upper jaw is wider, and the upper teeth overhang the lower at rest. Also look at how the upper teeth fit into the lower teeth-when in occlusion.

   It should be reasonably obvious that, when chewing, a horse must move its jaws from side to side, not just to bring the tooth rows into occlusion, but because forward movement of the cheek teeth against each other is restricted by the orientation of the tooth ridges.

   If you get the chance to watch a horse chewing, see if you can confirm these conclusions.

Herbivores III

(Order Artiodactyla, the roe deer, Capreolus capreolus)

1. The major difference between roe deer and horse dentition is the absence of teeth on the anterior upper jaw in roe deer. The front of the mouth is covered in life with a horny pad, against which the lower incisors bite. (Note that not all artiodactyls totally lack upper incisors and canines.) The dental formula of the roe deer is 10/3; C 0/0; PM 3/3; M 3/3.
2. The cheek teeth are again hypsodont with large open roots that broaden the sides of the face. The anterior premolars are simpler than the molars.
3. The crescent-shaped tooth ridges are taller than in horses, and the enamel ridge patterns are less convoluted. But the ridges are maintained by differential wear, as in horses.
4. Compare the lower jaws of these two herbivores—their proportions do differ, but they also have similarities. The, differences are mainly due to the greater specialisation of horses for eating grass.

The ungulate (i.e. hoofed) herbivores are adapted for grazing and browsing. They evolved alongside the expanding grasslands of the world, and are an example of close adaptation of predators to their prey (grass, in this case).

Grass is tough and requires a lot of mastication—hence the hypsodont teeth and the ridged wear patterns. Leaves require less mastication because of their lower fibre content. The major movement in mastication is from side to side, and the cheek teeth can slide across each other because of their complementary surfaces.

The major muscles involved are the masseter and pterygoideus muscles, which is why the jaw is so deep to house them. The temporalis is comparatively small, particularly in horses—hence the small coronoid process.

The diastema houses grass stems or leaves after they are bitten off and before passing them back to the cheek teeth for chewing. The fact that the incisors are at a distance from the bulky cheek teeth also means that the tip of the snout can be quite narrow, and so can penetrate into small spaces to crop food (as the roe deer does).

Finally, the major force to be borne by these herbivore jaws when feeding is that between the cheek teeth and the food during mastication, which proceeds by lateral movements. Thus, the jaw articulation must not be easily dislocated laterally.

Its long transverse shape prevents this. There are no large forces pulling it forwards' or back (unlike in carnivores), so it is unlikely to be dislocated in this direction. Not surprisingly, therefore, the condyle is not locked in place anteriorly or posteriorly, but simply rests against the glenoid, which is relatively flat.

MAMMALIAN DIGESTIVE SYSTEMS

To explain all the intricacies of mammalian digestion would be out of place in a book of this sort; but it is possible to observe some gross differences in the morphology of the gut in mammals with different diets. Some general conclusions can be reached about what these differences mean in functional terms.

We shall look at the guts of four very different mammals: the hedgehog, an insectivore; the fox (*Vulpes vulpes*), an unspecialised carnivore; the roe deer, a ruminant herbivore; and the rabbit, a non-ruminant herbivore. These are represented very diagrammatically in Figure elsewhere in this chapter.

All the guts were drawn from fresh-frozen specimens, and were unfolded and arranged linearly. Gut lengths are best expressed in relation to total body length.

Mammals that eat little vegetable matter (and hence fibre) tend to have relatively short intestines, which emphasise the small intestine where metabolites are absorbed. The caecum at the junction of the small intestine and colon is small and may be absent; for example, in

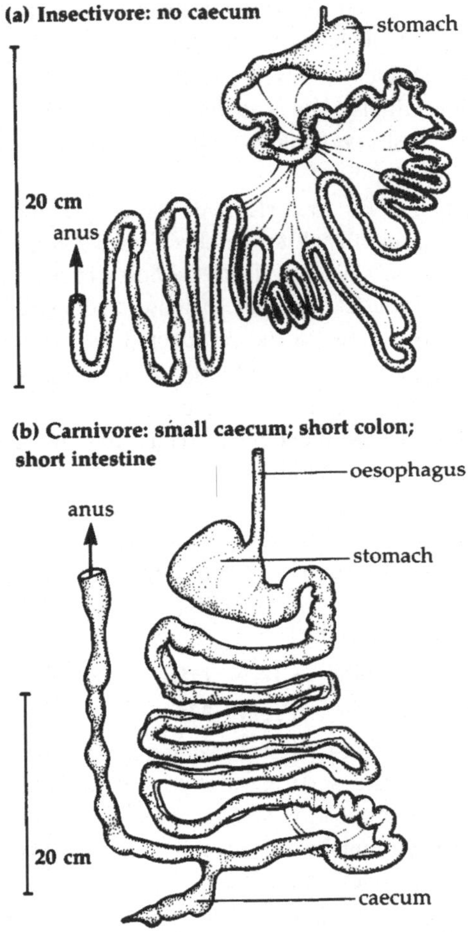

Figure 7.13: Digestive systems of (a) hedgehog, (b) fox, (c) roe deer, and (d) rabbit. (Figure Contd.)

members of the order Insectivora and in the marsupial carnivore *Dasyurus*. Carnivores have a particularly short colon.

In herbivores that feed on leaves and grass, fermentation of cellulose occurs, and the animals are host to bacteria and protozoa, of which the bacteria are the main fermenters.

Mammals cannot produce the enzyme cellulase themselves. There are two possible fermentation sites - the forestomach or the caecum. (Ruminants are not the only mammals with modified forestomachs; other examples are kangaroos and colobus monkeys.)

(c) Ruminant herbivore: rumen; long small & large intestine; caecum

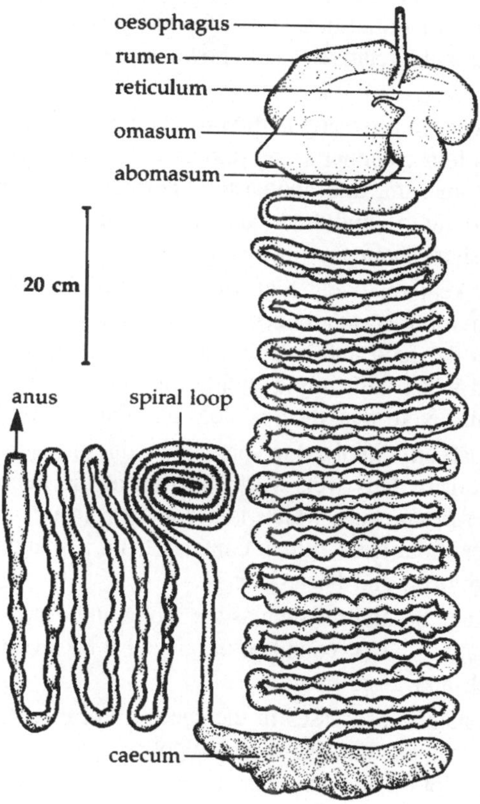

(d) Non-ruminant herbivore: simple stomach; relatively large caecum

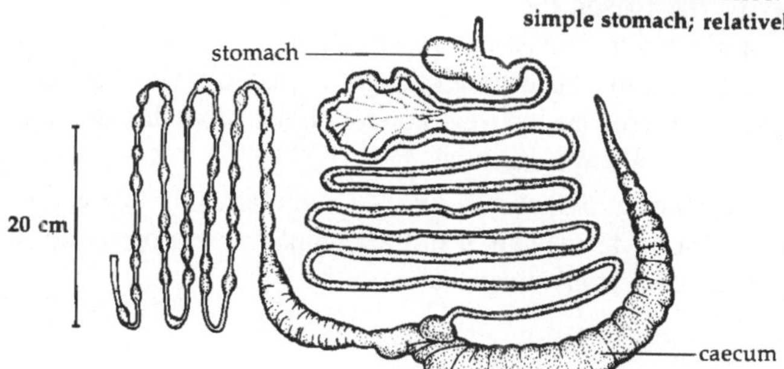

(Contd.) Figure 7.13: Digestive systems of (a) hedgehog, (b) fox, (c) roe deer, and (d) rabbit.

In addition, the intestine is very long- not just the small intestine, but the large intestine also. Diet seems to have a direct effect on intestinal length, for domesticated or laboratory mammals whose diets vary from their wild relatives may show marked differences in their guts.

In the roe deer, a browsing herbivore, the rumen is well developed. Note that it has four chambers—the rumen itself (much the largest), the reticulum, the omasum, and abomasum. Fermentation occurs in both rumen and reticulum, and both also absorb the main products of fermentation—short-chain fatty acids.

The pH is kept relatively high (why?) by the buffering action of saliva. The omasum is subdivided by many large, papillated folds, which partition the food and absorb water from it. In the abomasum, acid is secreted which kills any escaping micro-organisms, and protein digestion begins. Note that the roe deer also has a caecum.

This is apparently involved in some way with nitrogen and possibly mineral metabolism. It is well worth looking at the internal structure of a ruminant forestomach, which is a complex array of papillae and folds. Also, get some fresh rumen contents from a slaughterhouse and observe the protozoa and bacteria in it.

Non-ruminant herbivores such as the rabbit and perissodactyls have caecal fermentation; the proximal colon may also be involved. Note the simple stomach and large caecum.

The fermentation processes in the caecum are essentially identical to those in the rumen, but one might suppose that there is less scope for processing a lot of fibre, because there is no regurgitation and only the large intestine to follow.

This may be the reason for the practice of coprophagy in rabbits. Lagomorphs produce soft faeces in their burrows at night, which are eaten. Thus, material can pass through the gut a second time. But other mammals with caecal fermentation (e.g. horses) do not adopt this strategy, so it is certainly not always essential.

A very interesting discussion of the comparative virtues of forestomach and caecal fermentation in the ungulates is to be found in the paper by Christine Tanis eiven below.

8

Monotremes and Marsupials: Mammals with a Difference

Most of the mammals we are familiar with belong to the infraclass Eutheria, of the subclass Theria. However, there are two other groups of mammals which are less often seen by those of us who do not live either in Australasia or America.

These animals are the monotremes and marsupials. Although it may be difficult for most students to study them because of lack of material, yet they are so interesting for a variety of reasons that a whole chapter will be devoted to some of their more striking features.

Monotremes are the most primitive living mammals. They are considered primitive because they show an extraordinary mosaic of reptilian and mammalian characteristics. Unfortunately, there is virtually no fossil record of these animals to help unravel the evolutionary changes that led to their modern representatives

Monotremes seem to have evolved independently from marsupials and eutherian mammals, possibly since the Triassic period. But their divergence from the rest of the mammals may have occurred more recently than this—new studies of fossil material are suggesting that they may be more closely related to other mammals than was once thought.

Marsupials, on the other hand, evolved from the same group of Jurassic mammals as did eutherians, but they later diverged and evolved separately. Superficially, many marsupials have their eutherian counterparts (for example, there are marsupial 'wolves' and 'moles'), but closer inspection reveals their distinctiveness.

They provide an, excellent illustration of evolution in parallel. Much has been said and written in the past of marsupial 'inferiority', as if they were some cheap imitation of the 'real' mammals, namely the eutherians.

But recent work suggests this is far from so—marsupials are well adapted to their modes of life, and show how a different type of mammalian organisation has adapted to similar selection pressures. In other words, they are another way of being a mammal.

This chapter concentrates on some primitive and specialised features of monotremes; then illustrates the features which distinguish marsupials in general from eutherians; and finishes with some special marsupial adaptations.

It is, incidentally, not simply a matter of convenience to consider monotremes and marsupials together in the same chapter. They do share a number of characteristics, and although monotremes lay eggs and so seem radically different from all other mammals, yet their reproduction has several similarities with that of marsupials.

You will find it useful to refer back often to other chapter of this book, since a knowledge of topics discussed there is assumed, and will help you to interpret the stranger aspects of monotremes and marsupials.

Material Required

- Mounted skins and skeletons of the duck-billed platypus, *Ornithorhynchus,* and spiny anteater, *Tachyglossus.*
- Skull and skeleton of the Virginia opossum, *Didelphis virginiana*
- Preserved *Didelphis* for dissection.
- Skull and skeleton of the kangaroo, *Macropus.*
- Any other available marsupial material showing different feeding adaptations and/or locomotion.

THE MONOTREMES

The name 'monotreme' refers to the fact that urine, gametes, and faeces all pass to the outside through one cloacal sphincter and opening. This also occurs in reptiles and birds, not other mammals - though marsupials are close to this condition.

In this section, the idea is to appreciate those features of monotremes that are primitive and visible on a mounted skin or skeleton; and then to look for special adaptations using the same material.

There are three genera of monotremes: *Ornithorhynchus,* the duck-billed platypus; and *Tachyglossus* and *Zaglossus,* the spiny anteaters or echidnas. Each is highly specialised for a particular way of life.

General Features

1. Monotremes—have hair and suckle their young - two definitive mammalian features.
2. They also lay eggs—a reptilian characteristic. In *Ornithorhynchus* no pouch is present, whereas in female echidnas a pouch forms during the breeding season. Several marsupial species also only have pouches in the breeding season.
3. Monotremes retain some reptilian anatomical features too. One example is the structure of the pectoral girdle. This includes an interclavicle, coracoids and precoracoids—all bones that therian mammals do not have. Note that this confers great strength on the ventral part of the shoulder girdle, and its connection with the sternum is more rigid than in therian mammals.
4. Monotremes, like marsupials, have epipubic bones.
5. The neck vertebrae of monotremes carry separate ribs, unlike those of other mammals but like those of reptiles.
6. The monotreme jaw is articulated with the skull in a fully mammalian manner. A single dentary makes up each half of the lower jaw, and articulates with the squamosal. This implies that the middle ear contains three ossicles, which it does, but it is not enclosed in a tympanic bulla. Note that some marsupials also lack a tympanic bulla (see later).

Special Adaptations

The Duck-billed Platypus

The platypus, *Ornithorhynchus anatinus,* is adapted for digging and swimming; it gathers food under water and makes burrows along the banks of streams. Several characters are correlated with these habits—a dense pelage that traps air under water, webbed feet, claws, and robust limb girdles built to produce power, not speed.

1. The skull shows the large braincase and elongated flat bill. Sutures between the bones are not easy to see, but the bill's bony supports are extensions of the premaxillae dorsally and the dentary ventrally. The anterior parts of these bones are enclosed in extensive cartilage, which provides most of the

shape and substance of the front of the bill. In life the bill is covered in sensitive skin, which is the source of tactile stimuli when the animal is searching for food under water. Eyes, ears, and nostrils are closed off by flaps of skin during dives. So, the bill does not just pick up food, it also locates it.

2. The dentary is slender, suggesting small masticatory muscles, and there are no teeth in the adult. Instead, there are horny pads on the maxillary part of the zygomatic arch, and on the dentary below. Molariform teeth are present in young animals.
3. Note the shape of the limbs and limb girdles. Compare with mammalian limbs adapted for speed, like those of a horse. Note the proportions of the various bones and their shapes - particularly the flared humerus, and the large process on the proximal end of the fibula.

   Compare the latter with the shape of the olecranon process (elbow) on the ulna, which is a common mammalian feature. Suggest reasons for the large fibular process. Look at the limbs of other digging (or swimming?) mammals, such as the echidna and moles.
4. The humerus and femur are held more or less horizontal to the body axis. Note the position of their articulation with the scapula and pelvis.

   It is often stated that this is a 'reptilian' posture but, in fact,

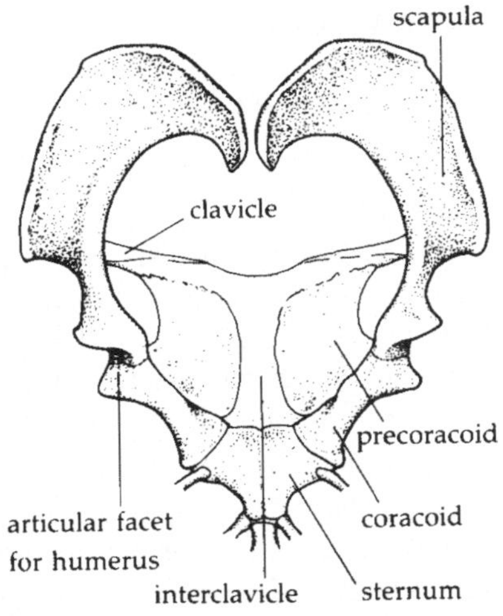

Figure 8.1: Pectoral girdle of Ornithorhynchus from above.

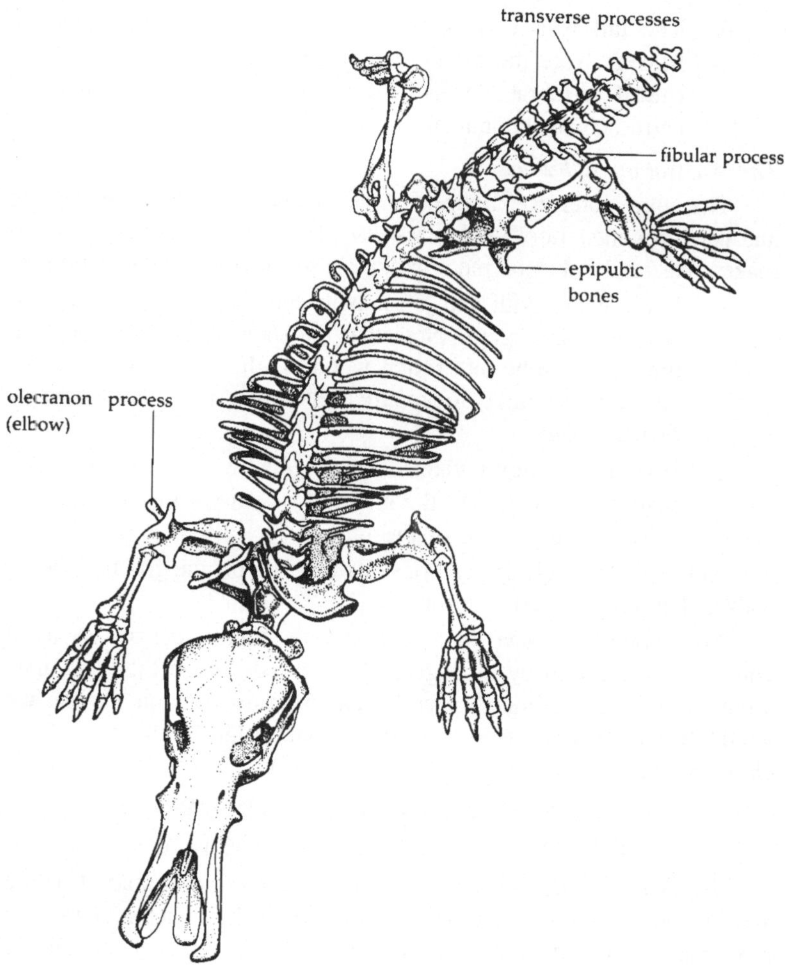

Figure 8.2: Skeleton of Ornithorhynchus.

mammals that swim and dig tend to have their limbs positioned more laterally for obvious reasons. Note that the platypus forelimbs provide the power in swimming—the hindlimbs are used as rudders.

5. Both hands and feet are pentadactyl with long claws on all digits. The webs extend beyond the ends of the digits, and can be folded back when not being used for swimming, so that the claws are then available for digging and traction when walking.

6. The tail is a remarkable structure, shaped like that of a beaver. Note the broad transverse processes on most of the caudal vertebrae. One of the tail's functions is to flatten the earth behind the animal during burrowing.

The Australian Echidna

The spiny anteater, *Tachyglossus aculeatus* is adapted for digging and catching ants. Look at figures elsewhere in this chapter so as to make notes on the skeletal modifications associated with these activities.

1. Look at the skull and jaws. Note the shape and proportions. Are there any teeth? Note that the snout is strong enough to break and probe into rotten wood, as the animal searches for ants and termites. Compare with other anteaters, such as *Myrmecophaga*.
2. How are the limbs adapted for digging? Note the proportions, shapes of bones, and the claws. Compare with the platypus. What is the posture of the limbs?

Although *Tachyglossus* can raise its body up off the ground when it walks, it is not a speedy mover.

You should now have some idea of why monotremes are regarded with such fascination by zoologists. Specialised though they are, they seem to provide a glimpse of early mammalian evolution - or so we would like to believe. However, their relationship to the rest of the class Mammalia remains tantalisingly unclear.

WHAT DISTINGUISHES MARSUPIALS FROM EUTHERIAN MAMMALS?

We shall concentrate here on two aspects of marsupial structure and function, namely certain unique features of the skeleton and of the reproductive system. For this, we shall use as a model animal the Virginia opossum, *Didelphis virginiana,* which is readily available for study in North America.

The Skull

It is instructive to compare the opossum skull with that of an unspecialised eutherian mammal, because it has certain features which are considered characteristic of primitive mammals in general. The family Didelphidae is one of the oldest of the marsupial families, and *Didelphis* itself is a relatively unspecialised marsupial. Concentrate on the features listed below.

1. Note the general proportions and shape of the skull. *Didelphis*

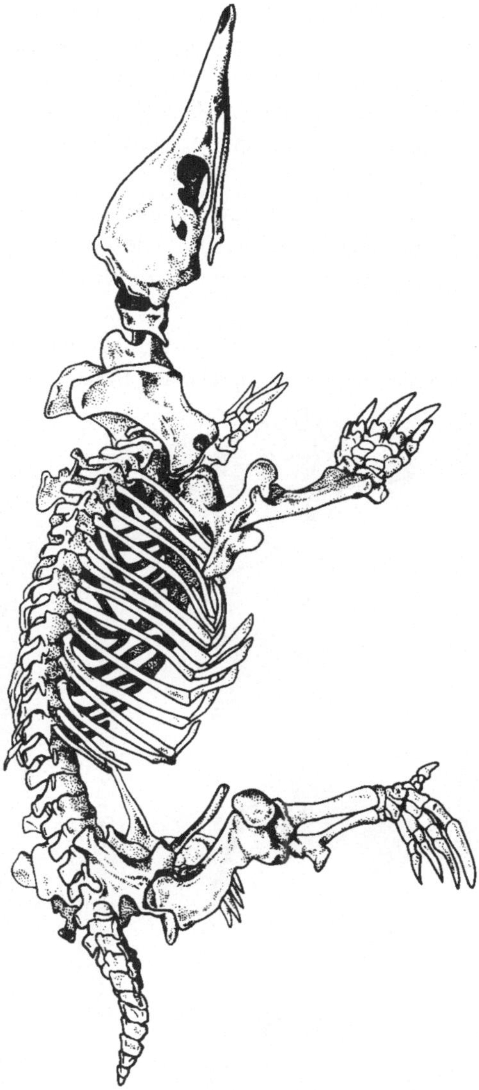

Figure 8.3: Skeleton of Tachnyglossus.

is a nocturnal omnivorous scavenger. Its sense of smell is well developed. How can you tell this? It also has all the usual mammalian tooth types, and the dentition suggests an omnivorous diet—why? Note the crests on the posterior dorsal surface of the skull, and around the rear of the braincase. What are the technical names for these crests? What is their function?

2. The opossum skull has all the main characteristics of mammal skulls, namely a large temporal opening, a flared zygomatic arch, an articulation between the squamosal and dentary bones, and a double occipital condyle. Can you recognise all these features? Note also that the sutures between the various skull bones are very clear.
3. One of the most obvious primitive features of marsupial skulls is the relatively small brain cavity. The best way to see this is to compare with a eutherian skull of similar size (see thylacine and dog later).
4. The lacrimal bone, which surrounds the tear duct in mammals, extends onto the face in marsupials, and the duct does not open

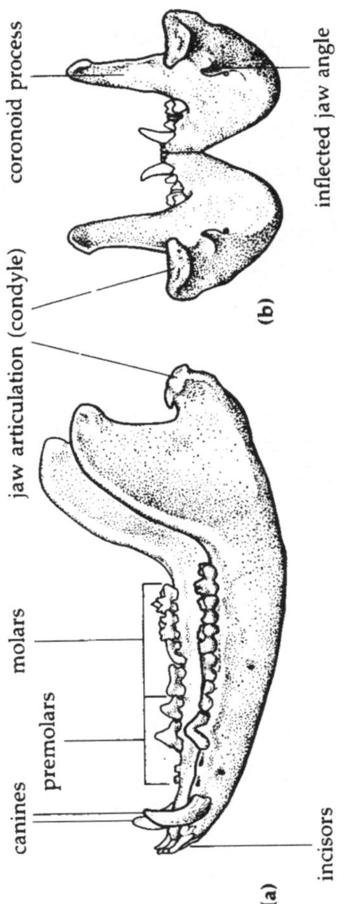

Figure 8.4: Lower jaw of Didelphis: (a) lateral and (b) posterior views.

within the orbit itself. Also, the jugal bone extends right back to the jaw articulation.

5. In the palatal region, two features are particularly noticeable. There are large vacuities in the posteror palate (covered over by tissue in life), and its posterior border is thickened below the inner opening of the nasal tubes. Palatal vacuities are associated with primitive mammals although they appear late in the embryological development of the palate. Check the skull of a hedgehog or other member of the order Insectivora for comparison.
6. Marsupials have a primitive ear region. The tympanic bone is small and ring-shaped, and is often missing from marsupial

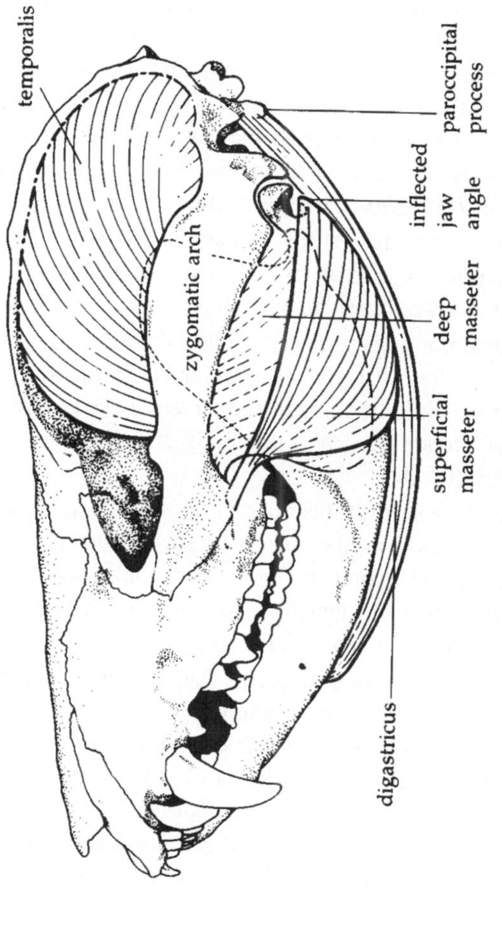

Figure 8.5: Diagram of Didelphis skull showing arrangement of jaw muscles.

skulls because it is not actually fused to the skull. Can you see a tympanic bulla? Many marsupials have none, and when a bulla is present, it is formed by a different bone than in eutherian mammals, and may be incomplete.

7. Now look at the teeth. The basic number of teeth in marsupials is different from that in eutherians, but the types of teeth are the same. What differences cay you see? Remember the basic eutherian dental formula (13/3; C 1/1; PM 4/4; M 3/3). How should it be altered to describe *Didelphis* teeth?

   If you have a *Didelphis* skull, look at the way in which the triangular upper molarss fit against the lower molars when the jaw is closed. The shape of *Didelphis* molars and their occlusion pattern is regarded as primitive, because the same features can be seen in the teeth of early fossil mammals.

   Are the lower tooth rows the same distance apart as the upper? What sort of movements do you think opossum jaws make during mastication? Could the jaw articulation allow lateral motion? References given at the end of this chapter include work on *Didelphis* masticatory movements.

8. The posterior edge of the dentary is turned inwards. This is usually referred to as an 'inflected jaw angle'. It is characteristic of, but not exclusive to, marsupials.

9. Once again, it helps in understanding skull shape and proportions to know where the jaw muscles are positioned, and how big they are. Just by looking at the *Didelphis* skull, you should be able to deduce that the temporalis and masseter muscles are well developed.

   Figure elsewhere in this chapter shows a diagram of the skull and lower jaw with the muscle origins, insertions, and relevant bones marked. Compare with other mammals. Note that this diagram does not include the hyoid muscles, which are important in jaw depression and tongue movements.

The above account is not exhaustive. Can you find any other features that seem to be characteristic of marsupial skulls? To end this section, we shall illustrate one of the most remarkable examples of convergent evolution among the vertebrates—the skulls of a dog and a thylacine (the Tasmanian wolf, *Thylacinus cynocephalus*).

Both are carnivores, but one is eutherian and the other marsupial. Although it is unlikely that you will have direct access to a thylacine skull, it is still worth looking carefully at Figure elsewhere in this chaprter. The two skulls are superficially extremely similar, and yet they can be distinguished by looking at the various features discussed above. Try explaining to someone else how you know which is the marsupial skull.

The Skeleton

This will not be a detailed description; look at the skeleton from the point of view of general adaptations and also special features.

1. Note the general proportions and stance of the animal *Didelphis* has the general mammalian features noted in other chatper of this book, with regard to limb posture, spinal flexures, types of vertebrae, and so on. Also, the pectoral and pelvic girdles are like those of other mammals. What is it about them that makes them 'mammalian'?
2. One feature in the pelvis is characteristic of marsupials and monotremes, and several fossil mammals. There are two epipubic bones articulating with the pelvis ventrally, just beside the pubic symphysis.

   The function of these bones is unclear. They used to be called 'marsupial' bones, because it was thought that they supported the pouch. But they do not seem to do so directly, although abdominal muscles are attached to them. They are, in any case, present in males as well as females, and in species that do not have a pouch.
3. Two features are interesting in the context of the opossum's mode of life. One is the tail, which is scaly, relatively hairless, and prehensile. Opossums climb trees, and use their tails to help hold on. What other groups of mammals have prehensile tails?
4. The other feature that is also an adaptation to climbing is an opposable first toe on the foot. Note that this toe does not have a claw on it but a flat nail. All digits in the forelimb have claws, and the thumb is not opposable.

   Both fore- and hindfeet in the opossum have thick, ridged, palmar pads—another useful adaptation for climbing. Note that prehensile tails and opposable first digits are also characteristic of many arboreal primates.

The Female Reproductive System

The most fundamental differences between marsupials and eutherian

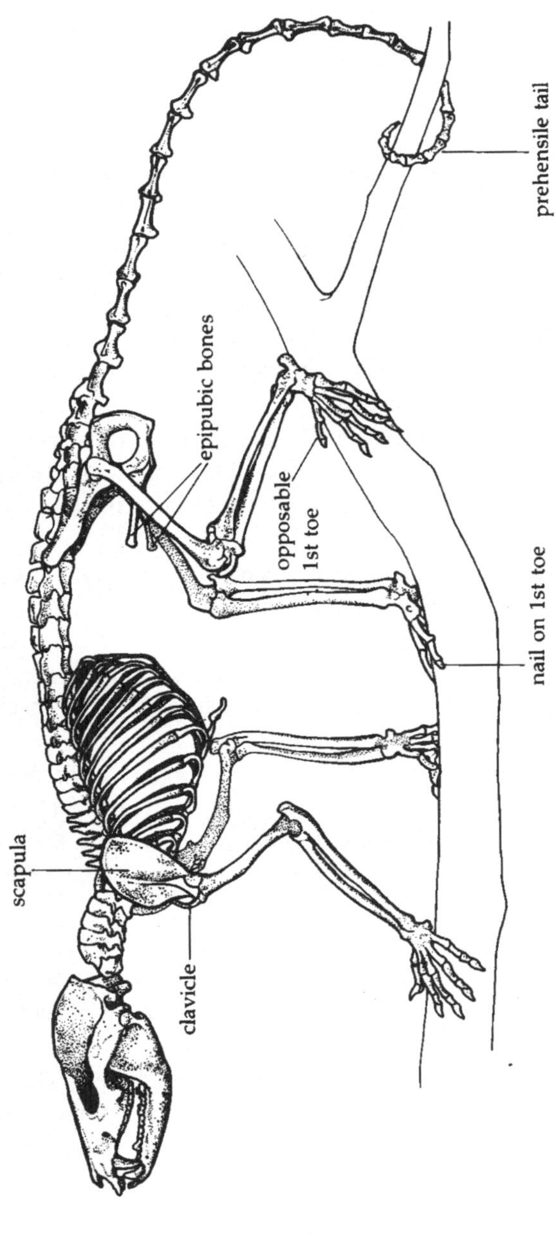

Figure 8.6: Skeleton of Didelphis.

mammals are to be found in their reproduction. When first discovered, marsupials were instantly amazing to everyone because of the pouch (marsupium), which was responsible for giving them their name.

However, there are marsupials that do not possess pouches, including male marsupials. Nevertheless, the female reproductive system is remarkable for another feature, which is less noticeable but is found in all marsupial species.

It is the presence of double uteri and vaginae. Also, all marsupial young are born at a very early stage of development, and undergo considerable growth while attached to their mother's teats. The equivalent period of development in a eutherian would mostly occur *in utero.* These features in-fallibly distinguish all marsupials from all eutherians.

1. The pouch in *Didelphis is* about two-thirds of the way down the body. It is much smaller in a female without young. In lactating females, the pouch is distended, and the teats become elongated during suckling.

   Underneath the pouch, which is a pocket of skin, is a flat sheet of mammary tissue, fat, and muscle fibres. The whole structure can be lifted away from the body wall underneath.

2. Young marsupials are tiny when they first enter the pouch. In *Didelphis* several are born at once, and may occupy all the teats, of which there are thirteen. More than thirteen young may be born, in which case some die immediately. Others may die laterit is common for about seven young to survive pouch life.

   The red kangaroo, *Macro pus rufus,* on the other hand, produces only one offspring at a time, can have young of very different ages suckling at the same time, and produces milk of different compositions from the teats suckling different individuals.

   Note that the forelimbs are better developed than the hindlimbs at birth, and are used to cling onto the mother's fur on the journey to the pouch.

3. Internally, the reproductive system of the opossum may be discovered dorsal to the bladder in the lower abdomen. Its various parts are not easy to distinguish, because tough connective tissue envelops them and binds them closely together. If you have an opossum to dissect, perseverance and care will reveal all the details illustrated here.

4. Short oviducts and fallopian tubes open into the uteri, which

are double throughout their length. The ovaries lie dorsal to the uteri, bound to them in connective tissue.

5. Posterior to the uteri are two large, horn-like structures. These are the lateral vaginae. The uteri enter them medially through tiny openings, surrounded by muscular folds. The vaginae then curve around posteriorly to join the urogenital sinus on its dorsal side.

   Careful dissection is necessary to distinguish the posterior parts of the lateral vaginae from the urogenital sinus, to which they are closely held by connective tissue. Note that there is no equivalent of the urogenital sinus in eutherians, where the duct from the bladder to the outside is separate from the vagina throughout its length.

6. The two lateral vaginae appear fused anteriorly; in fact, they are separated by a septum in this specimen. During parturition, a connection is made from the uteri, straight through the intervening connective tissue to the urogenital sinus, but this 'birth canal' subsequently closes off in *Didelphis* between births. The pouch also shrinks and the teats regress. This happens in many other marsupials too. In some, like the kangaroo, the median vagina remains open after the first birth.

7. Note the position of the bladder, and particularly the ureters. They pass between the lateral vaginae, not outside them. This is the reason for the presence of double vaginae in marsupials—their fusion is impeded throughout most of their length because of the position of the ureters. Male marsupials also have ureters entering the bladder ventral and medial to the sperm ducts.

8. A functional corollary of the double vaginae in female *Didelphis* is a bifurcated penis in males. Thus semen passes up both lateral vaginae—not up the urogenital sinus.

9. Compare all this with the reproductive system of, for example, a female rat or mouse. Note that the rat has double uteri, but a single vagina. Make a list of all the differences.

   It is now thought that, far from being inferior and in some sense incompetent, marsupial reproduction has developed in the way it has for sound adaptive reasons. The reference by J. A. W. Kirsch at the end of the chapter discusses the arguments in favour of this idea.

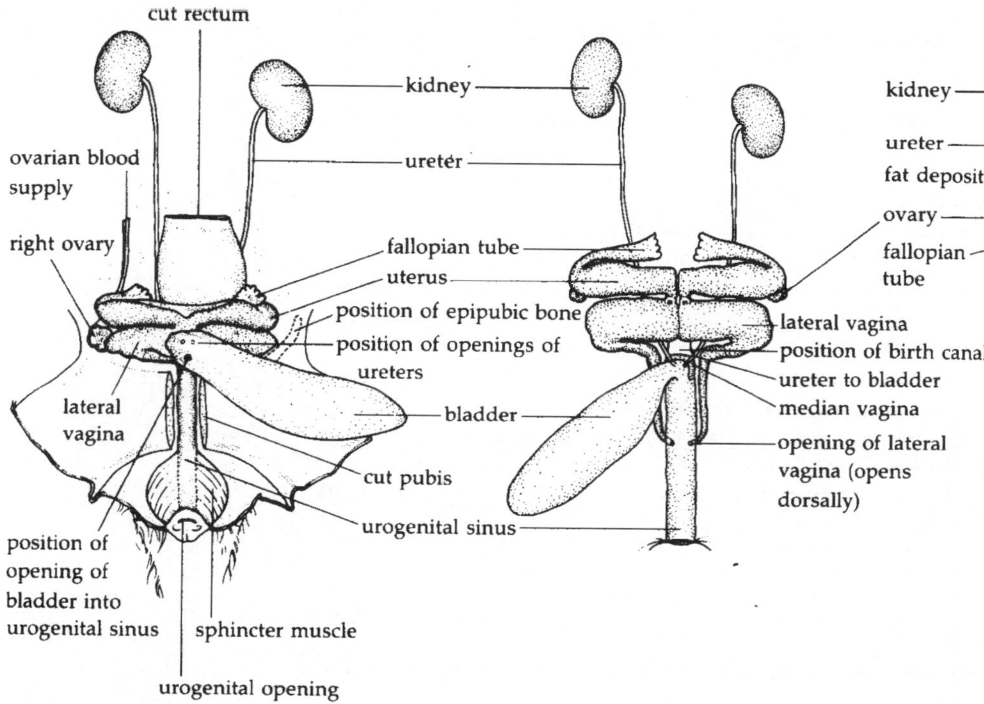

Figure 8.7: Didelphis, undisturbed female reproductive system.

Figure 8.8: Didelphis, dissected female Reproductive system.

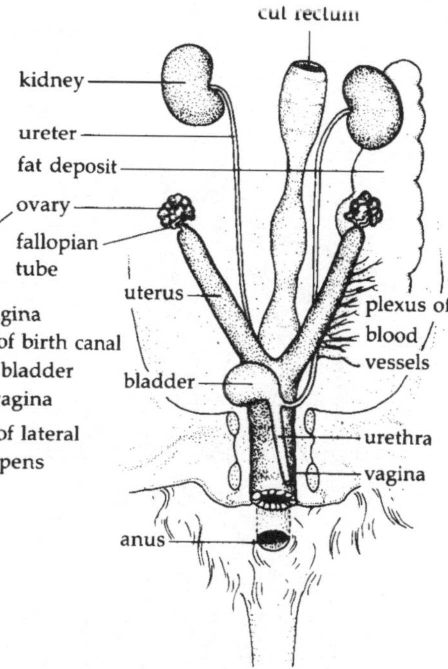

Figure 8.9: Rattus, dissected female reproductive system.

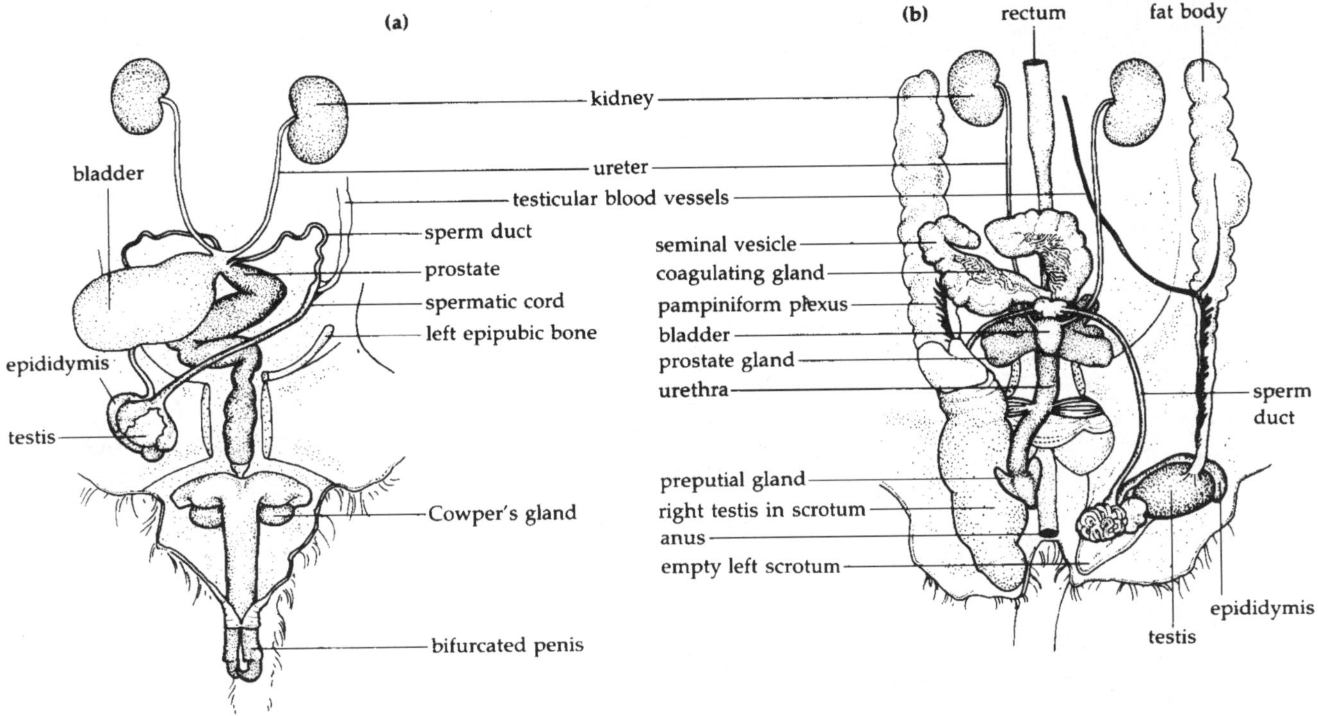

Figure 8.10: Male reproductive system of (a) Didelphis and (b) Rattus.

The Male Reproductive System

This also differs from the eutherian male system. The following are the major differences;

1. The testes and scrotum are anterior to the penis. Compare with the situation in a male eutherian.
2. The ureters pass medial to the sperm ducts, and so are in a position homologous to that in female *Didelphis*. In male eutherians, they pass outside the sperm ducts.
3. The prostate is diffuse and lengthy, consisting of many small glands. It is not restricted to the area around the urethra. This is very different from eutherian males. Note the presence of seminal vesicles and coagulating glands in the rat. These both contribute to the composition of seminal fluid - the seminal vesicles are not for sperm storage.
4. The penis is long and bifurcated.

This completes the discussion on the major ways in which marsupials differ from eutherians. It is now time to look at some particular ways in which certain marsupials have adapted to particular aspects of their mode of life. Consider the opossum as a generalised omnivorous marsupial, and compare it with the herbivorous kangaroo, and the highly specialised honey possum.

SOME OTHER MARSUPIAL ADAPTATIONS

During their evolution, marsupials have filled most of the ecological niches that eutherian mammals have occupied at one time or another. There are marsupial omnivores, carnivores, insectivores, herbivores, and nectarfeeders.

Their ways of getting about include running, hopping, swimming, and gliding through the air. The prehensile tail and opposable toes of the climbing *Didelphis* are just one example of the sorts of morphological adaptations to be seen in marsupials. A few other examples of their adaptive radiation follow.

A Ruminant-like Marsupial

(The kangaroo, Macropus)

The members of the family Macropodidae are grazers and browsers, showing several convergences, with eutherian ruminants. Kangaroos are adapted for living on vegetation in dry, desert habitats. Various aspects of their digestive physiology (including forestomach fermentation) allow them to process food which is often of poor quality, and their reproductive biology is beautifully adapted to cope with the harsh conditions in which they live.

Their method of locomotion allows them to cover large distances over open ground, and is unique in the sense that no other mammal of similar size moves in this fashion. Many smaller mammals hop.

When all there is to study is bones, none of the intricacies of kangaroo physiology will be obvious, but the skeleton does reflect the requirements of herbivory and hopping.

The Skull—Adaptations to Herbivory

Study the kangaroo skull alongside that of a eutherian mammal with a similar life style; for instance, an artiodactyl such as a deer or antelope. The roe deer skull illustrated in Chapter 6 would be a useful reference.

First, decide what adaptations to herbivory mammalian skulls generally show. Then make a list of all the similarities and differences between the kangaroo and eutherian skulls which you think relate to herbivorous adaptations. After that, you can see how your list compares with the features described below.

1. The skull of the red kangaroo has all the marsupial characteristics mentioned earlier. Look now only at the dentition, and the areas where jaw muscles would be attached.
2. Kangaroos have three incisors on each side of the upper jaw, and two procumbent incisors on the lower jaw. These can be moved to some extent independently of each other, because the jaw symphysis does not fuse.

   Kangaroos are said to be diprotodont, because of this arrangement of two lower incisors. *Didelphis* is polyprotodont, because it has several incisors in each half of its lower jaw. What is the function of the incisors in herbivores? Not all eutherian grazers have upper incisors. What is the situation in sheep, for example? And horses?
3. There is a gap or diastema between the incisors and cheek teeth. This is very characteristic of mammalian herbivores. What is its function?
4. There are no canines. The cheek teeth seem to be reduced in number. Look at their wear patterns; note that the teeth are relatively high crowned, and wear into *a* series of transverse ridges. The teeth near the front of the mouth are most worn, whereas those at the back still have high cusps.

What is the interpretation of this observation? Kangaroo molars actually erupt sequentially, as do elephant molars, and move forwards in the jaw as the anterior cheek teeth are shed. The skull illustrated in Figure elsewhere in this chapter still has premolars, so it cannot be very old. (Note that each half of both upper and lower jaws carries four molars.)

It is possible to age kangaroos approximately by looking at the number and position of the molars in relation to the bony process on the zygomatic arch. This skull would be from an animal around 4 years old.

5. Now try to work out where the jaw muscles would attach. With transverse ridges on the cheek teeth, it is likely that side to side motion is important in grinding up the food—as it is in ruminant herbivores.

   It is therefore reasonable to expect the masseter and pterygoideus muscles to be large. So where are they attached, and how is the shape of skull and jaw modified to accommodate them?

6. The masseter muscle has several layers: superficial, middle, and deep. It originates mostly on the zygomatic arch, and inserts on the outer surface of the dentary, as is usual in mammals.

   Unusual structures for its attachment are the prezygomatic process, and the deep pocket in the dentary, which houses the deep masseter and extends into a so-called masseteric canal. This canal is unique to the family Macropodidae.

7. The pterygoideus muscle runs from the pterygoid bone to the inner side of the dentary, as would be expected. But note that the pterygoid has a large surface area, and that the inflected angle of the dentary forms a large, bowlshaped shelf for the insertion of the muscle.

   So the skull is clearly modified to accommodate large masticatory muscles, and work has-shown that lateral movements are involved in chewing. The articulation between the dentary and the skull is flat and allows sliding.

8. The temporalis muscle is of moderate size, and has the same origin and insertion as it does in all other mammals. Note that the coronoid process on the dentary is well developed.

The Skeleton—Adaptations to Hopping

1. Note the relatively small head, relative lengths of limbs, and the long tail.

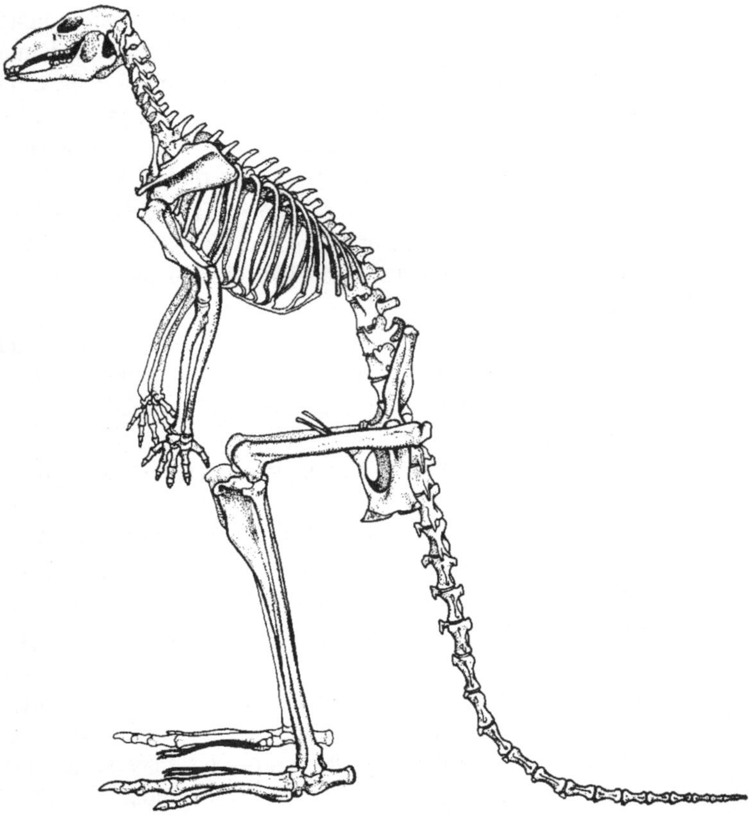

Figure 8.11: Skeleton of Macropus.

2. Much can be inferred about the locomotion of a mammal by looking at the length and morphology of the limbs. Kangaroos hop, so it is no surprise to see that their hindlimbs are long; but it is somewhat surprising to find that the forelimbs are also quite long.

   Most of the length is provided by the long forearm bones, which are considerably longer than the humerus. If the animal bends forwards, its forelimbs soon touch the ground. Do they have any function in locomotion?

   The fact is that they do, for kangaroos have a crawling gait, in which the forelimbs and tail are used as props. As the animal moves forwards, it shifts its weight onto the forelimb, and then brings its hindlimbs up alongside them—rather in the manner of a hopping rabbit. This slow 'crawl' is useful when the animal is grazing. Other functions of the forelimbs, which would also explain their length, are in holding food, holding open the pouch (e.g. when the female cleans it), and in sparring between two individuals. The forepaws are mobile, with fingers that can grasp objects.

3. A longer leg allows an animal to apply force to the ground for a longer time as it pushes off. This is important for animals that jump and run, and also for most birds when they take off. Long legs also increase stride length.

   Which bones provide most of the length in kangaroo legs? Compare with the frog, chicken, and rabbit legs. Even if you did not know how kangaroos move, the long hindlimbs would have given you an important clue.

4. Kangaroo feet are extraordinary, being modified for bearing the weight of the animal and for pushing off during hopping. They are the most extreme example of a foot structure which is characteristic of all diprotodont marsupials, and of the bandicoots. Which bones are elongated?

   One toe is particularly enlarged, and bears most of the weight. The foot must act as a rigid lever during hopping, and this is probably best achieved by strengthening along one toe. It is not easy to decide which toe this is.

   In fact, it is the fourth—toe five is smaller, and toes three and two are very slender. The first toe is missing. In life, the second and third toes are held together by skin, and are said to be syndactylous. They are used for grooming the fur.

5. Note the position of the foot pads. These tell you which parts of the foot carry weight. A kangaroo's foot is arched, and weight is transmitted to the ground via the heel, the proximal part of the metatarsals, and the toes.

   You can see from the whole skeleton that when a kangaroo is sitting it has a plantigrade posture. The question is whether it is plantigrade or digitigrade when it is moving. To find this out, look at the drawings of a hopping kangaroo.

   Among other vertebrates, the closest equivalent morphologically to the kangaroo foot is that of the ostrich. It also has two toes which carry its weight at all times, because birds are always digitigrade. Which toes carry the weight of the ostrich?

6. Note that none of the ankle bones is elongated, except for the

long heel bone (calcaneum). Is this also true of frog and bird ankle bones? What about the ankle of galagos, the leaping primates described in Chapter elsewhere in this chapter?

7. Look at the sacral region and the shape of the pelvis. Note the position of the acetabulum. How many vertebrae are fused to form the sacrum? Compare with other mammals and also with birds; look at a bipedal dinosaur skeleton.

   Note the length of the kangaroo's tail; how does its length compare with the length of the trunk? The tail is both counterbalance and prop.

Now look at the drawings of a kangaroo moving. The gait is a graceful springy bound. You should be able to answer the following questions:

- Do the forelimbs participate at all in sustained hopping? How are they held during hopping? Check back to what was said above about the slow, quadrupedal crawl which kangaroos sometimes use. Then, the forelimbs support the front end of the body, and they, together with the tail, act as props while the back legs swing forward.
- Where (approximately) is the centre of gravity of the animal as it hops? Look carefully at how the body is held at each phase of movement. Where does the centre of gravity fall in a sitting kangaroo?
- The kangaroo is completely off the ground at times during its movement. What other fast mammalian gait has a phase in which all legs are off the ground at once?
- How is balance maintained during movement, when the kangaroo is leaning far forwards? Remember, this is a bipedal animal. What are the major structural differences here between kangaroos and other bipedal movers such as birds and people? What about the bipedal dinosaurs, many of which seem to have been swift runners? What was their stance while running and how did they keep their balance?
- Does the kangaroo have a digitigrade posture when it is hopping? If it does, then the long metatarsals are effectively adding to the length of the leg.

Some work done on the mechanics and energetics of kangaroo hopping has shown two important things. One is that the oxygen consumption of a kangaroo does not rise as it hops faster—contrary to expectation. The second finding probably explains the first. It is that energy is stored during hopping through the elasticity of the gastrocnemius and plantaris tendons in the leg and foot. In one set of calculations, it was shown that a 40 per cent energy saving was being made. The details of this work are described in two papers referred to below.

Small Size and Nectar-Feeding

(The honey possum, Tarsipes)

To end this chapter, we will take a brief look at a very small marsupial, the honey possum, which lives in a restricted area of south western Australia. *Tarsipes* looks superficially like a mouse or shrew, but it feeds: on nectar and pollen.

The only eutherians to feed exclusively on nectar are bats, although other mammals do visit flowers occasionally for nectar, and may pollinate them in doing so. One of the flower genera on which *Tarsipes* feeds *is Banksia,* named after Sir Joseph Banks, who was the botanist on Captain James Cook's voyage to Australia in 1768.

The area in which it has been most recently studied is covered with *Banksia* thickets. It is thought that *Tarsipes* is the major pollinator for species of *Banksia* which are cryptically coloured and which have never been observed to be pollinated by birds.

Adaptations correlated with blossom-feeding are the elongated snout (which is pushed right down into flowers), reduced teeth and lower jaw, and long tongue with a brush-like tip. The lower jaw carries two procumbent incisors (diprotodont), and can be moved forwards to pierce objects. Look at the skull of *Tarsipes*, and note its specialisations.

A shrew skull of similar size is also illustrated for comparison. This chapter has described some aspects of the structure of monotremes and marsupials which relate to their position among the mammals, and to their own particular specialisations.

Our myopic European view of adaptive radiation in the mammals can now be extended to include these other dimensions of mammalian evolution. Although the position of monotremes remains unclear, the marsupials have become of consuming interest to zoologists as examples of a different type of mammalian organisation that arose after the fundamentals were established.

It is for this reason, regardless of whether we have any in our own backyard, that all of us should be interested in the subjects of this chapter.

9

Primates: The Consequences of Arboreal Living

The order Primates includes all those mammals most closely related to ourselves—that is, the monkeys and apes, and a whole range of less familiar animals such as the *lemurs*, *bushbabies*, and *pottos*. *Primates* are basically adapted to life in the trees, and although their later evolution has involved adaptation to life on the ground, even in these ground-living forms there is still evidence of descent from *arboreal ancestors*.

It is therefore fair to say that arboreal life has shaped the primates, including man. (The word 'man' is here used in its general *biological* sense, as a noun including both sexes of members of the family *Hominidae*.)

One question to ask is what it is about the *arboreal* environment that has led to the success of the higher primates, which seems to lie in their *amazing versatility* in adapting to different situations. This chapter will illustrate some features of primate *locomotion*, which is one *aspect* of primate biology that is *particularly versatile*.

There are a number of striking characteristics of primates which were all evolved initially in the trees. These include binocular vision, *grasping* hands and feet, and the tendency to hold the body erect. This combination of characteristics *subsequently* proved to be *supremely adaptable* to life on the ground.

As we look at the various different primates described in this chapter, we shall *concentrate* on these particular features, so as to show how they are reflected in skeletal anatomy, and then to correlate this with what is known of the *behaviour* of the animals in the wild. An example of each of the main *methods* of primate locomotion will be described.

Material Required

- Mounted skins or skeletons of different types of primates; even one monkey skeleton would be a great help in working through this chapter.
- Skulls and/or *skeletons* of dog or cat for comparison.
- Skeleton(s) of other *arboreal* mammals, e.g. squirrel.
- *Films* (or zoo visits) to show *primates* in action.

PROSIMIANS

One of the things that makes primates interesting animals to study is that the most primitive living primates resemble the earliest fossil primates. This means that by looking at the primates alive now, we can gain some insight into the paths that evolution followed within the group.

This is not possible with most other groups of mammals, where the early fossil forms bear little *resemblance* to the animals alive today. *Prosimians* retain more primitive features than other living primates. They live in *Madagascar*, *Africa*, and *South East Asia,* but were once much more widespread.

The lemurs, now restricted to *Madagascar*, form a useful starting point for our discussions, and are the most similar to the earliest known fossil primates. (The tree shrew, whose *taxonomic* position has been a source of considerable *argument*, is not any longer thought to be a primate.)

The Ring-tailed Lemur, *Lemur catta*

These lemurs are the size of a large cat. They walk and run quadrupedally along branches, using their tails for balance, and leaping from tree to tree. Lemur catta also spends time on the ground, walking *quadrupedally* and holding its tail erect.

The *conspicuous* tail is then being used as a visual signal and, at times, as a *transmitter* of scent. Ring-tailed lemurs eat mainly fruit, and are active mostly during the day. Lemurs show the basic primate features at a primitive stage: concentrate on the general *stance*, the *head*, *limbs*, and *tail*.

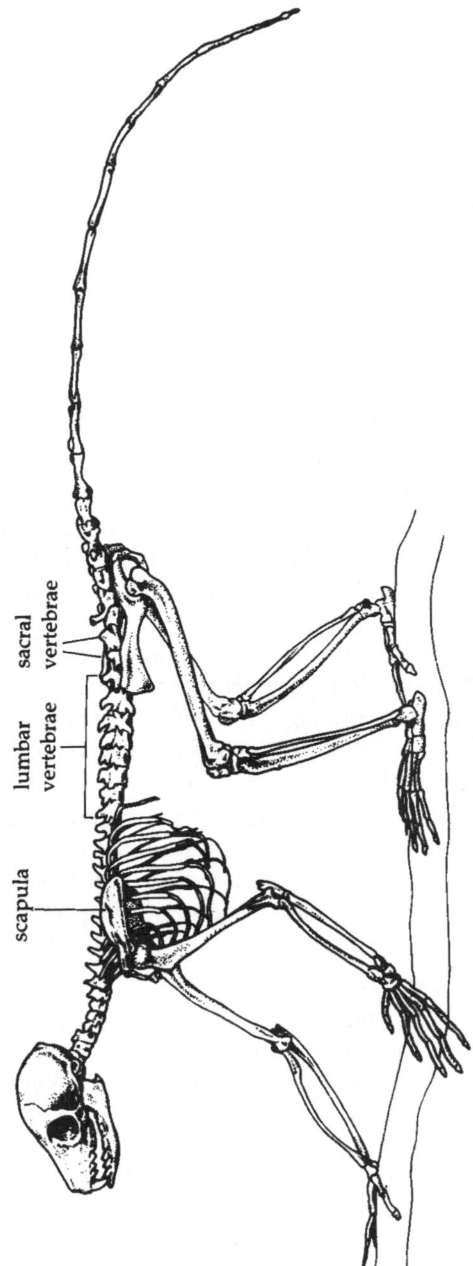

Figure 9.1: Skeleton of Lemur catta.

The Head

Proportionately, primates have large brains, and so the rear part of the skull is enlarged and becomes *globular*. Compare the shape of the lemur skull with that of, for instance, a dog or cat.

The part of the brain that is most enlarged is the cerebrum, and the cerebral hemispheres become so large in higher primates that they may *overgrow* other, more posterior, parts of the brain such as the cerebellum.

As you go through this chapter, you should be able to work out some of the reasons for this increase in brain size. Certain senses have become very well developed in primates. Their inputs require correspondingly large association areas in the brain, and so certain parts of the brain are enlarged.

What are these important primate senses? In the centre of the lemur skull are two large orbits. Note that they flare out to the sides of the head, and that a bony bar encircles the orbit completely. Compare this situation again with that in a dog or cat skull.

Do they have orbits pointing forwards or to the side? Is there a postorbital bar? One of the specialities of primates is full stereoscopic vision. If you look at a dog skull, you can see that the eye sockets do not point straight forwards.

Lines drawn through the axes of the two eyes would diverge at a wide angle. Dogs do not have binocular vision - the field of view of one eye does not overlap that of the other. Lines drawn through the axes of your own eyes would be nearly parallel, and close together—they point straight forwards and their fields of view overlap.

What about the lemur? Its eyes are, as it were, beginning to point forwards. Does it have binocular vision? Now look at the lemur snout. Primates evolved from small nocturnal insectivorous forms, as did all the mammals.

Their sense of smell was very important, as were the tactile hairs on the snout, which projected from the face and so touched objects first. Lemurs still have a well-developed sense of smell, whereas in higher primates smell becomes less important, and is used less in communication between individuals.

The snout tends to become reduced and the face is flatter. What effect might this have on vision? Are there mammals with long snouts and binocular vision? The use of scent as a signal to other individuals is important in lemurs, where males mark their territories by rubbing glandular secretions on branches and trunks, or by rubbing their tails against scent glands on their forearms, and then waving them about to disperse the scent. Females also mark with genital glands.

Teeth

Primates usually have fewer teeth than the basic mammalian number, which is 13/3; C 1/1; PM 4/4; M3/3. A common arrangement among prosimians is 12/2; C 1/1; PM 3/3; M 3/3, which is shown in lemurs. Two special features are worth noting.

The upper canines are large and blade-like (often larger in males), and overlap the lower jaw; they are used for piercing fruit. The lower incisors are almost horizontal (i.e. they are procumbent); so is the lower canine, which lies alongside them and is similar in shape.

Lower incisors and canines together form the so-called dental comb, which is used for grooming the fur and for feeding. The fur is also cleaned by licking and by a grooming claw on the second digit of the foot. Dental combs and grooming claws are another characteristic of prosimians generally.

Thorax, Vertebral Column, and Tail

Note the positionn of the foramen magnum, the opening in the skull through which the spinal cord emerges. Animals which habitually sit or walk upright will tend to have their heads positioned more vertically on top of the vertebral column.

Take some dividers and measure the width and depth of the ribcage. Compare your measurements on the lemur with those from other primate skeletons. It is characteristic of quadrupedal primates that the thorax is deeper dorsoventrally than it is wide from side to side.

This presumably reflects the type of forces it must withstand during locomotion. You will **see** that in galagos and gibbons, for example, the thorax is a different shape. Note also the position of the scapula (shoulder-blade); this also varies depending on the type of arm movements used during locomotion.

Primates that swing from their arms have the scapula in a different position. These lemurs have long tails; they are used for balance and are not prehensile. Notice the shape of individual caudal vertebrae. In life, the tail is completely covered in dense fur.

Even without any knowledge of the habits of living lemurs, would you predict that such a tail would be prehensile? Compare it with the tail of a spider monkey, for example. Look at the shape of the neural spines on the vertebrae in the lumbar region; they are laterally flattened and point forwards.

In the sacral region, and on the first few caudal vertebrae, the neural spines are shorter and point vertically. This is the area of the spine and tail which bears the weight of the body when the animal is sitting upright on a branch.

The Limbs

One of the features to notice about primates is the relative lengths of their fore- and hindlimbs, for this provides a key to how they move. Much has been written in primate literature of the intermembral index. This is:

$$\frac{\text{length of forelimb (humerus + radius)}}{\text{length of hindlimb (femur + tibia)}} \times 100$$

A figure greater than 100 denotes an animal with longer forelimbs. *Lemur catta* has longer hindlimbs. Some other lemurs have very long hindlimbs, and leap from tree to tree propelled by them (e.g. the sifaka).

Lemur catta mostly runs quadrupedally along larger horizontal branches, but also leaps. Compared with an animal such as a squirrel, which also runs along branches, it looks ungainly with its long limbs and larger size.

The centre of gravity is not as close to the substrate as is that of a squirrel; because of the longer limbs. A lemur could, therefore, overbalance more easily, and does not use small branches for moving along. How does it hold on?

Look at the hands and feet. Primates have opposable thumbs and first toes. These allow them to develop a power grip, such as we use when carrying a suitcase or grasping a door handle.

The manipulation of objects by the hands becomes a considerable skill in higher primates, particularly man, but the beginnings of this ability are present in the most primitive prosimians.

The uses of a power grip are numerous, but two major ones are to hold on more securely when moving, and to allow food to be held by one hand only (a squirrel must use two hands), so that the other hand can continue to give support—an important consideration for a relatively heavy animal feeding from an insecure perch in a tree.

Look at the position of the thumb and first toe (hallux). A saddle-shaped articulation between the base of the digit and the wrist or .ankle allows opposability to the other four digits. Lemurs use digits 2 to 5 in parallel to form a hook around branches, while the thumb can be used as a clamp on the other side.

The thumb is not mobile enough to manipulate very small objects, and lemurs cannot form a precision grip between the tips of thumb and index finger.

Primate hands and feet have two other special features. One is the presence of highly sensitive naked pads on the palms and soles, and on the ends of the digits. This nakedness enhances the sense of touch, and improves the grip because the pads are ridged and carry numerous sweat glands.

The sweat causes the ridges to swell, so increasing the area of contact. The other feature is the development of flat nails instead of claws, which reinforce the broad pads at the tips of the digits. Nails and claws differ in fine structure, but externally the main difference is in their shape and the extent to which they overlap the digital pads themselves.

Claws are the more primitive, but nails evolved after primates had developed their specialised digital grip. A few primates, like the marmosets, retain claws on all their digits, but most either have only nails or have a toilet claw only on their second toe. Compare with the claws on the foot of a dog or cat.

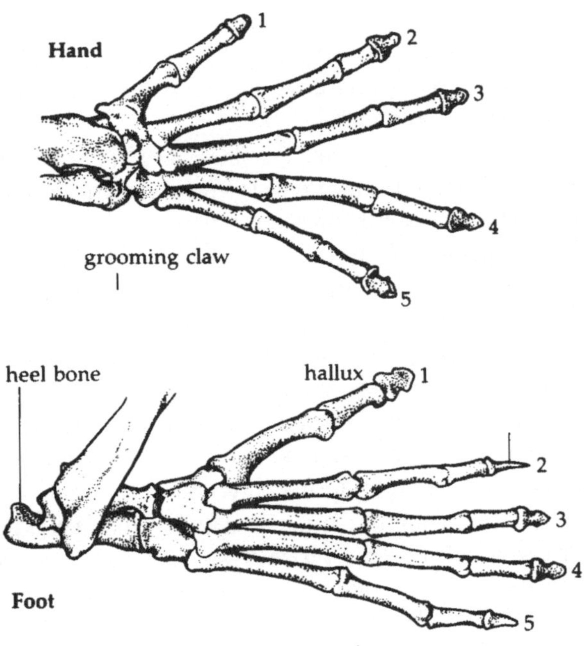

Figure 9.2: Hand and foot of Lemur catta.

How do cats or squirrels hold on when climbing trees? Is it with their digital pads or claws? Do they then have a digital grip? Consider whether the sensitivity of the digital grip and the development of the tactile function of the digital pads in primates could have been as great with clawed digits as with flat nails.

The shape of a nail is correlated with the shape of the pad under it—note that digits 2 to 5 on the lemur hand and foot have narrow pads, and therefore the nails are also narrow. In contrast the opposable hallux, for instance, has a broad pad, and a broad flat nail. Compare with the galago hand and foot.

This brief look at the lemur skeleton has introduced several fundamental features of primate structure and evolution, which will be referred to constantly in the rest of this chapter.

Large brains, binocular vision, and sensitive hands and feet that grip with the digits themselves, not with claws, are all central characteristics of the primates which can be seen in the most primitive living members of the group.

The ability to get about in the trees is a primate speciality, for although other groups of mammals are arboreal, none has evolved such versatility in arboreal movement. The quadrupedal branch-running and walking of the genus *Lemur* is the least unusual method of locomotion adopted by arboreal primates.

The potto, *Perodicticus potto*

a branch, sometimes holding on with hindlimbs alone when reaching for another branch. Their movement is slow, smooth and silent; limbs are moved either in diagonal pairs, or one at a time.

The animal is always well balanced, because its body is kept close to the branch, and the centre of gravity falls either in the middle of a tripod of limbs while the fourth is moved, or between the forelimb of one side and the opposing hindlimb.

This, combined with their firm grip, makes pottos extremely hard to dislodge. They can also creep up on insect prey without causing a disturbance, and simultaneously keep themselves inconspicuous to predators.

The Head

Pottos have the large cranium and eyes that are characteristic of all primates. Note the position of the eye sockets and the postorbital bar. Compare with the lemur. Could the potto have binocular vision? From observations in the wild, it is known that they see well and follow complex paths through the forest canopy. But pottos also mark their territories with scent, by spreading urine on their hands and feet, and so onto the branches as they move about.

Thus, smell is an important sense for them. Look at the length of the snout region in front of the eyes, and compare with the skulls of lemur and galago.

Teeth

Pottos have the same dental formula as lemurs. Note the small upper incisors, and the dental comb in the lower jaw, which incorporates both incisors and canines.

The dental comb, as in the lemur, is for grooming the fur, together with the tongue and toilet claw on the second toe. It can also be used as a scoop in feeding and for obtaining gum from trees.

Pottos have large upper canines for piercing insects or fruit, or for defence, as they will strike at an attacker with their teeth if severely provoked. They are omnivorous, the diet consisting of insects, resin, fruit, and various sorts of vegetable matter.

Thorax and Vertebral Column

Look at the back of the skull (occipital region), and the position of the foramen magnum. Compare with its position in galagos. Pottos are quadrupedal animals, which only occasionally stand up on their hindlegs to reach branches, and seldom sit upright for long periods.

The neck and trunk regions are long and flexible, allowing the potto to curl and extend itself into a variety of positions. Note the neck vertebrae; they have long spines.

Look at the lemur skeleton, and other primate skeletons; you will find that the cervical spines are unique to the potto. Note also the flared scapulae, which almost meet over the dorsal side of the vertebral column forming a shield.

Check that the lemur scapulae are not like this. Cervical spines and scapular shield are the structural basis for the potto's defence behaviour. When attacked, a potto bends its head downwards between its forelegs, exposing the shoulder region to the attacker.

The cervical spines are covered in life with horny skin and stick up from the surface of the body. It is possible that the spines could also injure a predator that picked a potto up by its neck. The whole area of the neck and scapular shield is covered with thick skin, muscle, sensory hairs, and glands.

The potto then lunges at the attacker with scapular shield foremost,

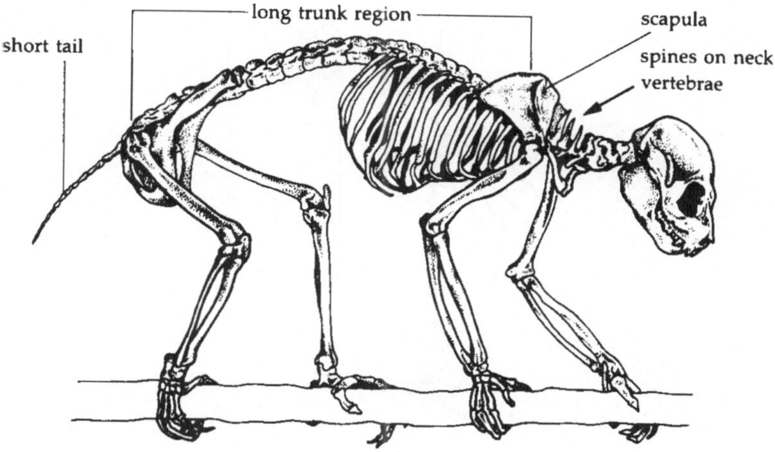

Figure 9.3: Skeleton of Perodicticus.

and without altering its grip on the branch. Bites aimed at the shield are deflected by the underlying bones and tissue, so preventing damage to the spinal cord. If provoked further the potto will bite at the attacker, again without altering its grip.

This whole complex of special structures and behaviour is unique among primates. The number of thoracolumbar vertebrae is high in pottos and all members of the family Lorisidae; they give the trunk its length. The tail, however, is short, unlike the lemur tail.

Two major functions of the tail in lemurs - balance and scent dispersal—are in the potto performed by the limbs themselves, and by the hands and feet.

Limbs

Pottos have fore- and hindlimbs that are almost equal in length. They do not leap or swing from their arms. However, their arms and legs are actually much longer than they appear in life, when their covering of thick fur makes them look deceptively short.

The length of the limbs, the long trunk, and the great flexibility of the limbs at wrist and ankle all allow the potto to assume a wide variety of positions during its daily life.

None of these would be possible, however, without a very strong grip. Look at the hands and feet. The thumb and first toe are widely opposable to the other four digits, so that on closing, a forceps-like grip is produced. This is particularly true of the foot.

It is reminiscent of the feet of a chameleon, at least in functional terms. Which digit is particularly reduced in pottos? Look at both hand

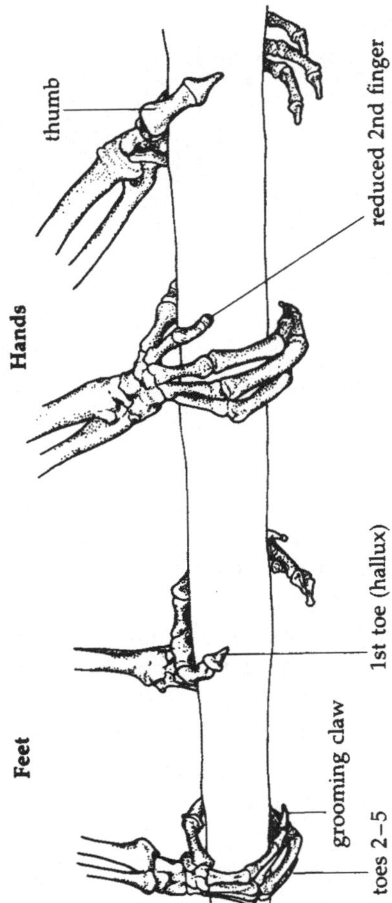

Figure 9.4: Hands and feet of Perodicticus.

and foot. Is there a toilet claw? Compare with the lemur, which could not produce a grip like that of the potto.

The pads on the palms and soles are also important in maintaining the grip, and the one between digits 1 and 2 is very prominent. Note again the difference between a digital grip and that of a cat, say, holding onto a tree trunk by its claws. The potto's grip is far stronger.

The Galago *Galago Senegalensis*

Galagos live in equatorial rainforest and savanna woodland, where they move through the canopy at night by running along branches and leaping between supports with great rapidity and precision. Their characteristic method of leaping is often referred to as 'vertical clinging

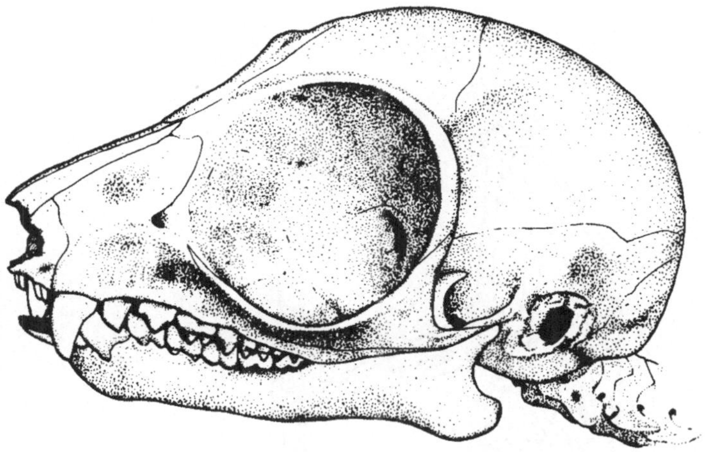

Figure 9.5: Skull and lower jaw of Galago.

and leaping', because the body is frequently held vertically. This habit seems to have evolved very early among the primates, and is possibly an important precursor to the various upright postures of the higher primates. There are several striking adaptations to leaping, particularly in the hindlimbs.

The Head

Galagos have very large ears and eyes. They can hunt insects by night and use both hearing and vision to do so. They can easily locate insects by the sounds they emit. Good vision is also of critical importance in their locomotion.

Leaping large distances between branches and trunks requires precise judgement of distance and depth perception. *Galago senegalensis is* known to have very good visual acuity, and the speed and precision of its movements are only inhibited on the darkest of nights.

Look at the skull and the whole skeleton. Note the position of the eyes and their size. Does this animal have binocular vision? Why would binocular vision be useful to an animal with the galago's mode of life?

The braincase is large and globular—compare the proportions of the skull with those of the lemur and potto skulls. Areas of the brain concerned with vision, hearing and tactile information (from the hands and feet) are particularly well developed.

Where are these areas located? Notice the position of the foramen magnum at the back of the skull. Remember that this animal regularly holds its body erect—in contrast, for instance, to the potto.

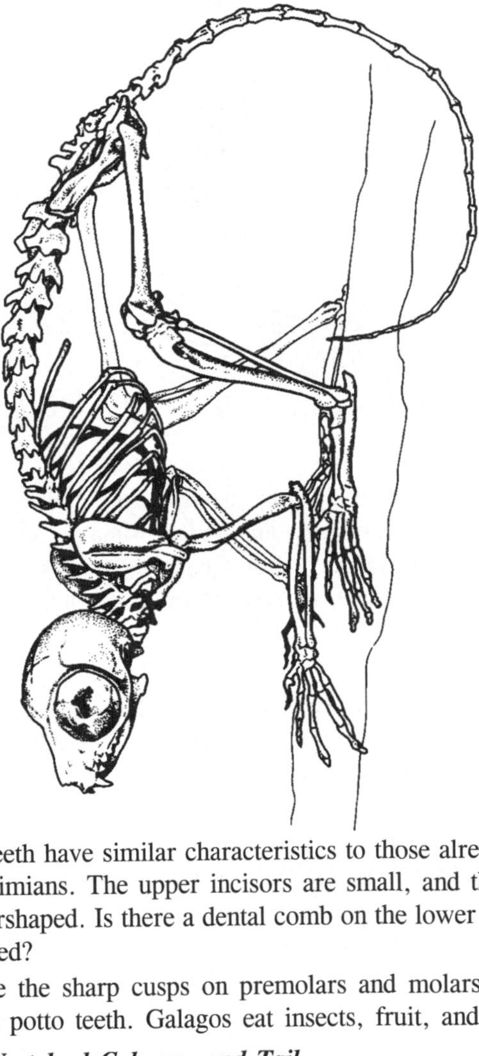

Figure 9.6: Skeleton of Galago.

The teeth have similar characteristics to those already described in other prosimians. The upper incisors are small, and the *canines* large and daggershaped. Is there a dental comb on the lower jaw? What teeth are involved?

Notice the sharp cusps on premolars and molars. Compare with lemur and potto teeth. Galagos eat insects, fruit, and gum.

Thorax, Vertebral Column, and Tail

Galagos do not have such long trunks as pottos—the number of lumbar and sacral vertebrae is lower. Look at the dimensions of the rib cage (depth versus width), and the position of the scapula. Do galagos have cervical spines or a scapular shield?

They do not have the same defensive behaviour as pottos. Notice the long tail; in life it is covered in fur. It is not prehensile, but has a very.. important role in *maintaining* balance and orientation, both when running and leaping (see drawings below). Note that this is another difference between galagos and pottos.

Limbs

Galago hindlimbs are much longer than the forelimbs. What has happened to produce this extra length? Is it simply that the femur and tibia/fibula are lengthened? Notice the projecting heel—a large heel is a feature of mammals that use their hindlimbs to provide the main propulsive force in their locomotion.

Now look at the ankle region: two ankle (tarsal) bones called the calcaneum and navicular, have become very long. The rest of the tarsal bones are small and lie at the distal ends of these bones.

The length ening of the tarsal region has provided the leg with an extra joint, which' produces extra leverage when the hindlimb pushes off from the support in a leap, or when the animal is hopping bipedally on the ground. What other vertebrates have long hindlimbs with similar characteristics?

When the galago is sitting, its hindlimbs are flexed at knee and ankle. When running quadrupedally, quick retraction of the hindleg could be a problem, because they are so much longer than the forelegs. The extra joint at the ankle probably facilitates this, because it makes the leg less cumbersome when folded.

Even so, some galagos must swing their hindlegs out from the branch when moving forwards. Now look at the hands and feet. The digits in *Galago senegalensis* are long and carry flat nails. Is there a toilet claw on the foot?

The hallux is much more opposable than the thumb; it forms a forceps-like grip with the other four toes. In the hand the fingers are more splayed out, but thumb and index finger—or thumb alone—may be opposed to the other three fingers.

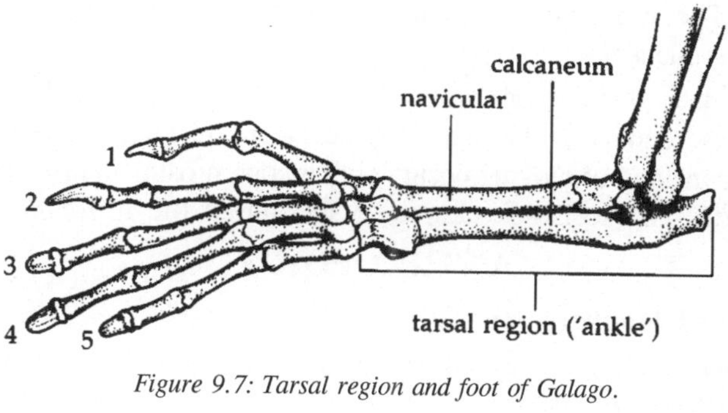

Figure 9.7: Tarsal region and foot of Galago.

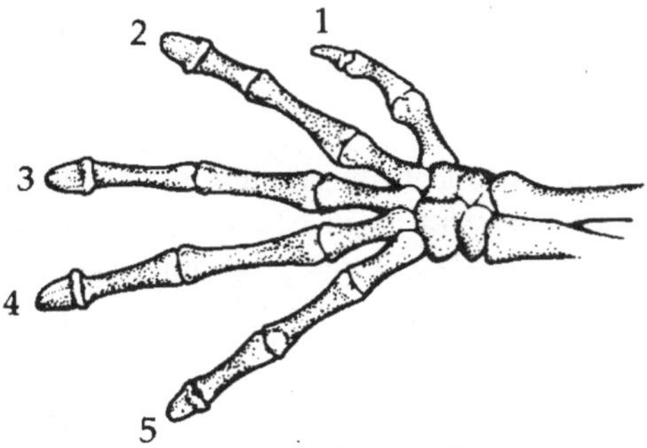

Figure 9.8: Hand of Galago.

Note that the index finger is quite short; compare with the potto hand. All digits carry fleshy pads at their tips, and they, together with the palmar pads, are very important in maintaining a grip.

The fingers are flexed when the hand is on a support, so that palmar and digital pads touch the surface, and the fingers are bent up between the first and second phalanges. These bent fingers are very striking in galagos—even when they are running along a branch, the palms of the forelimbs strike the branch first, and then the fingertips touch.

Similarly, when a galago pounces onto an insect, it touches it first with its palms; the fingers then close to grip against the palmar pads.

Vertical Clinging and Leaping

Look at the drawings from film of G. *senegalensis* leaping over a measured distance in the laboratory, and from tree to tree in the wild. Note:

- Which limbs push off for the leap.
- The angle at which the body is carried during the leap.
- Which limbs take the force of landing.
- The movements of the tail (not very pronounced in this sequence).

Correlate what you find with what you know of the skeletal structure. The precise details of the leap vary according to circumstances. This particular method of moving occurs only among prosimian primates, and so provides an excellent example of specialised life in trees.

ANTHROPOIDS

New World Monkeys: The Spider Monkey, *Ateles*

Spider monkeys are South American monkeys, which live up in the forest canopy. One feature sets them apart from all the prosimians and

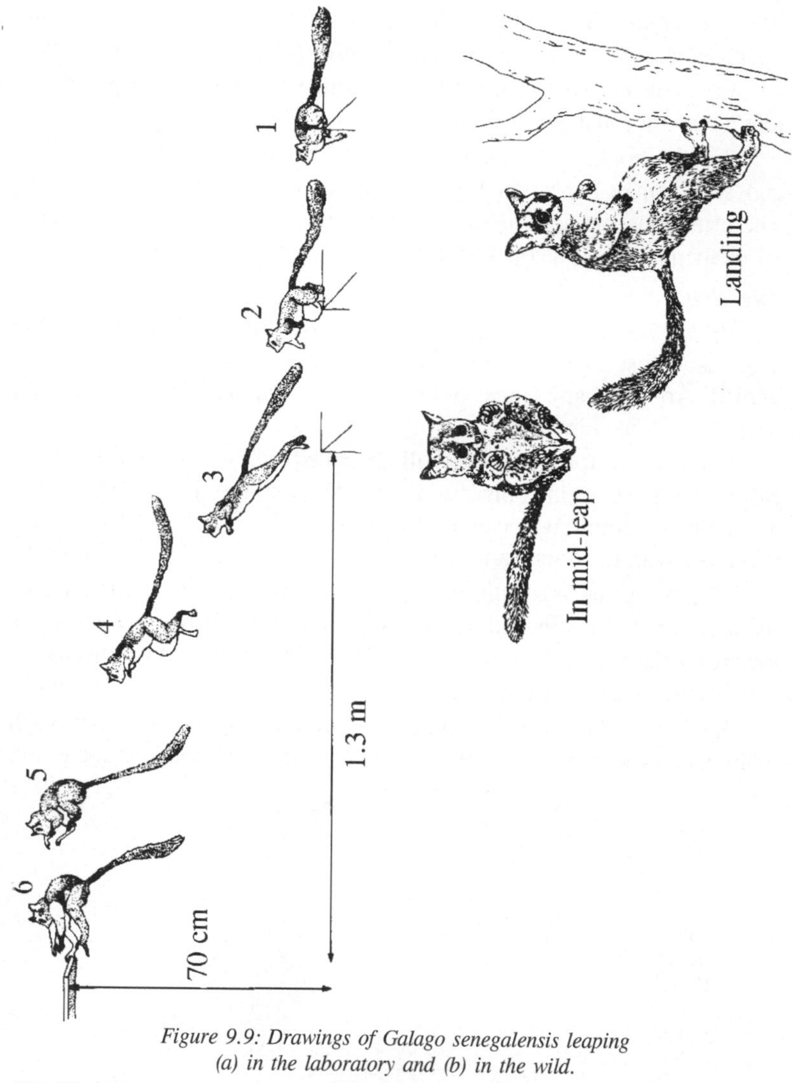

Figure 9.9: Drawings of Galago senegalensis leaping (a) in the laboratory and (b) in the wild.

Old World monkeys (even the arboreal ones), and that is their possession of a prehensile tail. Some New World monkeys lack this marvellous appendage.

The tail becomes a fifth member for holding on, and can support the whole weight of the animal, because it may hang from tail alone. How could you infer that the spider monkey tail was prehensile just from looking at it?

Are lemur tails like this? The highly sensitive naked patch near the tip provides grip and receives tactile information. The tail is otherwise covered with coarse fur. What other mammals have prehensile tails? Are they naked or furred?

Spider monkeys frequently move by swinging from their arms, and so we may expect to find adaptations correlated with this habit. The arms must be able to support the animal's weight, and contribute an element of propulsion to the body, at least occasionally.

The Head

Ateles has a large cranium, which is quite flat on top in the specimen illustrated. In some specimens, the frontal region is steeply domed. Are there any ridges of bone on the occiput or along the central part of the cranium?

Compare with the baboon skull described below; also look for brow ridges. Notice that, in comparison to the baboon, the spider monkey has a smooth cranium and occiput. Look at the face; it is relatively flat. Compare with the lemur and galago, and then look at the baboon skull.

The jaw projects a little in front of the nasal region, but the spider monkey is not very prognathous in comparison to the baboon. A tendency towards a flat face with close-set eyes is characteristic of many primates, and is correlated with the decreasing importance of the sense of smell.

Spider monkeys depend more on sight and sound. However, such other factors as the nature of the diet will affect the size of teeth and

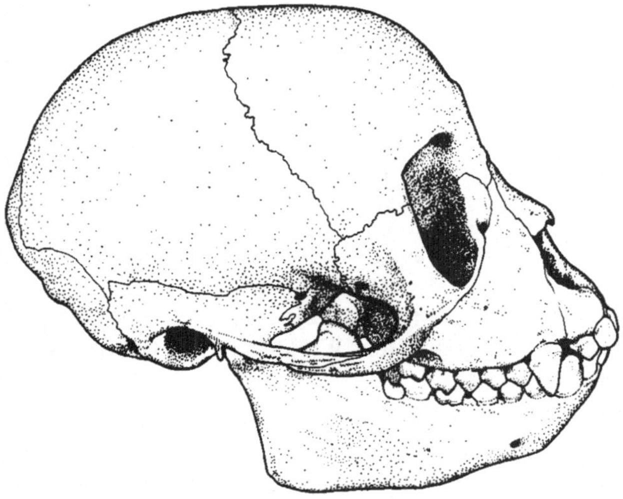

Figure 9.10: Skull and lower jaw of Ateles.

jaw muscles and hence the length and depth of the jaw. Look at the eye sockets—they are closed off behind the postorbital bar, except for openings carrying nerves and blood vessels.

Compare with the lemur and galago skulls. What do you think are the functional reasons for closure of the eye socket with bone? Note that the eyes are pointing directly forwards and are not obstructed in their field of view by a snout.

All monkeys and apes have binocular vision. The postorbital bar is the first accompaniment of the trend towards forward-pointing eyes in primate evolution, and as it continued, greater protection and support for the back of the eye was provided by filling in the socket with bone.

In all higher primates, the backs of the eyes are completely encased in bone. The teeth are adapted for a mainly fruit-eating diet. Is the dental formula the same as it is in prosimians?

The incisors bite or nip, together with canines, which are conical and occlude so that the tip of the lower canine fits into a space between the upper canine and its adjacent incisor. Premolars and molars are used mainly to crush fruit and extract the pulp, after piercing by the anterior teeth.

Thorax, Vertebral Column, and Tail

Note the general proportions. The trunk from shoulder to sacrum

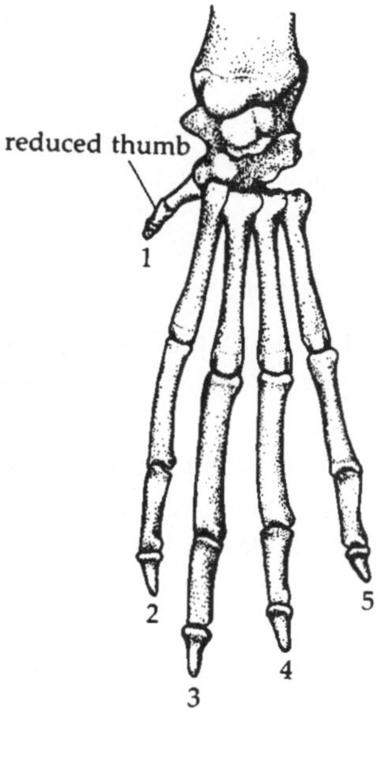

Figure 9.11: Hand of Ateles.

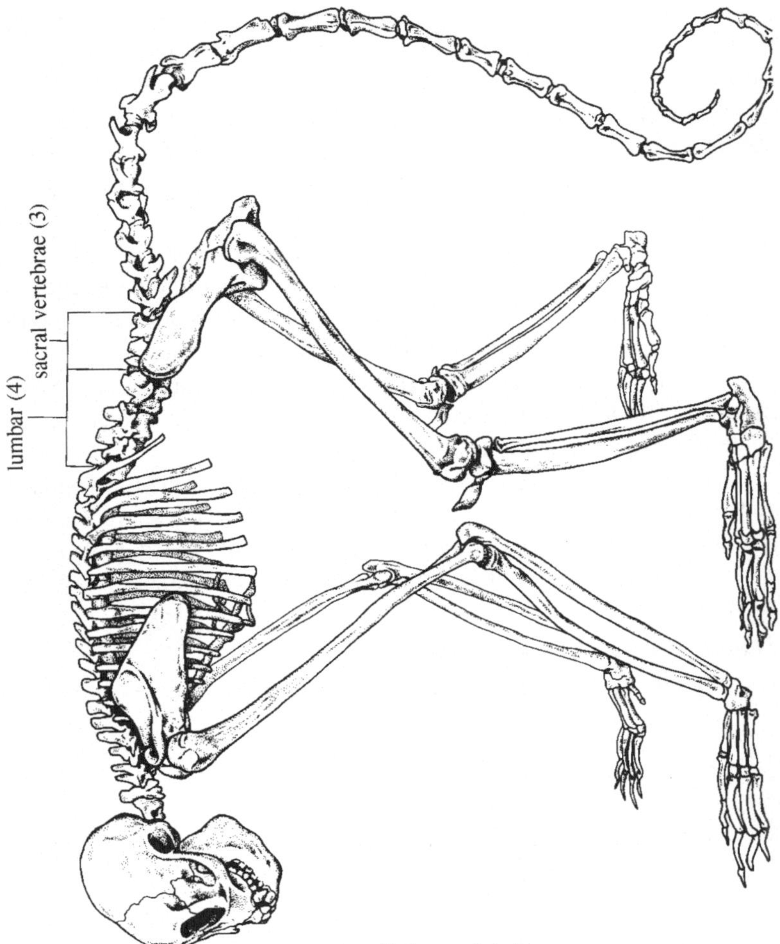

Figure 9.12: Skeleton of Ateles.

is much shorter than the limbs. Also, the thorax makes up most of the trunk, and the lumbar region is very short. Compare this situation with the proportions of the potto.

Measure the rib cage—it is slightly wider than it is deep; also note the position and shape of the scapula. The pelvic girdle is attached to three sacral vertebrae, and is essentially similar in shape to the girdles of other primates already discussed.

The main feature of these girdles is the long ilium, and the considerable distance separating the sacro-iliac joint from the hip. At least thirty (the exact number varies) caudal vertebrae form the long prehensile tail, which is much longer than either trunk or limbs, and has the highest number of postsacral vertebrae of any primate.

Check where along this series of vertebrae the naked pad is. The tip of the tail moves constantly during life, reaching out for supports and for objects to pick up, often without accompanying visual information. There is a special motor area in the brain for co-ordination of tail movements.

Limbs

Both fore- and hindlimbs are very long; measurements of their bones will show that the forelimbs are longer. With this information alone, you might predict that this monkey uses its arms in some way during locomotion—not just for holding on, but actually for propulsion.

Look at the hand; on a live animal or prepared skin, there appear to be only four fingers, which are used to form a large hook when it is hanging from branches. The thumb is very reduced, and may consist only of a metacarpal in the skin, invisible externally; in some animals it is completely absent.

This is quite unlike the hand of any other primate described in this chapter. Compare it with the gibbon hand, which is also used for swinging through the trees. How does the spider monkey get by without an opposable thumb?

It mostly progresses beneath branches, and a mobile, hook-shaped hand is evidently well suited to this. Perhaps a forceps-like grip (e.g. in the potto) is less adaptable to quick release and quick attachment under these circumstances.

Why might it be an advantage to be able to hang beneath branches when feeding? In contrast, the feet have a fully developed opposable hallux, which is nearly half the length of the longest toe. It allows the foot to grasp well. Note general proportions of the feet—there is no lengthening of the tarsal region (cf. galago), but the toes are long.

Locomotion

Spider monkeys are highly mobile animals, both within and between trees. They can also move on the ground, either quadrupedally or bipedally. They have five main methods of locomotion:

- Quadrupedalism, either along branches or on the ground.
- Climbing, which involves all four limbs and the tail.
- Bimanual progression, underneath branches or other supports.
- Bipedalism on the ground, very rarely along branches.
- Leaping, often over large distances (10 metres).

Ateles is thus the most versatile arboreal primate we have discussed so far. The fact that it spends so much of its time suspended from branches has a lot to do with its method of feeding.

It is a terminal branch feeder, and will tend to move along underneath a branch as soon as it becomes too flexible. Moving beneath such supports allows *Ateles* to reach food otherwise inaccessible to an animal of its weight.

The mobility of the shoulder and forearm allows a form of progression known as brachiation, in which *Ateles* swings forwards and round from one arm support to attach its other arm further along. The trunk may rotate through 180° between each hold.

The versatility of locomotion in *Ateles* allows the animal to exploit sources of ripe fruit on different trees with ease and speed; it is not restricted to robust supports, nor is it at a loss on the ground.

Thus it can forage far and wide—an advantage when exploiting an environment with a diversity of fruit all ripening at different times.

Old World Monkeys: The Baboon, *Papio*

Baboons are quadrupedal ground dwellers, which also climb trees. They live in a great range of habitats from woodland to open country with few trees. They are thus highly adaptable animals—probably more so than any other primate except man.

Their adaptability is also reflected in their diet, which is omnivorous and encompasses almost every conceivable item of food at one time or another. For the purposes of this discussion, baboons should be regarded as the main example of a grounddwelling, quadrupedal primate; but it should not be forgotten that they frequently climb as well, both to obtain food and for safety.

The Head

Baboons have a characteristically large snout. Note that it does not obstruct the field of view of the eyes, because of its pronounced downward flexure. The enormous development of the snout is due to differential growth of the nasal, maxillary, and premaxillary bones.

Baboons are not born with a large snout, but develop it as they grow—it is therefore an example of allometric growth. The snout is proportionately larger in male baboons, because male animals are larger than females.

The development of the snout overshadows that of the cranium in an adult male, for the distance from brow ridge to occiput is smaller than from brow ridge to tip of snout. The cranium usually bears a sagittal crest, and also nuchal crests. What is the function of these bony ridges? Think about the position and mass of jaw and neck muscles.

There are also pronounced brow ridges over the closely set eyes. Compare with the skull of *Ateles*. Note the teeth: the dental formula is 12/2; C 1/1; PM 2/2; M 3/3, which is characteristic of all Old World anthropoids, including ourselves. Male baboons have very large canines; why do you think they are so big?

There is a particular behaviour pattern associated with them. Otherwise, the teeth are adapted for an omnivorous diet that includes grasses, small hard objects (e.g. seeds), and large objects (e.g. fruit), which are opened by the large incisors. Compare the teeth with those of a fruit-eater such as *Ateles*.

Thorax, Vertebral Column, and Girdles

Note the stance of the baboon. Compare its general proportions with those of other primates. The baboon backbone is capable of flexion and extension during galloping, the fastest method of progression on the ground.

Look at the proportions of the trunk in the gibbon (see below), where flexion and extension during locomotion occur only in the limbs. As an adaptation to galloping, the gluteus medius muscles of baboons are very well developed to control lateral movement of the pelvis.

The ilium has a curved gluteal area to accommodate them. A more striking feature of the pelvis is the prominent ischial callosities. Look at the two ischia—their posterior edges are flared out into two bony pads.

In life, these are covered with horny skin, and baboons spend a lot of time sitting on them. The callosities and their skin are non-slip devices for sitting on surfaces such as rocks and branches, but not all monkeys have them. Spider monkeys, for example, do not.

Some baboons carry their tails bent upwards from the sacrum. The extent to which this is done depends on the species, and varies individually. Between the sixth and seventh caudal vertebrae, another flexion occurs and the tail bends down again to the tip.

Changes in the zygapophyses mark the flexion point. There are also chevron bones beneath the first few caudal vertebrae. Baboon tails are not prehensile and are not a major balancing device. What other roles might they have?

Limbs

Baboons have fore- and hindlimbs of nearly equal length. Measure

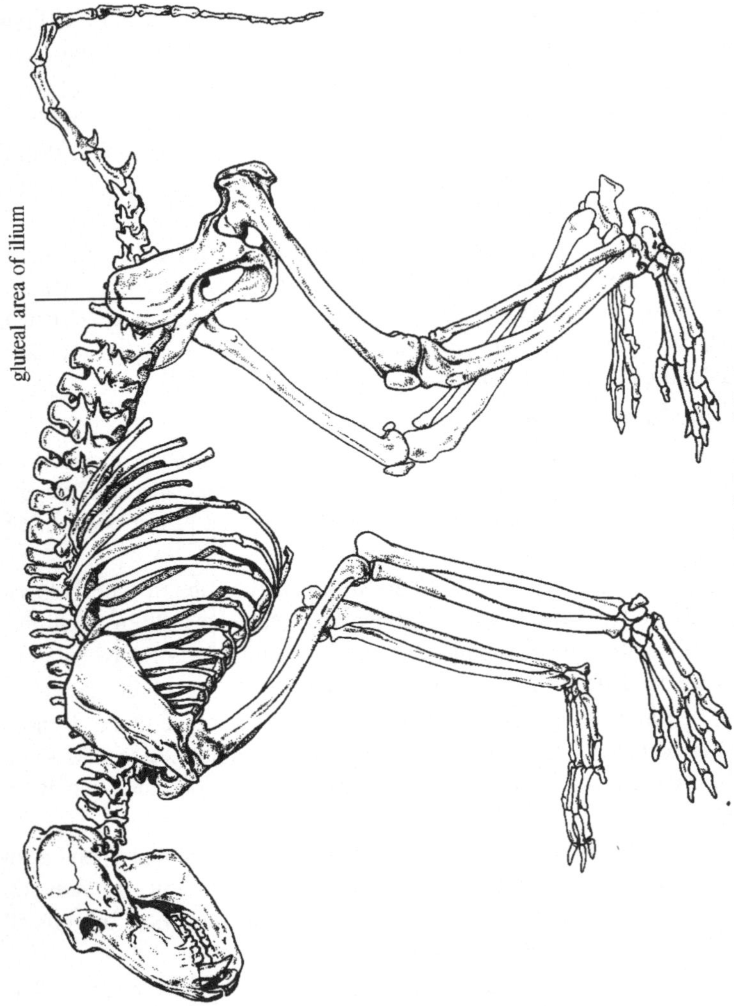

Figure 9.13: Skeleton of Papio.

the intermembral index if you can. Compare the proportions with those of the other primates.

Would you conclude that these proportions are a feature of quadrupedal primates generally, or just of those that live mostly on the ground? Now look at the hands and feet; the digits are very short.

To appreciate this, look at one finger; and compare the length of its metacarpal with the total length of all three of its phalanges. Repeat for the digits in the foot.

The overall phalangeal length is about equal to or shorter than the

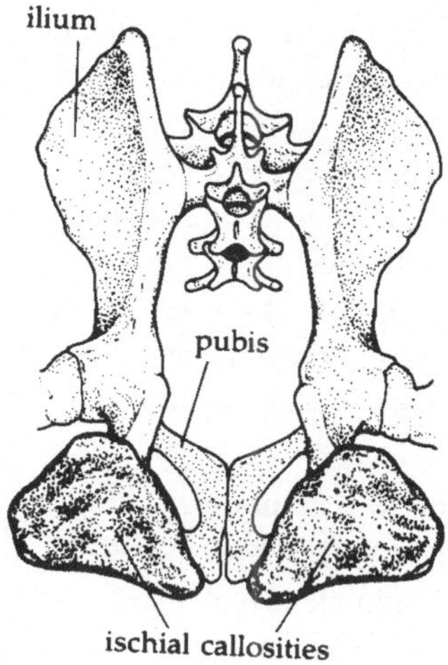

Figure 9.14: Ischial callosities of Papio.

length of the corresponding metapodial. Look at the hands and feet of other primates—the proportions are very different. Short digits are perhaps an adaptation for fast quadrupedal running.

Also, baboon hands are used more for walking on flat surfaces than for gripping branches, and they are used a great deal in feeding, as when grass is picked or roots excavated.

Baboons are very efficient at manipulating objects, because they have a fully opposable thumb and a precision grip, such that the tips of thumb and forefinger can be opposed. Compare with the human and

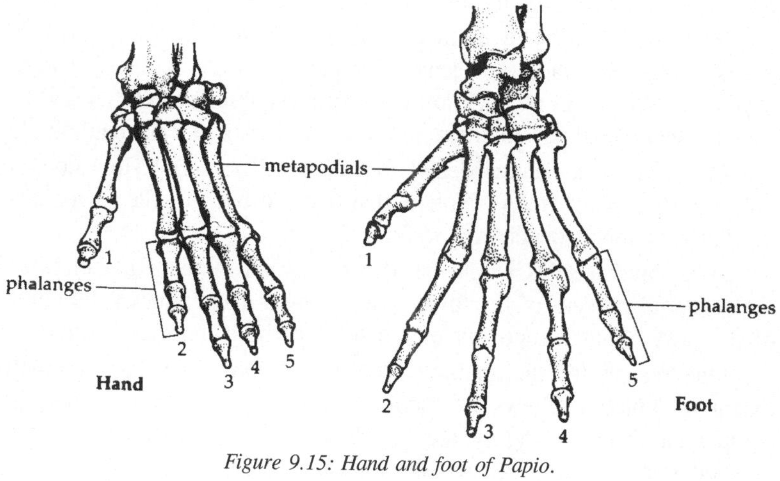

Figure 9.15: Hand and foot of Papio.

chimpanzee hand. During quadrupedal locomotion, the hands are often bent up at the knuckles, so that the weight is borne by the front of the palm.

This is a characteristic, semi-digitigrade posture of baboons. The foot tends to be placed more in a fully plantigrade position. Note the opposable hallux—also the heel.

Look carefully at Figures elsewhere in this chapter which show various baboon postures and movements. Compare the whole complex of anatomy and locomotion with what you know of other forms of primate locomotion.

Hominoids: the gibbon and siamang,
Hylobates* and *Symphalangus

Gibbons are highly mobile arboreal fruit- and leaf-eaters, living in the forests of South East Asia. The term 'brachiation' *was* first applied to their method of locomotion, for they have a striking way of swinging from their arms and propelling themselves rapidly along from one to the other, often taking off as they do so.

Their acrobatics are astounding, particularly during some display behaviour, but they are not always achieved without cost, for some skeletons do show repaired fractures.

The Head

Gibbons have flattened, globular braincases, which are usually smooth, without nuchal or sagittal crests (cf. baboon). The foramen magnum opens obliquely downwards from the base of the occiput. How does this compare with its position in the human skull?

You should now be familiar with the main features of primate skulls. Note eyes, face, and jaws. Compare with the skulls of *Ateles, Papio,* and *Homo*. Look back to the prosimians described earlier and be sure to understand the main trends in evolution of the primate skull.

Can you work out the dental formula of *Hylobates*? How does it differ from that of *Ateles?* Notice also that the back of the lower jaw is relatively much deeper in *Ateles*.

What jaw muscles would be affected by an increase in height of the coronoid process of the lower jaw, or by a deepening of the angle of the jaw? What component of the bite do these muscles control?

One reason for the shallow jaw in *Hylobates* may be the small extent to which it chews its food. Recent work has shown that, in comparison to leaf-eating monkeys such as langurs, *Hylobates* swallows its food relatively unprocessed by the cheek teeth.

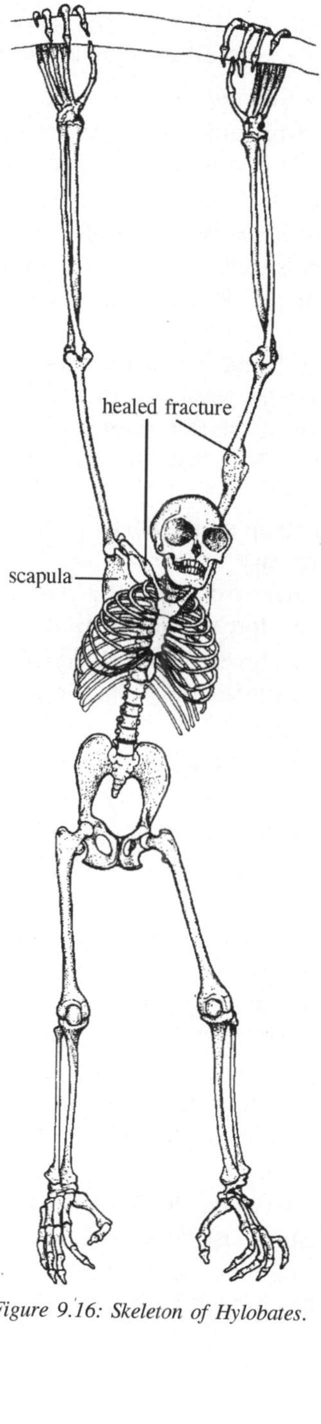

Figure 9.16: Skeleton of Hylobates.

A large proportion of the diet (50 per cent) is composed of fruit. The siamang, which eats more leaves, must chew its food more.

Thorax and Vertebral Column

Note the general proportions. Gibbons have very long arms, short trunks, and long legs. How does the intermembral index compare with that of *Ateles* and *Papio*?

As in *Ateles,* most of the trunk is made up of a large broad thorax, and the lumbar region is short. Compare the shape of the ribcage with that of *Papio,* for example. It is proportionately wider than the thorax of *Ateles*.

A wide ribcage is found in primates that swing from their arms, and perhaps is related to the tensile forces which the arms and shoulders have to bear. The gibbon skeleton illustrated is mounted as if it were hanging from its arms. Note that the arm can be raised right back behind the head.

The scapula is high up on the dorsal surface of the thorax and the humerus can move up and back on its articulation with the scapula. Note also the shape and position of the clavicles. A high degree of mobility in the shoulder, forearm, and wrist is essential for brachiation.

Compare with a nonbrachiator (e.g. *Papio).* Note that this gibbon specimen has had a fractured right clavicle and left humerus, which have subsequently healed.

In the sacral region, three vertebrae are fused together *so* that there is a rigid sacro-iliac joint. They are also fused to the caudal vertebrae behind. The ilium is long, and the sacro-iliac joint well separated from the hip. There is no functional tail.

Limbs

The most striking characteristic of the gibbon is its long limbs. In comparison, the trunk is short. The forelimbs are considerably longer than the hindlimbs (length of long bones = 40.5 cm versus 34 cm in this specimen). This great length is used for leverage during brachiation.

The metacarpals of digits 2 to 5 are also very long, and these fingers form a hook over branches, much as in *Ateles*, but gibbons also have a thumb which is only slightly longer than the metacarpal of the second digit.

It does not form part of the 'hook', and is kept out of the way when the animal is brachiating fast through the trees. The thumb is used, though, for gripping in other situations—for instance, during feeding, when fruit is not bitten off but hand picked.

An object is either gripped between fingers and palm, or, if small, between the thumb and the side of the index finger. Gibbons do not have a precision grip (see under *Papio* and *Homo*).

The hallux is considerably longer and more robust than the thumb. Note its length in comparison to the other four toes. It is used for holding on,in the numerous postures adopted by gibbons when they are not brachiating. The feet can also be used to hold objects such as fruit.

The secret of the mobility of the gibbons body about the forearm during brachiation lies in a joint in the wrist, which allows about 70° rotation. They joint is between the proximal and distal carpals, and so is called a midcarpal joint.

The radius can also rotate by 20°, thus producing with wrist rotation, a total body swing through 90°. Spider monkeys also have a ball-and-socket joint in their wrists, but non-brachiating monkeys do not.

Locomotion

There are four patterns of locomotion, some of which are illustrated in the accompanying drawings. They are brachiation, climbing, bipedalism, and leaping. Of these, bipedalism and leaping are least used.

Brachiation is normally used for covering distance through the trees, whereas a feeding siamang or gibbon will climb among smaller branches to reach fruit and young leaves at the tips. Note:

- Only the arms are involved in brachiation, whereas all four limbs participate in climbing.
- In virtually all situations, the trunk is held erect.
- The body rotates about the forearm which is held fully extended. The legs are flexed and extended during brachiation, which is important in maintaining momentum. No rotation of the body about the legs is involved.
- Brachiation may include a 'floating' phase, in which the animal takes off between handholds. This is more common in the smaller *Hylobates* than in *Symphalangus*.
- During bipedal walking the legs are flexed, and the arms have an essential role in maintaining balance. They are held up—one in front of and one behind the head. Compare this with the bipedal walking of *Ateles,* where the tail has a counterbalancing role, and the arms are lowered.

The locomotion of gibbons and siamangs allows them to exploit the small branch niche in the forest canopy. Even a relatively heavy animal like the siamang is able to distribute its weight over enough supports to feed from small branches.

The Chimpanzee and Man, *Pan*- and *Homo*

We shall discuss the chimpanzee and man together as a comparative exercise, rather than describing each separately, for this helps to emphasise their differences and so highlight particular adaptations.

Chimpanzees are at home in the trees and on the ground. In the trees they use all four appendages for holding on, but although they may swing from their arms, they do not brachiate as gibbons do.

They are, of course, much heavier animals than gibbons or spider monkeys. On the ground, they have a specialised form of quadrupedal walking called knuckle-walking, in which the weight of the anterior part of the body is borne by the second phalanges of the fingers, which are bent at the first finger joint.

In contrast, people are bipedal walkers, and more specialised for living on the ground. The upright posture of *Homo* imposes entirely different stresses on the skeleton, which has been modified accordingly in several quite dramatic and obvious ways.

Of course people can climb trees, and do use their climbing skills from time to time; when they climb, they use postures very like those used by great apes.

Heads

The major feature of the human skull, as we never get tired of reminding ourselves, is the enormous cranium. The increase in size of the cerebral hemispheres during human evolution has not simply been due to an increase in nerve cell number, but also to an increase in cell size, spacing, and in the number of intervening cells between neurones.

This much can be seen by comparing chimpanzee and human brains. Externally, the human cranium is smooth, domed, and rounded at the back. It sits on top of the vertebral column, and the foramen magnum points vertically downwards from under the skull.

Compare this arrangement with the chimpanzee skull. Here, the cranium is smaller, the occiput bears ridges, and the foramen magnum is not shifted so far underneath the skull.

Now look at the orbits and face. Modern man does not have pronounced brow ridges; the chimpanzee does. The forehead is also receding in chimpanzees. What part of the brain lies underneath the forehead? It is considerably enlarged in the human brain. The human face is flat vertically, but has a pronounced nose.

In contrast, chimpanzees have flatter noses and protruding jaws to accommodate large incisors and canines - they are 'prognathous'. Another feature is the human chin; chimpanzees have no chin.

The teeth show several striking differences. Both chimpanzees and people are omnivorous, but chimpanzees have a large vegetable component in their diet, particularly fruit. For this diet, they have large incisors and canines to pick and pierce, whereas their cheek teeth are comparatively small.

Note the large canines; as we have seen, most primates have relatively large canines—often larger in the males of a species. One of the ways of deciding whether fossil teeth and jaws belong to the family Hominidae (to which we belong) is to look at the size of the canines.

All adult apes have large canines, and are therefore readily distinguishable by this alone from all members of the Hominidae, which have relatively small incisiform canines. This allows the jaws to rotate more against each other.

The shape of the tooth row also differs. In man, the jaws have a parabolic shape around the front, whereas in the great apes the tooth arcade is more of an elongated U-shape. Check that you can see these differences in Figure elsewhere in this chapter.

Jaw shape is another feature used to identify hominid fossils. As the most common fossil remains are teeth and jaw fragments, their distinguishing features are of considerable significance to those studying the evolution of man and the apes.

The evolution of a short, flat face, and parabolic jaw arcade must have been correlated with changes in the diet. With the shifting of the jaws more underneath the skull, greater crushing power could have been developed during chewing.

How can you tell whether you are looking at an adult skull? The eruption of the molars is the key. The dental formula of man and the great apes is 12/2; C 1/1; PM 2/2; M 3/3.

Deciding whether a skull is from a mature animal can be of considerable importance, because the proportions may change dramatically during growth (as in baboons, for instance) and bony ridges may only appear in adults.

Thorax, Vertebral Column, and Limb Girdles

The forces acting on the trunk of a quadrupedal animal are quite different from those experienced when walking upright. The chimpanzee

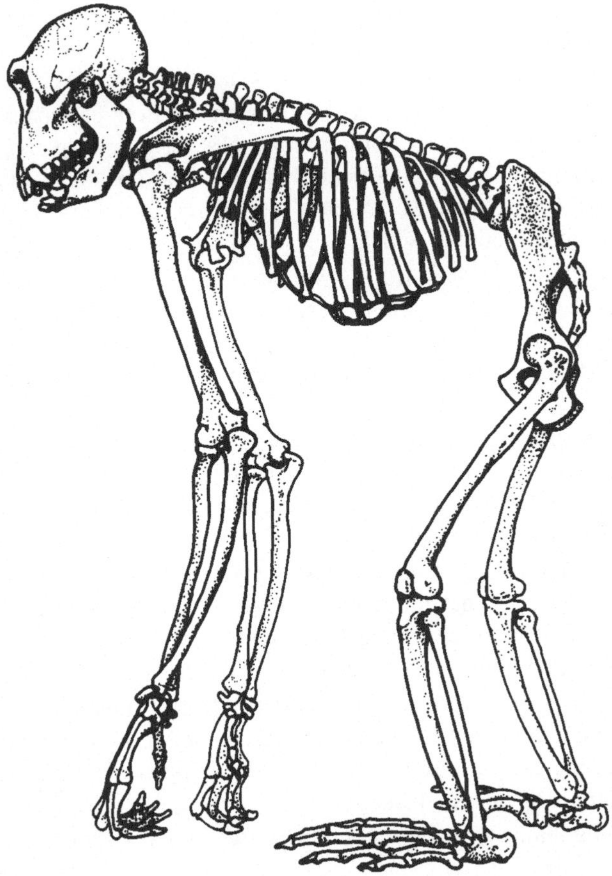

Figure 9.17: Skeletol of chimpanzee.

carries its thorax and abdominal organs slung from an inclined strut - the backbone - when it is walking quadrupedally.

In man, on the other hand, the weight of thorax and abdomen falls vertically downwards onto the pelvis and hindlimbs. The head must also be supported on top of the backbone.

To distribute these forces directly over the centre of the pelvis in a stable fashion, the human backbone is curved in the lumbar region, and to a lesser extent at shoulder level.

A straight backbone set above the back of the pelvis (which is where the sacro-iliac joint is necessarily situated) would be unbalanced, and tend to topple forwards, since most of the weight it must support is in front of its own axis.

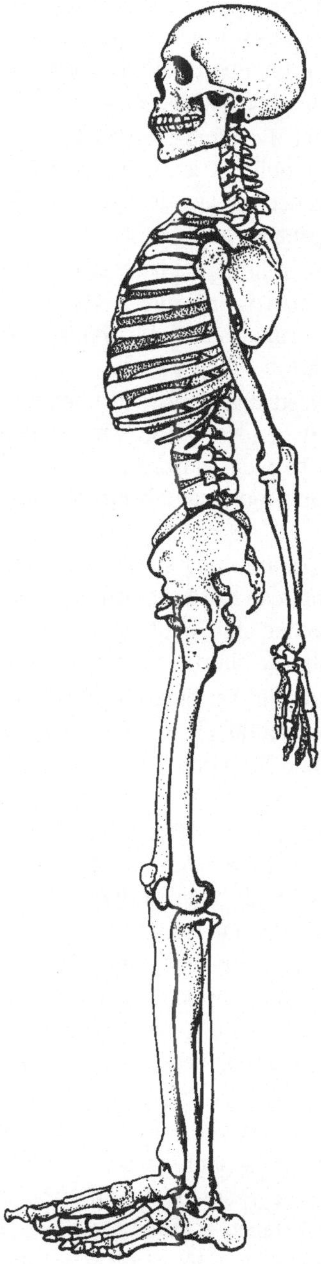

Figure 9.18: The human skeleton.

The shape of the human backbone, in contrast, allows the trunk to remain erect and balanced even when one leg is fully extended during walking. Compare the pronounced lumbar curve of the human vertebral column with the chimpanzee backbone, which has no such curve.

It is interesting that the lumbar curve develops during the life of each human individual only as an infant learns to walk. This again emphasises its importance as an adaptation to bipedalism. Thoracic shape differs in chimpanzees and people.

Compare the broad human chest with the narrow ribcage in chimpanzees. A long, narrow ribcage is characteristic of quadrupedal primates. Which other primates have broad chests (see earlier sections)? What sort of locomotion do they have?

It has been suggested that the broad human chest is derived from ancestors with this sort of locomotion. But, if that is the case, then a broad chest must also be well adapted for the stresses imposed during bipedal locomotion, for people have been standing upright for millions of years.

Look also at the position and shape of scapula and clavicle. Both chimpanzees and people can raise the arm well up above the head and shoulder—perhaps another sign of their arm-swinging ancestors. The lumbar region is relatively short; compare it in the two skeletons.

Are the same number of vertebrae involved? Look at the sacro-iliac joint. How many vertebrae are involved here? You might predict that the human sacrum would be more strongly built, because of the forces imposed on it.

An indication of strength in this joint is the number of vertebrae that are involved in it, and the extent to which they are fused with each other or with the lumbar and caudal vertebrae in front and behind. Note that the tail, as in the gibbon, is rudimentary.

Now concentrate on the pelvis itself. The human pelvis is unique among primates. It is shaped by its function in bipedal walking and by the weight of the torso, which it must bear and transmit to the legs. As a whole it is bowl-shaped, because of the characteristic expansion of the iliac blades.

Note that in the chimpanzee, the iliac blade is flat and much less flared. Also, the distance separating sacro-iliac and hip joints in the human pelvis is relatively small. In all the other primates so far described, this same distance is large.

Close proximity of the two joints increases the efficiency of weight transmission from the pelvis via the hips to the legs when the body is standing upright. But bipedalism is not simply a matter of balancing the head and trunk above the legs when stationary; they must remain balanced when the body moves.

Whereas people can walk without lurching from side to side, chimpanzees cannot do so. One reason is that their gluteal muscles perform different functions. The human gluteus medius and minimus prevent tilting of the pelvis towards the unsupported side when one leg is lifted off the ground.

The gluteus maximus is the hip extensor. These new functions are possible because the spatial relationship between gluteal muscles, hip joint, and femur has changed—and the human gluteal muscles are also much larger.

Check that you can see and understand all these adaptations to bipedalism in the human backbone and pelvis. Then look at the photographs of a chimpanzee walking and standing bipedally and decide why its balance is less stable.

Limbs

Chimpanzees and people both have arms and legs that are long relative to their trunks; look at the proportions. Are they the same in both skeletons?

Can you explain the differences? Measure the intermembral index for each skeleton if you can. Of the primates discussed here, which have high indices and which have low ones? What methods of locomotion are characteristic of each group?

Are there primates whose limbs are essentially equal in length? How do they move about? Note that the human arm is not primarily used in locomotion; it is mainly for manipulating things.

Note shape and proportion of the forelimb bones, and then compare the hands. Chimpanzees have long, curved fingers. How long is the thumb compared with the other fingers? What about the human thumb? Bring together the tips of your thumb and index finger.

This movement is the basis of the precision grip so characteristic of fine manipulations, and chimpanzees cannot do it. It could simply be a matter of manoeuvrability at the base of the thumb.

Look again at the chimpanzee hand; you should be able to see another reason why the precision grip is impossible. How do chimpanzees grip objects? What features of the chimpanzee hand are particularly associated with knuckle-walking? Again, it is helpful to have a basis for comparison.

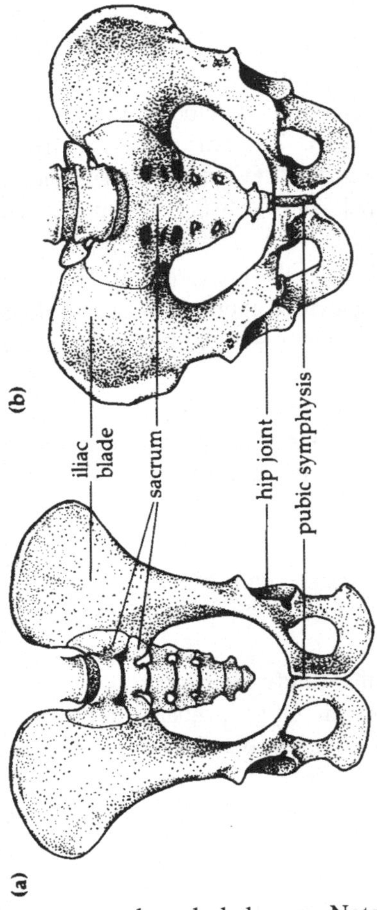

Figure 9.19: The sacrum and pelvis in (a) Pan and (b) Homo.

Look at the metacarpals and phalanges. Note which bones bear the weight during knuckle walking, and look at the same bones in the human hand. What are the differences? Finally, look at the terminal phalanges. They are much broader in man. Are chimpanzee nails and fingerpads the same shape as ours?

Sensitive fingerpads are just one feature of primate hands that has become highly developed during human evolution. Our manipulative skills are very extensive, and this is reflected not just in the immediate structure of the hand, but also in the brain.

There is a separate motor area in the cerebral cortex for each finger, which allows much more complicated movements and sophisticated controls. This is another way in which the human brain has increased

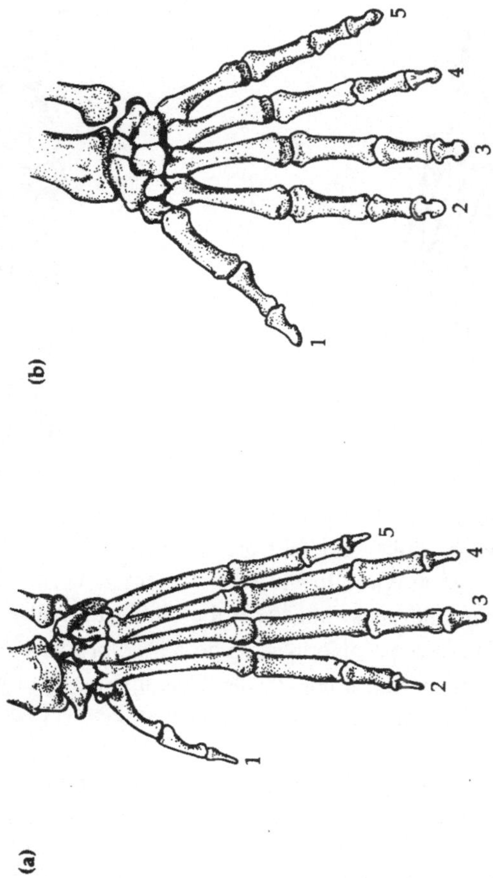

Figure 9.20: The hand of (a) Pan and (b) Homo.

in size and complexity over other primate brains. The hindlimbs provide other contrasts. Bipedalism has had far-reaching effects on the human leg and foot.

List all the differences that you can see; then check below for further description and explanation. Starting at the top, work out where weight falls down the leg.

In chimpanzees, the femur is vertical from hip to knee, and the knees are held as wide or slightly wider apart than the two hip joints. Weight is carried mainly by the inside of the knee.

The human femur is at an angle, so that the knees are closer together than the distance between the two hips. Weight is borne mainly by the outside of the knee. There are also differences in the shape of the tibia, which carries the weight in the lower leg.

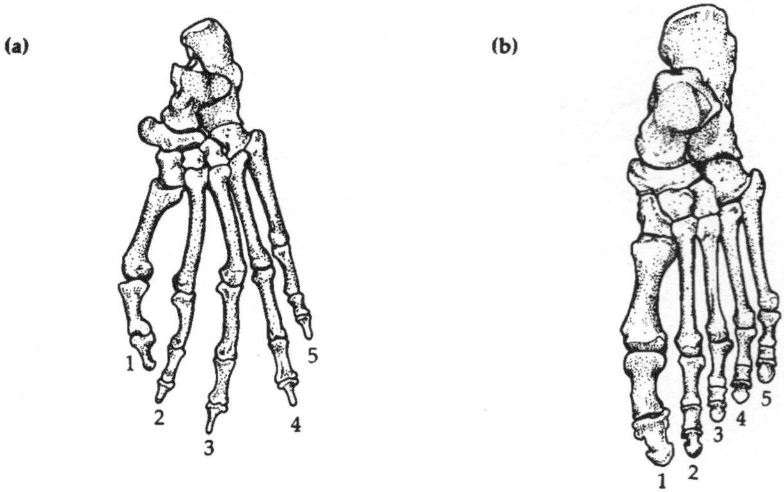

Figure 9.21: The foot of (a) Pan and (b) Homo.

The human knee, tibia, and foot are arranged in a straight line, close to the centre of gravity. In the foot, weight is borne along the outside in both man and apes; but there the similarity ends.

Chimpanzees have opposable toes, as do all the primates described here—but the human foot does not. In the great apes, a firm grip with the feet is essential to provide support for their heavy bodies while climbing.

The sole of the foot is also arched, to assist in gripping, and there is much more mobility in the foot. But in man, the prime consideration is to bear the weight of the upright body, and to provide a springy base for pushing it off from the ground during walking.

For, this, the big toe is large and lies alongside the other four—it cannot be opposed to them. During human walking, the heel lands first.

Weight is then transmitted along the outside of the foot, across the ball of the foot, and finally along the big toe, which pushes off again. Note the very robust human heel and the large bones of the hallux—its metatarsals and phalanges are massive. Note the relative lengths and arrangement of the toes in the human and chimpanzee foot.

Observe a friend walking, and follow the movements, posture, and weight distribution. As you walk yourself, notice how your foot hits the ground, and what happens as your weight shifts forwards to push off for the next stride. Measure your stride length and consider how length of leg affects it.

How might the human stride length compare with that of other primates? You have now studied several animals that have illustrated both the common characteristics of primates, and also their various specialisations.

Primate locomotion provides good examples of adaptative radiation within one order of mammals. Versatile movement seems to have been the key to primate success, and it arose in the trees. The origins of our posture, manipulative hands, and intelligence lie in our arboreal past.

INDEX

C

D

E